Advance Praise for

THE EXCELLENCE DIVIDEND

"*Wow* jumps off every page of Tom Peters's book *The Excellence Dividend,* delivering brilliant insights imploring business leaders to change before it's too late." —Cheryl Burgess, CEO of Blue Focus Marketing and author of *The Social Employee*

"Genius. . . . Tom Peters is a fearless thinker with a once-in-a-generation mind. Open this book to any page, start reading, and ten minutes later you will know this is true. . . . I'd rather hire someone who has studied his writings than someone who has an MBA." —Matthew Kelly, CEO of Floyd Consulting and *New York Times* bestselling author of *The Dream Manager*

"We spend our entire lives searching for purpose. Tom Peters found his early and never wavered. For the rest of us, thank God he did! . . . He inspired me to pursue joy, and decades later, he is still inspiring me with his writing and his passion. . . . If we are wise enough to listen, we will receive dividends that last a lifetime." —Richard Sheridan, CEO of Menlo Innovations and author of *Joy, Inc.*

"Peters has always been original, commanding, and cutting-edge. If you think you've heard or read it all, you'll be happily invigorated by *The Excellence Dividend*. . . . By turns amusing, stimulating, and complacency-disturbing, Peters provides true food for thought—the sort you'll mentally chew on through the day and which may gnaw on you through the night."

—Whitney Johnson, Thinkers50, author of *Build an A Team*

TOM PETERS

THE EXCELLENCE DIVIDEND

Tom Peters is a leading business management guru and founder of the Tom Peters Company. He continues to be in constant demand for lectures and seminars. In 2017, he received a Lifetime Achievement Award from Thinkers50 and the Jack Covert Award for Contribution to the Business Book Industry from 800-CEO-READ. Peters is the bestselling author of sixteen books, including *In Search of Excellence* (with Robert H. Waterman, Jr.), which is often cited as among the best business books ever written. He lives in Massachusetts.

THE EXCELLENCE DIVIDEND

Meeting the Tech Tide
with Work That Wows
and Jobs That Last

TOM PETERS

VINTAGE BOOKS

A Division of Penguin Random House LLC
New York

A VINTAGE BOOKS ORIGINAL, APRIL 2018

Library of Congress Cataloging-in-Publication Data
Names: Peters, Thomas J., author.
Title: The excellence dividend : meeting the tech tide with work that wows
and jobs that last / Tom Peters.
Description: New York : Vintage Books, [2018]
Identifiers: LCCN 2017031994 | ISBN 9780525434627 (trade pbk.)
Subjects: LCSH: Organizational change. | Organizational effectiveness. |
Strategic planning. | Automation—Economic aspects.
Classification: LCC HD58.8 .P4779 2018 | DDC 658.4—dc23
LC record available at https://lccn.loc.gov/2017031994

Vintage Books Trade Paperback ISBN: 978-0-525-43462-7
eBook ISBN: 978-0-525-43463-4

Book design by Christopher M. Zucker

www.vintagebooks.com

Printed in the United States of America
10 9 8 7 6 5 4 3 2 1

To

Susan Sargent, inspiration, prod, steadfast partner
Captain Richard E. Anderson, CEC, USN,
role model/mentor extraordinaire
Gene Webb, igniter-in-chief of intellectual fires
Bob Waterman, best mate in pursuit of Excellence
Harry Rhoads, faithful pal, game changer
Darl Kolb, Kiwi instigator
Herb Kelleher, the One and Only I
Richard Branson, the One and Only II
Anita Roddick, the One and Only III
Larry Janesky, king of basements
Jim Penman, loves the tasks we hate
"Jungle" Jim Bonaminio, offers customers "America's Best Restroom"
Vernon Hill, contrarian, WOW-meister, fan-maker, job creator
Esther Newberg, sine qua non
Sonny Mehta, sine qua non

EXCELLENCE: THE TRIUMPH OF HUMANITY

Janet Dugan, a health care architect, took inspiration from her recent experience having an MRI (magnetic resonance imaging) scan. While she was lying still and waiting, she noticed a small mirror that had been placed below the head support piece. It was angled so that she could see through the barrel to the radiology technician and make eye contact with him. "What a small thing," she told me. "And yet what a difference it made. I felt less alone. I was connected to another person at the very moment I needed support. And even though I'm not claustrophobic, it calmed me some to be able to see out of the barrel. . . . I [saw] that the technician was friendly and that the nurse went out of her way to make me laugh. . . . I firmly believe in the power of design to contribute to the healing process—that architecture can shape events and transform lives. But that day, in that experience, the thing that really gave me comfort was a tiny mirror about as big as a Band-Aid."

—Tim Leberecht, *The Business Romantic: Give Everything, Quantify Nothing, and Create Something Greater Than Yourself*

EXCELLENCE DIVIDEND: THE SCHEME

SECTION V: ADDING VALUE, A "TOP LINE" OBSESSION

SECTION VI: LEADERSHIP EXCELLENCE

THE PITCH: EXCELLENCE, NOW MORE THAN EVER

When *In Search of Excellence* was published in 1982, America's mood was dire. Recession raged, unemployment stood at 10.8 percent, the highest since the Great Depression, and Japan's mighty *keiretsu* was threatening a wide range of American industries, from automobile manufacturers and banks to electronics firms and steelmakers.

MBAs, and I was one, had ascended to the top in American business. They (we!) tended to relentlessly focus on abstractions—the spreadsheet, the bottom line, the strategic plan. Japanese business chiefs had a different emphasis: an unrelenting quest for continuous product improvement marked by the involvement of every employee every day. America's passionless obsession with numbers, numbers, and more numbers was the opening Japan needed to embarrass us. The automotive industry was especially vulnerable; compared to theirs, our cars were clunkers. (This quote from Honda founder Soichiro Honda overstates the case, but his point is all too well taken: "When Congress passes new emission standards, we hire fifty more engineers and GM hires fifty more lawyers." Ouch!)

The *In Search of Excellence* message was that some U.S. companies *did* focus on what was right—developing people, obsessing on product quality, seeking inspiring design, and listening to the engineers more intently than to the finance department staffers. As a result, they were scoring in the marketplace. All of us, my coauthor Bob Waterman and I argued, could learn from these *American* exemplars of excellence.

I consider this book, *The Excellence Dividend*, arriving at an equally troubling time, to be a sequel of sorts to *In Search of Excellence*—excellence II, if you will (more on that in a moment).

Today's economy is in surprisingly good shape, given the depth of the hole that we were in ten years ago. But there are big exceptions—in particular, growing income inequality and an enormous, and restless, underemployed class. However, there is a larger threat looming, one that has been building for a long time, and which, over the next five to fifteen or twenty years, is likely going to knock us back on our heels with once-in-a-century consequences.

It's not globalization.

It's not immigration.

It's technology.

Entrepreneur, venture capitalist, and Silicon Valley icon Marc Andreessen says, "Software is eating the world." An alarming Oxford University analysis claims that, in the next two decades, nearly 50 percent of American white-collar jobs are at risk, either to automation or artificial intelligence (AI). The first thirty years of advanced automation brought robots and mass layoffs to factories and, via software, eliminated the jobs of those who performed routine white-collar tasks. Says Daniel Huttenlocher, dean of Cornell Tech, "The industrial revolution was about augmenting and replacing physical labor, and the digital revolution has been about augmenting and replacing mental labor."

What's changed is that automation is no longer just occurring in the realm of repetitive tasks, whether blue collar *or* white. Instead, smarter machines learn on the job ("deep learning") and see patterns based on enormous data troves and draw conclusions that humans often cannot find. Artificial intelligence–driven devices can spot tumors on CT scans better than pathologists and radiologists. Machine learning pioneer Geoffrey Hinton said, "If you work as a radiologist, you are like Wile E. Coyote in the cartoon; you're already over the edge of the cliff, but you haven't looked down." *Hinton went so far as to recommend that med schools stop training radiologists right now.* AI also drives the overwhelming majority of trading in stocks and bonds. As Vasant Dhar, a New York University professor and developer of hedge-fund trading programs, noted, "At the end of the day, you have to ask yourself what will be left for humans to do that machines can't do as well or better?"

Can we fight back against this likely employment apocalypse? While I hardly dismiss the impending turmoil, I run to optimism. And it is that optimism that leads me to think in terms of "excellence II"—focusing on the human attributes that will, effectively deployed, likely remain beyond the realm of artificial intelligence. For example, the quality of fully engaged employees providing personalized service that makes you smile as it is delivered and creates fond memories that last. Or the design excellence that made Steve Jobs's Apple products, more driven by his months sitting quietly in Japanese gardens than by computer coding skills, worthy of the head-shaking amazement of hundreds of millions of customers.

Truth be told, I have had a love affair with excellence throughout my career. I believe—oh, how deeply I believe—that excellence is far more than just an organizing business principle that can be reduced to a series of "success traits." Excellence can be the way we live our lives, professional as well as personal, the way we support one another, particularly in difficult times. Excellence is the seemingly small acts that shout, "We care," and which linger in the memories of those we interact with—our own people, our communities, our suppliers, our customers.

Here's an example that is—literally—close to home. Not long ago, my wife and I had fifty trees planted on the border of our property in southern Massachusetts. She's the gardener in chief, and I was the designated waterer in chief. That translated into an hour-a-day task that entailed dragging about two hundred yards of heavy-duty hose hither and thither. The person who helps us with the lawn and my wife's gardens has to move that bulky hose out of his way when he cuts the grass. To do so, he thoughtfully coiled it with the utmost care so that when I had to drag it back out to water the trees, there were no kinks, a smooth flow, and the chore was made easy. It was a small, but critical, act of, yes, excellence. It's tempting to dismiss hose coiling as unimportant when compared with the precision needed to design a computer or run a global business. But that is dead wrong. I've spent my adult life studying excellence, marveling at all its myriad manifestations, and this seemingly tiny display of attention and care is precisely the sort I will remember, not just when I water our new trees but when I lecture to business leaders around the world about how to build organizations that do things differently, that do things in ways that engender fond and lasting memories in their customers' heads and hearts.

So what is this Excellence Dividend? In short, businesses that are committed to excellence in every aspect of their internal and external dealings are likely to be survivors. They are better and more spirited places to work. Their employees are engaged and growing and preparing for tomorrow. Their customers are happier and inclined to spread tales of their excellence far and wide. Their communities welcome them as good neighbors. Their vendors welcome them as reliable partners. That in turn translates directly into bottom-line results and growth. And, AI and robotics notwithstanding, it translates into jobs that last and the likely creation of new jobs as well.

To observe the Excellence Dividend at work, let's move beyond garden hoses and talk about dog biscuits and a global retail banking revolution. Or, rather, let's turn to Vernon Hill, founder of Commerce Bank in the United States and now Metro Bank in the United Kingdom. For years, the retail banking model, as software moved to every desktop and countertop, and then to every pocket, has been to abandon bricks-and-mortar branches and compel customers to use ATMs, and now smartphones, and to perform as many transactions as possible online. Hill, the contrarian, opened Commerce Bank and said in effect, "*We want 'em in the branches where we can get beyond soulless 'transactions' and turn an inhuman account number into a fully engaged member of our family.*" His plan was to build gorgeous, colorful, pulsating "stores" (the Commerce/Metro term for branches); pay good wages; train like crazy; and fill the stores with enthusiastic employees who would provide sterling service and convert customers into "fans"—one of Hill's favorite terms.

Very long hours have been one signature of the Commerce/Metro experience—his branches are open a previously unheard-of seven days a week (and until midnight on Fridays!). The most complex transactions are completed in a flash. No problem is too convoluted that it can't be solved autonomously by frontline staffers taught literally never to say "no." (*When a computer glitch occurred at one point, an employee went so far as to put a customer's plane ticket charge on her personal credit card in order to preserve that customer's deeply discounted, time-sensitive airfare; her imaginative act earned kudos from bank management, let alone the shock and awe of the customer.*)

To top it off, the bank has always advertised itself as "dog friendly." Its ubiquitous mascot, Duffy ("Sir Duffield" in the United Kingdom), is featured in every promotion. Come to the bank, and you'll likely leave, as I did in London, with a bright red dog bowl emblazoned with the bank's logo, a pooper scooper (also with logo), and, of course, dog biscuits. The biscuit giveaway count—featured in the annual report a few years ago—totaled two million.

In 2007, Hill sold Commerce Bank to TD Bank for $8.6 billion, a rousing testament to the effectiveness of his contrarian, fan-generating approach. He rested for a while but couldn't remain idle for long; so he took his "WOW-bank" philosophy, captured in his book *Fans Not Customers*, across the Atlantic. The innovative Metro Bank became the first new, major chartered bank in the United Kingdom in 150 years. Hill put on his version of the Greatest Show on Earth, the British bought the whole act (thousands come out for branch/store openings), joined in the fun, and in short order Metro had more than one million accounts—oh, and his UK customers took to "dog friendly" even more avidly than their American counterparts.

In a nutshell, what Hill and his associates brought to the staid, stagnant banking business was bold, brash, colorful, fun, energetic excellence. And they delivered it in a human-centered way that created memorable, emotion-laden experiences that earned millions of loyal fans. But it's not just customers who have benefited. Hill and his management team, first at Commerce, now at Metro, have created more than seventeen thousand good new jobs while traditional banks, consumed by technology's efficiency-first approach, closed branches, left empty buildings behind, and slashed jobs by the tens of thousands.

THE COMMERCE BANK/METRO BANK MANTRA

"Are you going to cost cut your way to prosperity? Or are you going to spend your way to prosperity?"

"Over-invest in our people, over-invest in our facilities."

"Cost cutting is a death spiral. Our whole story is growing revenue."

As Hill and associates have demonstrated, excellence that sticks *is* achievable in 2018 and achievable in big arenas where the herd is moving, obsessed with technology for technology's sake, in the polar opposite direction. But, as you'll find in the pages that follow, there is an implicit warning accompanying this heartening story: Excellence is damned hard work, and the pursuit thereof is unrelenting. Excellence, Commerce- and Metro-flavor, cannot be turned over to the code writers; and it is definitely not for the faint of heart. Maintaining the banks' culture is a minute-at-a-time, hour-at-a-time, forever affair.

This book is about hard work and unrelenting development and maintenance of a culture of excellence. But it is not a guide to "defending" yourself in the midst of the "disruptions" that have become commonplace and will be so for the foreseeable future. No, it is decidedly *not* about defense. It is about going on the offensive—creating, right now, excellence anywhere and everywhere, delighting customers with dog bowls, dog biscuits, a never-say-no attitude. Recruiting a team of optimists, then showering them with training and development opportunities that prepare them for an uncertain future and keep them in a mood consistent with providing service that invariably "Wows"—seven days a week and 'til midnight on Fridays.

As software replaces jobs, all industries all over the world are at risk. The technology is there already; the only issue is timing. Five years? Ten years? Fifteen? How long will it be before technology guts the job market? And are we, in the end, fighting a losing battle?

My response to that question is an unequivocal no. My bottom line is that there *is* an effective way to master and profit from the madness. And, yes, the answer *is* excellence: excellence reflected in the staff's attitude toward the coming day, excellence that translates into an emotional bond with customers and communities in a way that cannot—and I predict will not—be replaceable by algorithms in the foreseeable future. Excellence, to repeat, is a human-driven affair, a state of mind, not a computer-generated exercise.

EXCELLENCE is a perfectly coiled hose (coiled with care!) that makes my hillside watering task a lark, or at least easier.

EXCELLENCE is two million dog biscuits and a staff of thousands who never say "No" and live to produce a "Wow" in any and all transactions.

EXCELLENCE, per Steve Jobs, is a design so good that "you want to lick it" and a design-mindedness translated as fully to the care that goes into creating *boxes* in which Apple products come as to the software that powers them.

Hose, dog biscuits, lickability: EXCELLENCE 2018.

It is hard work.

But it is eminently doable.

And infinitely rewarding at a personal as well as professional level.

The basis for no less than economic revival at both local and national levels.

At least as true, or more so, for the millions upon millions working in the likes of two-person lawn and garden businesses as for those in the giant firms that grab the headlines.

Oh, and please trust me on this, a helluva lot of fun—witness customer smiles, employee growth, and the community's applause.

Excellence is profitable.

Excellence is security.

Excellence is a kick.

Believe it.

EXCELLENCE DIVIDEND: THE PLOT

Excellence, always.
If not excellence, what?
If not excellence now, when?

Excellence!

The story comes in fifteen parts.

Each stands alone.

Each is an integral and integrated part of a larger whole called EXCELLENCE.

The *why*: Excellence in all we do at this madcap moment in particular and for a variety of reasons is the best—I'm tempted to say *only*—high-probability strategy for personal and enterprise success.

I repeat:

The excellence story herein is *not* about "defense" and "surviving."

This excellence story *is* about offense and thriving!

On a very personal note, I'd add that this book, though fully engaged with the tumultuous times circa 2018, took fifty-plus years to write, starting in 1966 with my first management job and the lucky break of a boss who would accept no less than excellence.

The saga:

You suffer through a hundred-slide PowerPoint presentation. The first ninety-five slides focus on market analysis, competitors' strengths, and numbers, numbers, numbers (i.e., abstractions, abstractions, abstractions). The finale, if we even get there, is a rush through five dense pages of "To-dos." Well, damn it, I want the "To-dos"—*and* the processes and people associated therewith—to be the last fifty slides in the presentation. (Better yet, a twenty-slide presentation, with the last ten [or so] devoted to How to/To do/Who do.) I approvingly quote Omar Bradley, the commander of U.S. troops at the World War II D-day landing: "Amateurs talk about strategy. Professionals talk about logistics." In this book, you'd better believe that I talk about logistics and that execution comes precisely where it belongs: first! Execution is front, center, and first, not AWOL; it is the sole topic of section 1 and chapter 1.

The book's second section is, what else, "Excellence." The first excellence examination—chapter 2—consists of fourteen takes on excellence. We begin with the purposefully soaring notion that "excellence in management is a grand human achievement." That is, effectively organizing and energizing our fellow human beings to attain extraordinary ends—on a soccer team, in a symphonic production, in an ICU, in a training department—is the highest of arts. Effectively organizing is what humans did to move beyond our prehuman ancestors. My aim is pointing out that this organizational pursuit of service through excellence is an enormous and soul-filling opportunity. A second snapshot worth singling out here is the one that begets the chapter title: "Excellence Is the Next Five Minutes." Excellence is typically seen as a grand aspiration, an Olympian mountaintop to be reached, the acme of a ten-year plan. Not so. I will argue as stridently as I can that excellence is the boss's next chance meeting in the hall, the next phone call, and, yup, the next ten-line e-mail or two-line instant message. Excellence is a moment-to-moment way of life. Or it is nothing at all. There's no tomorrow in excellence; there is only right now.

Excellence is sustained by one (and only one) thing: a culture of excellence. And that culture of excellence is the topic of chapter 3. MIT's longtime organizational effectiveness guru, Ed Schein, famously said, "Culture eats strategy for breakfast." Culture, pure and simple, is the bedrock of any and all of the manifestations of excellence described above in chapter 2. Implication #1: Cultural development and maintenance is CEO Job #1. Moreover, tending to the culture is a full-time job.

Chapter 4 takes a turn particularly important for the times. The topic is SMEs/Small- and Medium-sized Enterprises. To deal with the forces descending upon us, we need energy, verve, imagination, and artistry—and a source of new jobs. Fact is, these positives are rarely associated with giant firms, and I present unassailable data to support that unsettling assertion. Smaller outfits are unequivocally the job producers (about 80 percent of new jobs, all around the world) and premier innovators. A special effort is made in this chapter to demonstrate that Enterprise Excellence is most decidedly *not* the exclusive domain of the likes of the denizens of Silicon Valley. Our exemplars will include Basement Systems Inc., a fast-growing Connecticut firm that logs $100 million in revenue drying out residential basements and turning them into family rooms or extra bedrooms. And a parking garage—yes, a parking garage—in Miami, 1111 Lincoln Road, that has become a cultural icon and center for everything from morning yoga classes to major entertainment events. Excellence here, there, and everywhere.

Section 3 is "the people stuff." As I repeatedly say (and have said) in every one of my roughly three thousand presentations spanning four decades, why in the world must I shout "People first!" at the top of my lungs again and again and then again? Why isn't it as obvious as the end of your nose and down to your toenails? I don't know, but here I go again.

We start with chapter 5, "One More (Damn) Time: Putting People First." By my accounting, "people first" has always ranked #1 on the Basis-for-Excellence scorecard. But it is "more #1" in 2018 than ever before—in fact, by a long shot. The headlines these days are chockablock with tales about replacing people (by the millions) with robots and advanced AI. All this book's headlines are about pursuing excellence with imagination and vigor through turned-on, growth-obsessed people.

(Note: The AI is there, to be sure, but its primary role is to abet workers' efforts to deliver excellent customer experiences—not to replace those workers.)

So in my book (and this damn well is my book), "People *First*" is far more intensely the message today than it was in our first excellence effort in 1982. And, as then, I never understand why businesspeople so rarely get it—in the same way a symphony or ballet or theater company leader, sports coach, or lab boss does. If a football team, though assisted these days by "Big Data" analytics, is obviously the sum of its players and their effectiveness as a team, why is that not equally the case at my corner grocery store in Westport, Massachusetts? In this instance it is. The local store's staff attitude is in fact a joy to behold.

New England Patriots.

Westport, Massachusetts, grocer.

Same-same.

People first.

Chapter 6 singles out training. It most logically should have been a part of the prior chapter, but I believe there is a compelling need to make a standalone/standout argument—and to use a strong word in doing so—namely, *mania*. You want the customer to experience excellence and delight and become a fan and *stay* a fan? Then you need each and every employee to be part of a fully engaged team and to be devoted to growth. Matthew Kelly, in his book *The Dream Manager*, based upon a housekeeping services company, contends that if you want employees to contribute heart and mind to the enterprise, then you must commit heart and mind to helping them achieve their dreams—to develop as persons who not only serve today's customer with verve but are in a position to move on and move forward in the crazy-getting-crazier world in which they are imbedded.

Chapter 7, next up in the "People" section, directly confronts and examines the new technologies. Titled "Tech Tsunami, White-Collar Apocalypse, the New Moral Imperative," it lays out the story of, indeed, highly likely apocalyptic change, and I also lay down the law. Or, rather, Richard Branson lays down *his* law: "Business has to give people enriching, rewarding lives . . . or it's simply not worth doing." Then I lay down *my* law, which I call "Corporate Mandate 2018"—namely, *Your principal moral obligation as a leader is to develop the skill set of every one of the people in your charge (temporary as well as semipermanent) to the maximum extent of your abilities and consistent with their "revolutionary" needs in the years ahead. The bonus: This is also the #1 profit maximization strategy!* In short, the idea of contemporary business's *moral imperative* is the bedrock of this book.

In chapter 8, "Job Security in an Insecure World," we turn to the individual's mandate—or, rather, opportunity. In 1999, I offered up a book titled *The Brand You 50: Fifty Ways to Transform Yourself from an "Employee" into a Brand That Shouts Distinction, Commitment, and Passion!* What was, I felt, a good idea then is a mandate today. It also underscores my earlier "defense versus offense" argument. I do not see Brand You as a defense *against* AI. I see it as an offensive strategy *for* you and your peers to build exciting lives that in fact take full advantage of the new technology.

Next up: "Innovation," section 4 and, first up, chapter 9, "Whoever Tries the Most Stuff Wins/Whoever Screws the Most Stuff Up Wins." There is lots to say about innovation, and I've said a lot over the years. But in this section, I limit myself to two principal ideas. WTTMSW (remember, whoever tries the most stuff wins) is the first. I've long been a vociferous enemy of spending an inordinate amount of time on planning. For example, #1 among the "Eight Basics" featured in *In Search of Excellence* was "A Bias For Action." 3M, my favorite company in that 1982 book—and a superstar almost forty years later—was one giant *playground*. And in this chapter, among other things, I tout a superb book appropriately titled *Serious Play* (e.g., "You can't be a serious innovator unless and until you are ready, willing, and able to seriously play").

Serious play. No big planning departments. Damn little formality. Zestfully jump in and then see what happens. Folks in every nook and every cranny of the organization talking about something for a short while, then turning out a half-assed prototype in a flash; then fiddling with it and playing some more. Mistakes (WSTMSUW, whoever screws the most stuff up wins) are regularly celebrated (not "tolerated") as essential steps on the path to progress; one successful CEO-innovator says he owes his success to a three-word motto: "Fail. Forward. Fast."

The catch with all this: The wildly accelerating pace of change circa 2018 requires a wholly animated, all-hands WTTMSW/WSTMSUW *culture*; as I'll examine in depth. Though popularized in Silicon Valley, establishing such a rockin'-and-rollin' culture goes against the grain in most settings, and breaking that case-hardened mold is no walk in the park.

Chapter 10 encompasses the second of the two big ideas in this section on innovation, "We Are Who We Hang Out With." The story can be condensed as follows: Weird times require hanging out (obsessively!) with weird people who relentlessly challenge our views and say the strangest things. Motto: Same-same kills in 2018. If you recognize all the folks wandering in the hall at your workplace, or if three-quarters of your team have the same background and same point of view, which is all too commonplace, well, you are in deep trouble. We'll also see that the war on same-same extends from the front line to, especially, the boardroom. Low board diversity = *VERY* common = life-threatening.

Section 5. In an age of AI-abetted, friction-free supply chains—and AI-abetted, soulless transactions—efficiency and cost minimization are de facto the beginning and end of the regnant story. But hold on for a beat and remember the Metro Bank axiom: *"Cost cutting is a death spiral. Our whole story is growing revenue."* In precisely that spirit, this section, "Adding Value, a 'Top Line' Obsession," is devoted to nine sources of top line enhancement.

In chapter 11, "A Passion for Design, Differentiator #1," I single out engaging design as first among equals in the value-added tale. There is a special angle to this story. Design is great functionality. Yes. Design is appealing aesthetics. Yes. But the essence of Design Excellence goes much further. It's all about lasting emotional connection. Starbucks' Howard Schultz wants us to have a "romance" with his shops—damned if I know why, but I do, on the road in Saudi Arabia as well as at home in Boston. Notions such as Schultz's animate this chapter. And, of the most importance, such notions apply as much to the local service station or a six-person purchasing department or the twenty-seven-year-old independent contractor making her way in the "gig economy" as they do to Starbucks!

The other eight value-added sources are covered in chapter 12. They include an abiding emphasis on services added. Rolls-Royce, for example, now makes more money from adjunct services than from producing aircraft engines; UPS in 2018 is more about logistics systems management than tossing packages on the back porch. The hell-bent use of social media by one and all is also front and center. Among other things, you will be introduced to a financial services CEO who insists he would rather have a Twitter conversation with one customer than spend millions of dollars on the purchase of a Super Bowl ad! Also on the new technology front, the game-changing impact of Big Data and IoT, the Internet of Things, are given their due.

Two gigantic and absurdly underserved, absurdly financially endowed markets will be examined in detail. Women are effectively the premier purchasers of, well, everything. Too few companies, even in 2018, get it. Among other things, the most surefire way to take advantage of the women's market is to have a top team that looks like the market (i.e., a senior management team and board with female majorities). The other underserved behemoth market is seniors. Their total purchasing power is staggering and dramatically exceeds that of their younger cohorts who are, absurdly, the focus of most marketing efforts.

Section 6, the finale, is a journey toward Leadership Excellence. I describe it as "some stuff." The point of that odd and seemingly lightweight designation is that I am not offering a grand design or a mystical formula for organizational or individual transformation. In fact, I avoid like the plague such words as *vision*, *authenticity*, *disruption*, and *transformation*. My aim here is tactical and practical. I will offer you proven (over and over and over again) ideas to increase your leadership effectiveness today and ignite your march toward Excellence today. (Remember the bedrock: Excellence is the next five minutes.)

Tactics that work.

Tactics you can begin to apply this afternoon.

Tactics that, taken together, and applied repetitively, will move you many steps down the road to Leadership Excellence.

The first of the three leadership chapters, chapter 13, is titled, "Listening, the Bedrock of Leadership Excellence." I gave serious thought to making *listening* chapter 1—if so, I would have been following the lead of Richard Branson, who devoted the entire first third, over one hundred pages, of his recent leadership book, *The Virgin Way: How to Listen, Learn, Laugh, and Lead*, to listening. Instead, I chose to single out listening as Item #1 in this leadership section, worthy beyond doubt of a stand-alone chapter. Along the way, I will also argue that an enterprise-wide commitment to what one leadership expert calls "fierce listening" is the top candidate for Core Value #1.

The second topic to be singled out in the leadership section, as chapter 14, is the abiding importance of an organization's full complement of first-line managers. Sergeants run the army and chief petty officers run the navy, and the armed services damn well understand that and act accordingly. Likewise, first-line leaders are, as I see it, a business organization's Asset #1, but most businesses do not behave accordingly. In this chapter, I dearly hope to make a rock-solid case for changing that.

The principal leadership chapter, chapter 15, offers up some twenty-six tactics, ranging from the (staggering) power of "Thank you" and "I'm sorry" to an analysis of the many cognitive biases that severely cloud our judgments (and some suggestions for diminishing the power of those biases). My goal is to have you dip in and get on with giving several of these tactical tips a try. Right now. To repeat, applied relentlessly, these nuggets are almost guaranteed to speed up your journey toward excellence.

The book's epilogue is titled "Coda 2018." It adds up to a simple plea for immoderate action fit for immoderate times. Only leaps and bounds and spirited play and the relentless pursuit of Excellence and Wow will add up to that offensive, rather than defensive, approach to mastering the trials of these times.

So that's it, fifteen chapters, fifteen ideas. Each, in fact, is a necessary way stop on the path to Excellence and surviving and thriving in the unruly times ahead.

Good luck!

ORGANIZING PRINCIPLE I

ON THE SHOULDERS OF GIANTS

Three years ago, I began an effort to pull everything together—to capture my thoughts over the past five-plus decades about people in organizations getting things done with excellence. The effort resulted in a monster—a seventeen-chapter, 4,094-slide Power-Point product that included one hundred thousand words of annotation. I called it THE WORKS. (You'll find it at http://excellencenow.com/.) What follows is significantly derived from that seventeen-chapter blockbuster. Specifically, before starting this book, I went through the entire slide set and extracted three hundred or so quotes from Hall of Fame performers that I have found most illuminating. I use these gems as my raw material. The reasoning is simple and consistent with a view I've long held. While I have observed thousands of organizations and ceaselessly wrestled with the ups and downs of my own small business, the simple fact is that I have *not* run a Fortune 500 company, and I have *not* birthed a "unicorn." Hence, virtually everything I've done has been done, indirectly, by standing upon the shoulders of giants. So what if Tom Peters thinks your employees should be your number-one customer? Forget my view; but I hope you *will* pay attention to the likes of Southwest Airlines founder and CEO

Herb Kelleher and the inimitable Richard Branson when *they* say precisely that. Frankly, this is their book far more than mine, and I delightedly acknowledge and offer my thanks for the lessons these often contrarian exemplars of excellence have pounded into my head and heart and which I hope, with my assistance, they pound into you.

ORGANIZING PRINCIPLE II

ON YOUR SHOULDERS

When I wrote my first book, I was working as a consultant at McKinsey & Co., and I first thought that my most important readers were our big-league clients or clients-to-be. But the letters of thanks I received that moved me the most were from elementary school principals, police chiefs and police lieutenants, fire chiefs, and department heads at big firms. Well, let me repeat the lesson of those letters here. *The Excellence Dividend* is aimed primarily at the boss of a six-person training unit in a $1 billion behemoth, the proprietor of a four-person construction firm in my hometown of Dartmouth, Massachusetts, or the likes of the police lieutenant cited immediately above. Frankly, it is their (*your!*) devotion to relentlessly developing their (*your!*) team members and turning their (*your!*) customers or community members into fans that makes the difference in creating a vibrant local and national economy. I do dearly hope these pages inspire you to renew your passion for and commitment to excellence; it matters now more than ever before.

EXECUTION

 **EXECUTION,
FIRST AMONG
EQUALS**

MY STORY*

HOW TWO SIMPLE WORDS—CAN DO—
STARTED ME ON A FIFTY-YEAR CAPER.

Too many business books offer "marketing secrets that sizzle" or give us a surefire formula for "coping with permanent disruption" or offer how-tos for creating a "knock 'em dead strategy." The peerless strategy is codified and approved to much applause. And then NOTHING. (Or at least, not much.) And the pattern is repeated time and again.

To frame my response to this sorry state of affairs, let's step back for a moment some seventy-five years. After Pearl Harbor,

---

* Each chapter begins with a personal reflection that aims to explain how the essential idea first got under my skin, followed by a linear narrative that fleshes out the notion under consideration.

the United States started its pushback trek across the Pacific. That meant hopping from island to island in the middle of nowhere. At home, Admiral Ben Moreell, the chief of the U.S. Navy's Bureau of Yards and Docks and Civil Engineer Corps, also started hopping. In his case, from one construction trade union hall to another. He was recruiting for the navy's new construction battalions, which would build the roads and airstrips and whatever else was needed to support the troops fighting their way across the Pacific.

Admiral Moreell told the union members that he had a job for them, a damned important job. They wouldn't have to worry about saluting, keeping shoes polished until they gleam, and standing at attention on parade grounds. They were being recruited for one and only one thing: to build stuff fast, using whatever equipment in whatever condition was on hand, with no excuses tolerated. And build they did. They completed airstrips carved out of rock that were operational in as little as twelve days from start to finish. Working all night under fire, they made major airfield repairs after the strips had been bombed into a moonscape during the daylight hours. The motto of the U.S. Navy's no-frills builders, or Seabees (for Construction Battalions), was two words: *can do*. The Seabees time and again, month after month, casualty after casualty, worked miracles. No bullshit. No crisp salutes. A bridge. A road. An airstrip. Just build it. *Now*. (John Wayne even starred in a famous 1944 movie titled *The Fighting Seabees*.)

In 1966, twenty years after the end of World War II, I landed on a hot August night in Danang, Vietnam, and debarked from a C-141 aircraft along with a hundred or so of my new Naval Mobile Construction Battalion 9 (NMCB9) mates. I was a twenty-three-year-old U.S. Navy ensign, greener than green. After giving us no more than a half hour to settle in, our commanding officer, a hardened World War II Seabee, gathered the contingent of young officers who'd just arrived and gave us our orders. For the next nine months, he said, we would be responsible for building stuff. Seven days a week. Dawn to dusk. And all night if necessary. Vietnam's four-month monsoon would not be a problem. Bad guys mining the roads we were building would not be a problem. Nothing would be a problem. We were there to build, build, build. The material would never be what we needed. The earthmoving equipment would be inadequate and often on its last legs. No matter. No formalities. No spit, no polish.

Just build stuff.

And build it fast. And build it right. End of story. We saluted and de facto said in unison, "CAN DO."

My two tours and fourteen months in Vietnam were my first management assignments. And they left an indelible impression: Cut the bullshit. Can the excuses. Forget the fancy reports. Get moving now. Get the job done. On this score, nothing has changed in fifty years, including the maddening fact that all too often the strategy *is* inspiring, but the execution mania is largely AWOL.

Lesson 1966.

Lesson 2018.

Forget that glossy strategy.

JUST BUILD IT.
NOW.
CAN DO.

THE EXECUTION NARRATIVE

1.1 EXECUTION IN A NUTSHELL

THE SHOWER CURTAIN AXIOM

Conrad Hilton, at a gala celebrating his remarkable career, was called to the podium and asked, "What were the most important lessons you learned in your long and distinguished career?"

His answer, in full:

> **Remember to tuck the shower curtain inside the bathtub.**

This Hiltonism earns pride of place in *The Excellence Dividend*; in fact, it has been the first slide in virtually every presentation I've given in the last five years. In the hotel business, "location, location, location" (and a great architect) matter; they entice me through the door. But it's the tucked-in shower curtain that brings me back and induces me to recommend the hotel to my friends. And as businesspeople know so well, you typically lose money on the first transaction and rake in the $$$ on #18, #19, #20 and via that vital (and one hopes viral) word of mouth and mouse.

And what holds for hotels holds, well, universally.

1.2 EXECUTION: FIVE TAKES

1.2.1
EXECUTION = STRATEGY

Execution *is* strategy.   —Fred Malek

Fred Malek was my White House/Office of Management and Budget boss in 1973–74. (Prior to public service, he'd been a very successful entrepreneur.) I owe him a lot for passing on his dogmatic, get-it-done approach to life. Every conversation with Fred featured relentless, impatient, even rude questioning about next steps, starting with next steps to be taken today, and tomorrow you'd damn well better be able to report concrete progress.

Maybe we did miss some strategic opportunities as a result of this overwhelming "bias for action," as I later called it, but Fred's team had an almost awe-inspiring reputation for somehow making the impossible actually happen in the labyrinth of a tangle of federal bureaucracies and even in the halls of Congress. While I am an avowed enemy of management by intimidation, I will admit that contemplating giving Fred a "not sure what so-and-so thinks" was enough to, at one point, spur me to take a body-busting, forty-eight-hour round trip from Washington to Bangkok and back so I could provide him with an eyewitness account of our ambassador's reaction to a drug-interdiction policy we were on the verge of taking public.

1.2.2
KEEP IT SIMPLE

Costco figured out the big, simple things and executed with total fanaticism.

— Charles Munger, vice chairman, Berkshire Hathaway

Concise: Simple. Execute. Fanaticism.

Spot-on.

(FYI: Costco's performance has been exceptional.)

1.2.3
JACK WELCH'S MANTRA

In real life, strategy is actually very straightforward. Pick a general direction . . . and implement like hell.

— Jack Welch

Former GE chief executive Welch and *strategic genius* were synonymous in the telling by management gurus. But the conventional narrative was almost total fiction. Welch was an "executionist" of the first order. You got an assignment at GE, and you delivered. Or not. The "or nots" were not long for GE.

Do also note Welch's definition of strategy: "general direction." My response would be, "Amen." A detailed strategy is stuff and nonsense. You head off in that general direction, and as you go the environment shifts shape again and again and then again. Going with the shape-shifting is the key to success, and only rarely, if you are open-minded to opportunities, do you end up anywhere near where you first imagined. And in nine of ten cases, that is a good thing.

(Incidentally, when Welch took the helm at GE, one of his first steps was to slash the headquarters strategic planning staff; the thick staffer-written tome of yore was to be replaced with no more than a page or two drafted by the line executive responsible for implementation.)

1.2.4
AMATEURS AND PROFESSIONALS

Recall from the introduction:

Amateurs talk about strategy. Professionals talk about logistics.   —General Omar Bradley,
Commander of American troops on D-day

Again: AMEN.

General Bradley's axiom always makes me smile/grin/weep/ leap with joy! I'd add that I consider it practical guidance, not a clever saying. The Bradley Axiom has long been bedrock military dogma. Getting the fuel for the tanks to the right place at the right time is Success Key #1 on the battlefield and concern #1 for generals who win battles. The private sector story, big business or small, is precisely the same.

1.2.5
THE THRILL OF GETTING THINGS DONE

Execution is the job of the business leader. . . . The first things I look for [in a job candidate] are energy and enthusiasm for execution. Does the candidate talk about the thrill of getting things done, or does she keep wandering back to strategy or philosophy? Does she detail the obstacles that she has to overcome . . . the roles played by the people assigned to her. —Larry Bossidy and Ram Charan,
Execution: The Discipline of Getting Things Done

> *(Bossidy was a former GE vice chairman and subsequently CEO of AlliedSignal. Charan is a longtime business consultant and author.)*

This is deceptively simple. And to simplify even further: People who talk about execution are more likely than others to spend their time on execution. And vice versa. This is a great story *and* a first-order hiring suggestion. Theoretician? Or pragmatist? People person? Or not? If a candidate does not talk about his or her team with pride and fondness, I advise you to run like hell in the opposite direction.

Strong advice:

Read this quote twice.

Act on it.

Turn it into policy and action.

1.3 NO TURNING BACK: ULYSSES S. GRANT

One of my superstitions had always been when I started to go anywhere or to do anything, not to turn back, or stop, until the thing intended was accomplished.

—Ulysses S. Grant

The art of war is simple enough. Find out where your enemy is. Get at him as soon as you can. Strike at him as hard as you can and as often as you can, and keep moving on.

—Ulysses S. Grant

Grant had an extreme, almost phobic dislike of turning back and retracing his steps. If he set out for somewhere, he would get there somehow, whatever the difficulties that lay in his way. This idiosyncrasy would turn out to be one of the factors that made him such a formidable general. Grant would always, always press on—turning back was not an option for him.

—Michael Korda, *Ulysses S. Grant: The Unlikely Hero*

Grant kept the enemy off balance—his armies were constantly on the move. As author Josiah Bunting said in *Ulysses S. Grant*, the general had "*an almost inhuman disinterest in strategy.*"

SUMMARY
- No interest in grand strategy.
- Do the thing until it is done.
- Do not overcomplicate.
- Do the next thing.

Grant, for whom my admiration knows virtually no bounds, was a man of action amid a sea of procrastinators (such as his predecessor, General George McClellan). Grant's obsession for perpetual forward movement was matched by a reputation for untrammeled relentlessness. In effect, those twin traits, which defined him and made him President Lincoln's favorite general, won the war for the Union. It wasn't always pretty; in fact, at times it was downright ugly, but Grant persevered, never stopped pushing, always kept moving, never turned back as much as an inch, no matter how dire the circumstances, and got the job done.

1.4 INTERVIEWS: *WE* BEATS *I*

Observed closely and quantitatively the use of *I* or *we* in the course of a job interview.
—Leonard Berry and Kent Seltman's chapter 6, "Hiring for Values," in *Management Lessons from Mayo Clinic* (The book is a masterpiece concerning health care practices and in general!)

Such a simple idea, literally counting the number of times a person says *I* or *we* in a hiring interview. But how extraordinarily important. The practitioner in this instance, Mayo Clinic, has differentiated itself in general and in medicine in particular with its century-old (first stated by William Mayo in 1914) abiding emphasis on cooperative medicine. And Mayo's leaders have discovered that, for one thing, using more *we* than *I* in an interview is a pretty darn good indicator of a future proclivity for focusing on teammates rather than oneself. All of this is crucial to execution, the ultimate "we-business."

Note: This I/we metric applies across the board (e.g., interviews of star M.D.s seeking a position at Mayo)!

I am hundreds of times better here [than in my prior hospital assignment] because of the support system. It's like you are working in an organism; you are not a single cell when you are out there practicing.
—Dr. Nina Schwenk, in chapter 3, "Practicing Team Medicine," from Leonard Berry and Kent Seltman,
Management Lessons from Mayo Clinic

One hundred times better if you are an unyielding literalist, doubtless exaggerated, but in any case one Damn Big Deal—and one Damn Big Endorsement of Dr. Mayo's "cooperative medicine" (alas, AWOL in most hospitals in 2018).

1.5 WORDS FROM THE MASTER: PETER DRUCKER ON TRUE "TOP MANAGEMENT"

The head of one of the large management consulting firms asks, "And what do you do that justifies your being on the payroll?" The great majority answer, "I run the accounting department," or "I am in charge of the sales force." . . . Only a few say, "It's my job to give our managers the information they need to make the right decisions," or "I am responsible for finding out what products the customer will want tomorrow." The man who stresses his downward authority

is a subordinate no matter how exalted his rank or title. But the man who focuses on contributions and who takes responsibility for results, no matter how junior, is in the most literal sense of the phrase, "top management." He holds himself responsible for the performance of the whole.

—Peter Drucker

Attitude and sense of responsibility matters *way* more than rank. It is a profoundly important comment; in fact, it's my favorite Druckerism. (And that's saying something since I am a pretty good student of Drucker.) I am particularly keen on the notion that focusing on contributions and results vaults even the lowest-level manager into top management in Mr. Drucker's assessment.

1.6 FIXING EXECUTION ROADBLOCK #1

1.6.1
CROSS-FUNCTIONAL EXCELLENCE/XFX

Poor cross-functional coordination and communication IS THE PRINCIPAL ELEMENT IN THE DELAY OF EVERYTHING.

A dogmatic statement, to be sure, but after my fifty years of practice and observation, said with certainty. Hence, it is axiomatic that the pursuit of "XFX"/Cross Functional Excellence is of surpassing importance:

I fervently believe that in most any organization of, say, more than a dozen people, the #1 issue that causes delays, implementation failures in general, employee angst, and customer ire is failures of cross-functional communication and integration.

IMPORTANT ADDENDA I: New-style organization forms, regardless of their fancy monikers and supporting software architecture, have not and will not come within a mile of eliminating functional units like finance or engineering. Believe it. In fact, the new software can make things worse—attendant depersonalization ("Let the software do it") is the kiss of death when it comes to truly value-adding cross-functional coordination.

IMPORTANT ADDENDA II: The commonplace argument, circa 2018, is that fluid, project-team-driven enterprises of tomorrow will eliminate the need for departments. While I dislike the term *department* (and prefer internal professional service firm/ PSF—see section 12.2.9), I believe the opposite is true. Enterprises today are, appropriately, in relentless pursuit of increasing intellectual property. To a significant extent, that is dependent upon collections of specialized talent—another term for *department* or *PSF*.

It is, alas, fair to say that our INTERNAL barriers, not our competitors' cleverness, are the principal impediment to effective execution and, hence, competitiveness. I suspect you'd mostly agree with that in a theoretical way. But do you see that a daily obsession with achieving cross-functional EXCELLENCE/XFX is what I call, with no hyperbole, *SO1/Strategic Opportunity #1*? I'd add that achieving XFX is not so much about dealing with negatives (fixing coordination problems) as it is about creating a basis for sustainable competitive advantage—the ultimate positive. (To perhaps unnecessarily repeat: XFX is *not* primarily about "Let's stop this damn feuding between purchasing and finance"; the goal *is* to be able to say, "Purchasing and finance teams supporting one another are improving operational performance and profitability alike through innovation and spirited, coordinated execution.")

1.6.2
AND IF XFX IS SUCH A PEERLESS OPPORTUNITY, WHERE DO YOU START?

Simple: NEVER WASTE A LUNCH!

Lunch = Cross-Functional Friction Reduction Agent #1

Lunch?
Strategic importance?
Yes!

IMPLICATION/TASK: Initiate a Formal Strategic LDP/Lunch Diversification Program

ACTION ITEM/PERCENTAGE OF XF LUNCHES: Measure your number of cross-functional lunches (lunches with people outside your unit) monthly! Make that measurement part of everyone's formal evaluations!

Exceptions notwithstanding (see commentary above), superior systems software *can* abet cross-functional coordination. But XFX/Cross-Functional Excellence is primarily a "people/relationship thing." Lunch is a big part of a set of what I call "Cross-Functional Social Accelerators." That is, winning the game is a lot more about soft/social/cultural factors than it is about upping software investment by, say, $5 million.

1.6.3
XFX = PERSONAL

Personal relationships are the fertile soil from which all advancement, all success, all achievement in real life grow.
                    —Ben Stein, investment/economics guru

True in 1718, 1818, 1918, 2018.

(And so often treated as catch-as-catch-can rather than the by-product of care and sustained—and, yes, even calculated—effort.)

XFX = Personal Relationships

1.6.4
XFX IS SOCIAL/THE SOCIAL ACCELERATORS UNDERPINNING XFX

Lunch. Personal relationships. XFX is, was, and will be a *social* affair. And in that spirit, I offer here a list of what I call *social accelerators*—a set of "soft" ideas that, taken together, would go a long, long way down the path to achieving long-lasting cross-functional excellence. To wit:

1. **EVERYONE'S JOB #1:** Make friends in other functions!
2. Do lunch with people in other functions frequently!
3. Religiously invite counterparts in other functions to your team meetings, and actively include them in your discussions. Ask them to present cool stuff from their world to your group. (Useful. Mark of respect.)

4. Proactively seek examples of tiny acts of XFX to acknowledge privately and publicly.

5. Present counterparts in other functions awards for service to your group—tiny awards at least weekly and an annual all-star supporters banquet.

6. When someone in another function asks for assistance, respond with *more* alacrity than you would if it were the person in the cubicle next to yours or even more than you would for an external customer.

7. **DO NOT BAD-MOUTH** "the damned accountants," "the bloody HR guy." Ever.

8. Establish "adhocracy" as SOP. Small XF teams should be formed on the spot to deal with an urgent issue.

9. Within days of coming aboard, the newbie should be running some bit of a bit of a bit project, working with people from other functions. Hence, working together becomes as natural as breathing.

10. Try your darnedest to arrange a temporary assignment for each of your people somewhere in the finance department. (Get to know the "numbers people"—perhaps career advice tip #1.)

11. "Get 'em out with the customer." Give everyone more or less regular physical customer-facing experiences. Such experiences are peerless motivators; one gets to literally see the impact of one's work.

12. Everyone, starting with the receptionist, should have a XF rating component in his or her evaluation. *XFX Performance* should be among the Top 3 items in *all* managerial evaluations.

13. Every unit should be formally evaluated by other func-
    tions concerning its usefulness and effectiveness and
    value added to the enterprise as a whole.
14. Demand sustained XF experience for, especially, senior
    jobs. For example, the U.S. military requires all would-
    be generals and admirals to have served a full tour of
    duty in a job whose only goals were cross-functional
    achievements.
15. *Excellence!* There is a sublime state of XF Excellence.
    Talk it up constantly. Pursue it. Aspire to nothing less.

1.6.5
XFX: SUGGESTED ADDITION TO STATEMENT OF CORE VALUES

If the importance of XFX is as I suggest, then it is a candidate for
membership in the stratosphere, part of no less than the set of
Enterprise Core Values. Consider:

> **We will not rest until seamless cross-functional integration/communication has become a primary source of value added. EXCELLENCE in cross-functional integration shall become a daily operational passion for 100 percent of us.**

REPEAT: The whole point here is that XFX is almost surely
the **#1** opportunity for strategic differentiation. While many

might agree with that statement, in our moment-to-moment affairs, XFX is not so often visibly and perpetually at the top of *every* agenda. I argue here for no less than . . .

VISIBLE.
CONSTANT.
MEASURABLE.
OBSESSION.

1.7

1.7.1
EXECUTION/PARTING THOUGHTS I: MEASURABLE TIME SPENT ON HOW-TOS

Execution is a SYSTEMATIC PROCESS of rigorously discussing hows and whats, questioning, tenaciously following through, and ensuring accountability.
—Larry Bossidy and Ram Charan, *Execution*

One implication: Will, for example, the next presentation you give allot more time to implementing than to the analysis of the problem? (Measure this!)

1.7.2
EXECUTION/PARTING THOUGHTS II: REVEL IN THE POLITICS

Implementation of anything is all about politics. If you don't like politics, forget about leading anything of any size at any time. *Politics* is not a dirty word about a dirty topic. "Politics," in the words of Otto von Bismarck, "is the art of the possible, the attainable."

The day I put this section together, I happened to chat with a friend who runs an exceptionally successful tech-based company in LA. Customers include the hyper-hard-nosed Walt Disney Company. He's not a kid by a long shot, and I asked him why he kept going; he makes two cross-country round trips from the East Coast each month. He said he loved the challenge, driven by the changing tech scene, of staying ahead of the game. Then he surprised me by adding, "You know, Tom, the fact is that I really enjoy the back-and-forth with our clients, and I like putting things together and figuring out how to wiggle my way through their internal politics."

In other words, he gets off on the politics of getting his thing done.

Sound absurd? Not at all to me. Many of the most successful folks I know get a buzz from the fray; putting the human/political puzzle together is their true talent. Consider this long and hard in your promotion decisions in particular: Does she or he enjoy the great game of getting things done in messy political environments? Or does she or he bitch and moan that "every damn thing is political around here"?

Corollary: In the Real World of Execution . . .

EQ >>> IQ.

That is, the EQ (emotional intelligence quotient) is more important to mastering the execution process than the standard IQ (intelligence quotient). This is obviously not to dismiss the book-learning flavor of intelligence, but which is to say that all effective leadership is primarily about feeling your way through the people-and-politics puzzle.

1.7.3
EXECUTION/PARTING THOUGHTS III: TALK THE TALK

The Iron Law of Execution

When you talk all the time about execution, it's likely to happen. When you don't, it doesn't.

Q: "Could it be this simple?"
A: "To a significant degree, yes."

FYI: This in fact translates into a practical action item and starts today. Monitor and assess your conversations and meetings: Is the execution/implementation/who-what-when-next-milestones discussion front and center and dominant and committed to paper and reiterated more or less immediately in follow-up written communications?

1.7.4
EXECUTION/PARTING THOUGHTS IV:
ONE FOR THE AGES

This vignette, from an NPR broadcast, was posted on my blog, tompeters.com:

A man approached J. P. Morgan, held up an envelope, and said, "Sir, in my hand I hold a guaranteed formula for success, which I will gladly sell you for $25,000."

"Sir," J. P. Morgan replied, "I do not know what is in the envelope; however, if you show me, and I like it, I give you my word as a gentleman that I will pay you what you ask."

The man agreed to the terms and handed over the envelope. J. P. Morgan opened it and extracted a single sheet of paper. He gave it one look, a mere glance, then handed the piece of paper back to the gent.

And paid him the agreed-upon $25,000.

On the paper . . .

1. Every morning, write a list of the things that need to be done that day.
2. Do them.

1.7.5
EXECUTION/PARTING THOUGHTS V:
VERY LITTLE = VERY BIG

For want of a nail, the shoe was lost,
For want of a shoe, the horse was lost,
For want of a horse, the rider was lost,

For want of a rider, the message was lost,
For want of a message, the battle was lost,
For want of a battle, the war was lost,
For want of a war, the kingdom fell,
And all for the want of a nail.

—Fourteenth-century proverb

(Shades of Conrad Hilton, who launched this chapter with tucked-in shower curtains, eh?)

SECTION II
EXCELLENCE

2 EXCELLENCE IS THE NEXT FIVE MINUTES

MY STORY

CALL IT "THE SAGA OF THE GOOD FRIDAY COMPUTER CRASH," OR "BALLET COMES TO BUSINESS."

It was Easter week 1978. The main computer in the San Francisco office of McKinsey & Co., where I worked as a consultant, chose to crash thirty-six hours before our managing director was scheduled to give a report on an important project to the top team at Dart Industries in Los Angeles.

With the computer down, his team was unable to prepare the sort of presentation he wished to make. I, meanwhile, was working frantically and independently on a project commissioned by the powers that be in the firm's New York headquarters. Though I was psyched by the project, it had the uninspiring title of

"Improving Organizational Effectiveness." John Larson (the S. F. McKinsey boss) came to me in desperation (Dart was a core client) and said, in effect, "*Can you put something short but somewhat sweet together and fob it off on Dart and save my ass?*"

"*Sure*," I said in a flash; one dreams of saving one's boss's ass, right?

The time frame was more or less instant, and I was desperate to get on with it immediately. However, my wife and I had tickets for the San Francisco Ballet the night the assignment landed in my lap. So wishing to avoid yet another fight over "once again missing something that matters to me," I reluctantly traipsed off to the opera house, where the ballet company performed. Though a ballet novice and stressed to the breaking point, I was mesmerized by the beauty and grace of the performance.

I got home about 10:30 p.m. and, in a daze, dutifully went to my home office and started pulling material together for Dart. I honestly have no idea what next transpired, but I do know, Bic pen in hand, the emotion stirred by the glory of the ballet in my psyche, I crafted a draft cover page with but one word, in all capital letters: EXCELLENCE.

You see, I got off on this stuff about organizations that don't work very well and what we might do about it; it was the topic of my then recently completed (1977) Stanford business school Ph.D. thesis. And I think that what went through my mind was something like this: "Hey, we spend the lion's share of our days—our lives, actually—in organizations. What if that organizational experience was an upper instead of a downer (polls show that about 30 percent of people enjoy their job)?" Mind-blowing ballet in front of mind, my reasoning went:

Ballet is an organized human endeavor that produces beauty and grace and, at its best, excellence and blows the minds of its customers. Why the heck can't life at work mimic ballet? Why must "amazing performance" be the exclusive provenance of ballet companies and football teams and the likes of an MIT science lab but not the twenty-four-person purchasing department?

That is . . .

Why can't *excellence* and *business* be uttered in the same sentence?

Absurd question!

(In retrospect.)

Of course they can!

So on Good Friday 1978, I gave my presentation. It was well received, and my boss was happy. I'm not going to imply that one heard the sounds of angels playing harps in Dart's LA boardroom. But I *will* tell you that somehow a switch had been tripped in *my* head. Yup, "*excellent business organization*" need not be an oxymoron.

The business-can-be-EXCELLENT notion percolated for years and influenced my extensive McKinsey research. Eventually, it made the cover of Bob Waterman's and my 1982 book, *In Search of Excellence: Lessons from America's Best-Run Companies.* To make a long story very short, a lot of people bought the book. There were numerous reasons for that, including good timing; American business was hurting, and businesspeople were tired of hearing from bestselling books like *The Art of Japanese Management* that the only answer was to copy the Japanese. (For God's sake, at that time, 1982, virtually all the CEOs' dads had fought in World War II.) However, I'm convinced that one other very big reason for our success was our decision to pair those two words, *business* and *excellence*.

Business (and work) can be exciting.
Business (and work) can be an upper.
Business (and work) can be EXCELLENT.

My *passion for excellence*—the title of my second book, in 1985, with Nancy Austin—has remained unabated for forty years. You'll see several manifestations thereof in this chapter. There is no linear plotline that ends with an aha moment. Instead, I offer fourteen snapshots of excellence, some of the best ways I've found of describing enterprise—and, for that matter, individual behavior—at its tip-top (excellent!) best.

(FYI: In 1999, a book was published by AMACOM, titled *The 75 Greatest Management Decisions Ever Made*, featuring Julius Caesar, Ted Turner, Henry Ford, Warren Buffett, and others of their ilk. Number forty-eight on the list, to my astonishment, was the spur-of-the-moment decision by John Larson to ask me to give a presentation to Dart Industries on Good Friday 1978: Welcome excellence to the world of business!)

THE EXCELLENCE NARRATIVE

2.1

2.1.1
EXCELLENCE IN MANAGEMENT IS
A GRAND HUMAN ACHIEVEMENT

Management as conventionally perceived is a dreary, mechanical, constrained word. Consider, please, a more encompassing, more accurate, more fulfilling definition:

Management *is the arrangement and animation of human affairs in pursuit of desired and societally worthy outcomes.*

Management is not about Theory X versus Theory Y, "top down" versus "bottom up." Management is about the essence of human behavior, how we fundamentally arrange our collective efforts in order to survive, adapt, and, one hopes, thrive and achieve excellence individually and organizationally.

Why start the excellence chapter with this riff? Odd as it may sound, I'm attempting to stress the abiding importance of and moral and artistic nature of management—that is, to make it clear that in fact good management and EXCELLENCE in management *are* the pinnacles of human achievement (i.e., accomplishing remarkable and worthy things through development of one's fellow humans). Sound grand? Sure, but I'd really like you, boss, to think about your next day at the office as an opportunity to pursue no less than excellence in the arrangement of human affairs, thus making your employees and the world a bit better off. It also turns out to be the best way to grow, create relatively stable jobs, and turn a profit.

2.1.2
EXCELLENCE. OR NOT.

WHAT IS MANAGEMENT TO YOU? YOUR CALL . . .

MANAGING: AS A PAIN IN THE ASS. Somebody's got to do it: punching bag for higher-ups on one end, grouchy employees on the other; blame

management if things go wrong, big bosses abscond with the credit if things go right.

MANAGING: AS THE PINNACLE OF HUMAN ACHIEVEMENT. The greatest life opportunity one can have; mid- to long-term success is no more and no less than a function of one's dedication to and effectiveness at helping team members grow and flourish as individuals and as contributing members to an energetic, self-renewing organization dedicated to the relentless pursuit of excellence.

Picking up from the prior section, I am aware that "pinnacle of human achievement" sounds quite grand. In fact, it *is* quite grand. And I mean it. My goal is to suggest that a management job, every management job, is anything but humdrum. It is a peerless opportunity to dramatically change the life trajectory of every employee in your charge and also to provide services of the greatest value imaginable to your customers and your community.

I got into a bit of a spat over this; well, to be honest, it was my intention. I said in a presentation, with numerous health care personnel in attendance, that a manager could de facto save more lives than a surgeon. I am not diminishing the lifesaving acts of a surgeon. But over the course of a managerial career, one can alter, sometimes dramatically, the life direction of thousands upon thousands of people. You can, in short, provide growth opportunities that can turn night into day for an extraordinary number of individuals.

I intend through this assertion to toss the ball squarely into your arms. The opportunity is there—"pinnacle of human achievement"—for the taking.

Corroboration: In an Oscar acceptance speech, the late director Robert Altman said:

> **The role of the director is to create a space where the actors and actresses can become more than they have ever been before, more than they've dreamed of being.**

Such a view squares with mine almost word for word. Please reread. Pause. Reflect. I'd be willing to assign the word *profound* to Mr. Altman's "more than they've dreamed of being."

2.2 EXCELLENCE: MANAGEMENT IS A LIBERAL ART

The discussion immediately above suggests that pursuing excellence in management is ultimately a humanistic endeavor. Such a descriptor is, alas, hardly what pops to mind when one thinks of management education, the MBA in particular.

2.2.1
LIBERALLY SUCCESSFUL: A TWO-DECADE REPORT CARD

Henry Mintzberg knows few if any peers in his decades-long effort to understand the sources of organization effectiveness. Among other things, in his masterpiece, *Managers Not MBAs: A Hard*

Look at the Soft Practice of Managing and Management Development, Mintzberg cites research that counters much of conventional wisdom—that is, over a two-decade period, the value of the MBA is eclipsed by the value of a liberal arts education.

AT GRADUATION: Business and professional degree holders in general (MBAs, engineers, lawyers, etc.) have higher interview and hire rates and higher starting salaries than new liberal arts grads.

YEAR TWENTY: By year twenty, liberal arts grads have risen further than their biz- and professional-degree-holder peers. At one giant tech firm, 43 percent of liberal arts grads had made it to upper-middle management compared to 32 percent of engineering grads. At one giant financial services firm, 60 percent of the worst managers, according to company evaluations, had MBAs, while 60 percent of the best had only BAs.

I recall my Ph.D. adviser at Stanford once saying, "Tom, when our students are getting their MBAs, all they want is 'more finance,' 'more marketing.' When they come back for executive courses fifteen years later, their goal is to get help on 'the people part' and organization effectiveness." It is presumably in such arenas that the liberal arts majors excel, thanks to their more catholic background, from the start, hence the results reported above.

(Mintzberg in fact suggests that a *philosophy degree* is the best prep for business leadership, tongue nowhere near cheek. I, for one, think he's got a damn good point.)

2.2.2
PETER DRUCKER'S ASSESSMENT OF HIS MOST IMPORTANT CONTRIBUTION: MANAGEMENT AS A LIBERAL ART

At a seminar in 1999, the moderator asked Peter Drucker, generally considered the father of modern management thinking, what he thought was his most important contribution to the field of management. Drucker replied:

> **I focused this discipline on people and power; on values, structure, and constitution; and above all, on responsibilities—that is, I focused the discipline of management on management as a truly liberal art.**

I think that is no less than a staggering pronouncement. Typical MBA programs focus on quantitative analytics, which is what their clients (students) ask for. The "soft stuff"—people practices, organizational arrangements—are typically seen by those students as an annoying distraction from the main event.

In recent years, consistent with Drucker's view, I have focused on shifting the MBA from **Master of Business Administration** to **Master of Business Arts**. I can hardly claim any great success, but in several instances I have at least ignited some soul searching on the part of business school deans and faculties.

2.3 EXCELLENCE: ENTERPRISE RESPONSIBILITY—INCREASE THE SUM TOTAL OF HUMAN WELL-BEING

In *Good Business*, Mihaly Csikszentmihalyi (best known for his book *Flow: The Psychology of Optimal Experience*) argues persuasively that business has become the center of society. As such, an obligation to community is front and center. Business as societal bedrock, per Csikszentmihalyi, has the **"responsibility to increase the sum of human well-being."**

Business is not "part of the community." In terms of how adults collectively spend their waking hours, business *is* the community. And businesses and those in them should act accordingly. The really good news (and I repeat myself and will unabashedly continue to repeat myself): Community-mindedness writ large is a great way (arguably the best way) to have a spirited, committed, customer-centric workforce and, ultimately, increase (maximize?) innovation, growth, and profitability.

The Excellence Dividend is directly predicated on Csikszentmihalyi's idea. In the face of the likely dislocations steaming toward us, business's moral role relative to its employees and community moves front and center; it should not and cannot be evaded.

2.4 EXCELLENCE: WORK RECONSIDERED. WHY NOT JOY?

It may sound radical, unconventional, and bordering on being a crazy business idea. However—as ridiculous as it

sounds—joy is the core belief of our workplace. Joy is the reason my company, Menlo Innovations, a customer software design and development firm in Ann Arbor, Michigan, exists. It defines what we do and how we do it. It is the single shared belief of our entire team.

—Richard Sheridan, *Joy, Inc.: How We Built a Workplace People Love*

Could there be a tougher or more competitive business than systems software? No! Yet Menlo Innovations founder Richard Sheridan's weapon of choice for successfully competing in this bare-knuckles arena is **JOY**.

Talk about stretching the imagination and laying down an exhilarating challenge! FYI: Menlo's performance is sterling.

"Empower" workers.

Fine.

"Engage" workers.

Fine.

Create "team spirit."

Fine.

Fine. Fine. Fine. Topics near and dear to my heart for many a decade. But Mr. Sheridan upped the ante by many a notch . . .

Joy is the reason my company exists.

It's easy to read this, give it a nod, and move on. I hope you don't do that. I hope you pause and think, *What if . . . maybe it's not over the top. Hmmm . . . I'll think on it, I'll talk to the team about it. Hey, it would be cool. Well, the guy (Richard Sheridan) is pulling it off in the most unlikely context.* Would you please do that, think about it? As a personal favor to me and Mr. Sheridan?

2.5

2.5.1
EXCELLENCE: ANYWHERE/EVERYWHERE

Enterprise (*at its best*):

An emotional, vital, innovative, joyful, creative, entrepreneurial endeavor that elicits maximum concerted human potential in the wholehearted pursuit of EXCELLENCE in service to others (e.g., employees, customers, suppliers, communities, owners, temporary partners).

I'm at the end of the world—Siberia. My typically exuberant, American-flavor message may miss the mark by a country mile or ten or ten thousand. But I decide not to pull any punches, and, absurd as it sounds, the challenging, optimistic statement above more or less magically emerged from my jet-lagged mind.

Is the statement above a common state of affairs in Siberia or, for that matter, anywhere else? Of course it's not. But, in the spirit of Richard Sheridan—joy as aspiration—I must ask . . .

WHY NOT?

Before dismissing this as pie in the sky and moving on, consider each of these words:

- *Emotional*
- *Vital*
- *Innovative*
- *Joyful*
- *Creative*
- *Entrepreneurial*
- *Excellent*

And then consider their opposites. Do we want an **un**emotional, **joyless**, **un**creative, **un**-excellent workplace? Of course not. So, I say again:

WHY NOT?

Why not shoot for the moon?

Sadly, in my experience, the average manager or enterprise boss doesn't even consider creating an *emotional, vital, innovative, joyful, creative, entrepreneurial, excellent* environment; she or he is often as not too busy focusing on cost-cutting or short-term "metrics" to let her or his imagination run wild.

So.
Please.
Today.
This morning.
Take a deep breath.
Let your imagination soar!

2.5.2
EXCELLENCE: ANYWHERE. EVERYWHERE. A FOOD TRUCK IN BRATTLEBORO, VERMONT.

Excellence may well be Silicon Valley's top coders, Madison Avenue's renowned fashion retailers, a soul-rending balletic performance, and yes, you may even find it in Siberia.

But I unapologetically believe **excellence** can be just as manifest in a food truck in Brattleboro, Vermont.

To wit, courtesy of the summer 2017 edition of *SO Vermont Arts & Living* . . .

SOUTHERN VERMONT'S TOP 10 FOOD TRUCKS
There's something about ordering your menu selection from a sandwich board, watching the chef prepare your meal, and enjoying it picnic-style in nature. . . .

- Andrzej's Polish Kitchen (Brattleboro, Vermont: "Former New York City Russian Tea Room chef Andrzej Mikijaniec cooks the traditional food of his homeland at his stand.")
- Bert's Chuck Wagon
- Dosa Kitchen
- Ro's Petite Fête
- Tito's Taqueria ("Tito Garza learned to cook authentic Mexican food from his grandmother . . .")
- Jamaican Jewelz (Westminster, Vermont: Caribbean chef Julian "Jewelz" Perkins)
- Mio Bistro (Dorset, Vermont: "A favorite is the crab and corn chowder. 'We sell out of it.'")
- Smokin' Bowls (Bellows Falls, Vermont: "Meats, which

come from Ephraim Farm in Springfield, are smoked in a
kitchen a few miles away and go into the popular pulled
pork sandwich . . .")

- Taste of Thai, Brattleboro
- Two Neanderthals Smokin' BBQ

Excellence.
Food truck.
Brattleboro, Vermont.
Westminster, Vermont
Dorset, Vermont
Why not?

2.6

2.6.1
EXCELLENCE: "OF SERVICE"

Organizations exist to SERVE.
PERIOD.
LEADERS LIVE TO SERVE.
PERIOD.
SERVICE is a beautiful word.
SERVICE is character, community, commitment.
  (And profit.)
SERVICE is *not* "Wow."
SERVICE is *not* "raving fans."
SERVICE is *not* "a great experience."
Service *is* "just" that—SERVICE.

2.6.2
SERVICE IS THE HIGHEST HUMAN CALLING

This all-powerful idea is directly derived from Robert Greenleaf's extraordinary book *Servant Leadership*.

Here are two "exam questions" that Greenleaf urges leaders to ask concerning the people on their team:

1. Do those served grow as persons?
2. Do they, while being served, become healthier, wiser, freer, more autonomous, more likely themselves to become servants?

Well?

Tough test, eh?

And if you buy my act and the logic of this book in general, a self-test that must be performed . . . daily.

(Of course I still love the word and notion of, say, "Wow!" But the idea here is to ask you to pause and reflect on this beautiful word in its purest sense: SERVICE. I ask you to reflect a lot in this chapter. That is purposeful.

Excellence is not a metric. It is a state of mind, a way of being—the marvel and magic of the San Francisco Ballet. The animating idea powering this book is excellence-as-the-best-antidote-to-the-tech-tsunami. It is, as I see it, the best antidote because it is ultimately human, spiritual, know-it-when-I-see-it. So, yes, the clarion call of this chapter is, in a word, REFLECT.)

2.7

2.7.1
EXCELLENCE = THE NEXT FIVE MINUTES

EXCELLENCE is *not* a long-term aspiration.
EXCELLENCE *is* the ultimate short-term strategy.
EXCELLENCE *IS* THE NEXT FIVE MINUTES.
(Or not.)

EXCELLENCE is your next conversation.
Or not.
EXCELLENCE is your next meeting.
Or not.
EXCELLENCE is shutting up and listening—really listening.
Or not.
EXCELLENCE is your next customer contact.
Or not.
EXCELLENCE is saying "Thank you" for something "small."
Or not.
EXCELLENCE is the next time you shoulder responsibility and apologize.
Or not.
EXCELLENCE is pulling out all the stops at warp speed to respond to a screwup.
Or not.
EXCELLENCE is the flowers you brought to work today.
Or not.
EXCELLENCE is lending a hand to an "outsider" who's fallen behind schedule.

Or not.

EXCELLENCE is bothering to learn the way folks in finance (or IS or HR) think.

Or not.

EXCELLENCE is waaay "over"-preparing for a three-minute presentation.

Or not.

EXCELLENCE is turning "insignificant" tasks into models of EXCELLENCE.

Or not.

Excellence is conventionally—in fact, almost without fail—seen as a long-term aspiration. I disagree. Vehemently disagree. Excellence is not a destination at which you arrive on a glorious sunny day after years of brutally hard work.

Excellence is a way of life that sustains us and inspires us day in and day out, minute in and minute out. There is no "long term." There is only the way we act when we step out into the corridor after a meeting—or, yes, the quality of your next four-line e-mail.

(Yes, damn it, the quality of that next e-mail. Leaders are always "onstage" [always = always = always], and even the tiniest manifestation of leader behavior reinforces—or diminishes—the commitment of the enterprise as a whole to excellence. You can call me a nutcase if you wish, but I insist that lousy grammar, poor word choice, carelessness of any sort is a direct reflection of the level of your commitment to excellence.)

The manifestation of excellence—or not—in our moment-to-moment behavior is the bedrock beneath the bedrock.

2.7.2
EXCELLENCE = ONE-MINUTE EXCELLENCE

A tale is told about the fabled IBM founding chairman Thomas Watson:

"Mr. Watson, how long does it take to achieve excellence?"
Watson: "One minute. You make up your mind to never again consciously do something that is less than excellent."

Hence, if you are so inclined, your journey toward excellence can begin . . .

IN THE NEXT SIXTY SECONDS.

2.7.3
EXCELLENCE = *LESS* THAN A MINUTE

Rance Crain of *Advertising Age* interviewed Linda Kaplan Thaler, founder of the ad agency Kaplan Thaler, upon her induction into the Advertising Hall of Fame:

Linda said the reason her agency grew so fast was because "We never concentrated one minute on the future. We always focused on what can we do today. I always tell people don't spend one second thinking about a vision, forget about it. Don't dream your way to success. . . . We never thought about becoming too big or hugely successful, we just did the best we could every day."

Forget the future—not worth even a minute.

Forget "vision"—not worth even a second.

Forget "dreams."

Do the best you can right now.

(Please consider.)

2.8 EXCELLENCE: BIGGEST LIFE DECISION!

Everything can be taken from a man but one thing: the last of the human freedoms—to choose one's attitude in any given set of circumstances, to choose one's own way.

—Viktor Frankl, one of the world's greatest psychologists and a survivor of a Nazi concentration camp

Message: You can take any damned attitude you choose to work today!

In fact, choosing your attitude this morning is your . . .

Biggest
Life
Decision!

This is in no way an exaggeration**!**

And this is another golden opportunity to express my commitment to excellence-as-short-term-ism. Something so seemingly simple as walking into the office with a smile can launch the entire day in a positive direction. One *more* time: This is not an exaggeration.

Of course, there's actually nothing simple about it. If you have a thousand items on your plate—the norm for most bosses—then bucking yourself up to smile and exchange a few pleasantries is not easy or automatic. But I beg you to think explicitly about it and act accordingly. Working on that "opening smile" may be the most important investment you make today.

2.9

2.9.1
EXCELLENCE: PROFIT IS DERIVATIVE

OUR MISSION
To develop and manage *talent*
To apply that talent throughout the world for the benefit
   of clients
To do so in partnership
To do so with profit.
    —WPP, the giant UK-based marketing services firm

Generally, I cringe when confronted with a mission statement—boilerplate invented by the few (top management) at a boozy off-site, foisted on the many (ten or ten thousand employees)—and invariably honored in the breech.

However, the WPP mission statement passes my muster. Here's why . . .

Profit *damn well* matters!

But . . .

Profit is DERIVATIVE.

And, first and foremost, the sine qua non, profit is derived through a primary and wholesale and continuous commitment to develop **TALENT.**

The WPP recitation inspired me to take a crack at this. Herewith my proposed mission statement—once more, fifty years in the making:

PEOPLE first.
TRY IT now.
LISTEN aggressively.
WOW or bust.
EXCELLENCE always.

2.9.2
EXCELLENCE: MORE THAN SHAREHOLDER VALUE

"Maximize shareholder value as Unforsakeable Commandment"?

Sez who?

Jack Welch! That's who!

Time and time and time again.

The aim was the centerpiece of his fabled twenty-year reign at GE.

But hold on . . .

Here's Welch, after retiring from GE, in the *Financial Times*:

> **On the face of it, shareholder value is the dumbest idea in the world. Shareholder value is a result, not**

a strategy. . . . Your main constituencies are your employees, your customers, and your products.

Yes, *the* Jack Welch, for so many years Vehement/Uncompromising Spokesman #1 for the Absolute Primacy of Shareholder Value Maximization.

Hmmm . . .

While increasing shareholder value is indeed an honorable end and is indeed demanded by some shareholders, shareholder value maximization at all costs is at the very least questionable as a be-all and end-all.

And, as it turns out, certainly not a legal requisite.

Lynn Stout is a professor of corporate and business law at the Cornell Law School.

She cuts to the chase in her short-but-very-sweet book *The Shareholder Value Myth: How Putting Shareholders First Harms Investors, Corporations, and the Public*:

The notion that corporate law requires directors, executives, and employees to maximize shareholder wealth simply isn't true. There is no solid legal support for the claim that directors and executives in U.S. public corporations have an enforceable legal duty to maximize shareholder wealth. THE IDEA IS FABLE.

Oddly, soon after reading Professor Stout's book, I gave a presentation to the leadership team of a major ($10 billion+), publicly traded electronic components company. With the book very much at top of mind, I was at one point in conversation with the CEO and mentioned Professor Stout's assertion. His response went like this:

> **I told my board that if they want to get the share price up 50 percent in the next twelve to eighteen months, I could do it without raising a sweat. *But it would destroy the long-term prospects of the company*. I made it clear I wouldn't tread that path and they'd need to find someone else to do the job.**

Harvard Business School Dean Nitin Nohria and Rakesh Khurana get to the same point in an article in the *Harvard Business Review* titled "It's Time to Make Management a True Profession." It includes this passage:

> **Managers have lost legitimacy over the past decade in the face of widespread institutional breakdown of trust and self-policing in business. To regain society's trust, we believe that business leaders must embrace a way of looking at their role that goes beyond their responsibility to the shareholder to include a civic and personal commitment to their duty as institutional custodians. In other words, it is time that management finally became a profession.**

The idea of management as an encompassing profession is intriguing. More intriguing, to me at least, is the implication that management in its current incarnation is *not* a broad-based profession. I would assume Nohria's response would be something like "Today's top managers are simply shareholder value maximization mechanics. There is more to life."

(Suddenly, in mid-2017, this topic caught fire. Duff McDonald came down on the Harvard Business School like a ton of bricks with his 657-page opus, *The Golden Passport: Harvard Business School, the Limits of Capitalism, and the Moral Failure of the MBA Elite.* He argued that the HBS was started for the right reasons—to improve the quality of management in general. But in the 1970s, it went off the rails when the idea that business chiefs should ignore all but shareholder value took hold at the HBS and effectively suppressed other aims. The world in general, McDonald argues, suffered as a result.

At the same time McDonald's book appeared, the business school's in-house journal, the *Harvard Business Review*, jumped into the fray as well with a scathing article by perhaps its most prominent professor, Joseph Bower, titled, "The Error at the Heart of Corporate Leadership"—that error is, per professor Bower, the presumed duty to maximize shareholder value.

What's the upshot of all this? Only time will tell; but, alas, I'm afraid I'd bet on the shareholder value maximizers holding their own—and along the way the lion's share of our giant firms, with their innovation funds minimized by the short-term cost cutters and tech-firsters, will become less and less able to deal with the revolutionary forces heading our way. Which in turn is why I'd put *my* money on SMEs/small- and medium-sized enterprises—see chapter 4.)

2.9.3
EXCELLENCE: ENOUGH!

The spirit of "more than shareholder value" is captured by Vanguard Funds founder Jack Bogle in the introduction to his refreshing book *Enough:*

At a party given by a billionaire on Shelter Island, Kurt Vonnegut informs his pal, Joseph Heller, that their host, a hedge fund manager, had made more money in a single day than Heller had earned from his wildly popular novel *Catch-22* over its whole history. Heller responds, "Yes, but I have something he will never have . . . ENOUGH."

To get a flavor of Bogle's book, one need do no more than peruse the chapter titles:

"Too Much Cost, Not Enough Value"

"Too Much Speculation, Not Enough Investment"

"Too Much Complexity, Not Enough Simplicity"

"Too Much Counting, Not Enough Trust"

"Too Much Business Conduct, Not Enough Professional Conduct"

"Too Much Salesmanship, Not Enough Stewardship"

"Too Much Focus on Things, Not Enough Focus on Commitment"

"Too Many Twenty-First-Century Values, Not Enough Eighteenth-Century Values"

"Too Much 'Success,' Not Enough Character"

Jack Bogle's passion shines through on every page of the book. The founder of the world's largest investment firm ($4 trillion under management in January 2017) and father of Index funds, says that there surely is—or damn well ought to be—more to life than shareholder value!

2.10 EXCELLENCE: "GIVE-A-SHIT-ISM" TOPS ANY FANCY TECHNIQUE

I didn't have a mission statement at Burger King. I had a dream. Very simple. It was something like "Burger King is 250,000 people, every one of whom gives a shit." Every one. Accounting. Systems. Not just the drive-through. Everyone is in the brand. That's what we're talking about, nothing less.
—Barry Gibbons, former Burger King CEO and architect of an extraordinary turnaround; I know Barry well, and this is a true bedrock belief.

Mr. Gibbons's formulation inspired me to generate a related tweetstream. Here are a couple of entries, @tom_peters :

1. Suddenly realized how sick/tired I am of this technique (six sigma, agile, etc.) vs. that technique. Get respect/listening/acknowledgement/civility "stuff" right, screw technique.
2. If you really really (really) give a shit about people, then other "miracle" systems of management are secondary.
3. If you do *not* have a culture of respect/caring/give-a-shit-ism, applying "good" techniques often make things worse—more bureaucracy, less democracy.

My (personal) bottom line:
RESPECT beats technique.
LISTENING beats technique.
"GIVE A SHIT" beats technique.

"Give-a-shit-ism" (my rather awkward adaptation of the Gibbons's mantra) is arguably Key #1 for an environment featuring productive, innovative employees and, thence, happy customers.

2.11

2.11.1
EXCELLENCE BEATS SUCCESS:
EXCELLENCE BEATS HAPPINESS

Strive for excellence. Ignore success.

—Bill Young, race car driver

Auto racing and producing a museum-worthy piece of art are one and the same as I see it. I believe that most any activity, at its very peak, deserves to be called art. In fact, the fundamental premise of this book is that to avoid the grasp of artificial intelligence and the like, we must move past commodities (and the short-term profits associated therewith, the all-too-common measure of "success") and introduce art into our products and services, which in turn will only occur if every employee is a wholehearted part of the endeavor.

The graduates are also told to pursue happiness and joy. But, of course, when you read a biography of someone you

admire, it's rarely the things that made them happy that compel your admiration. It's the things they did to court unhappiness—the things they did that were arduous and miserable, which sometimes cost them friends and aroused hatred. It's excellence, not happiness, that we admire most.
—David Brooks, "It's Not About You,"
op-ed, *The New York Times*

Mr. Brooks is spot-on, even if the formulation causes discomfort. It certainly is worthy of contemplation. At the very least, one must acknowledge that the attainment of excellence at anything is a product of extreme exertion and constant frustration, not just in the long hours required to reach the level of stellar performance, but in the even greater and perpetual exertions required to stay at or even near the performance peak.

2.11.2
EXCELLENCE—TO ME—IS SPIRITUAL

Apropos of the two quotes immediately above:

EXCELLENCE, by my definition, is first and foremost a way of life, a way of behaving with care and respect toward one's fellow human beings day in and day out, moment in and moment out.
    EXCELLENCE is, in short, spiritual.

And, again, for after all this book is mostly about business, EXCELLENCE through care and attention to each other and to our customers and to our communities also turns out to be a profit builder and profit sustainer and job maintainer or creator of surpassing importance, especially in uncertain times.

2.12 THE EIGHTEEN E's OF EXCELLENCE

Exuberance. (Vibrate—cause earthquakes!)

Energy. (Be fire! Light fires!)

Execution. (Do it! Now! Get it done!)

Empowerment. (Respect and appreciation! Always ask, "What do you think?" Then: Listen! Liberate! Celebrate! One hundred percent innovators or bust!)

Edginess. (Perpetually dance at the frontier and a little or a lot beyond.)

Enraged. (Be determined to challenge and change the status quo!)

Engaged. (Be addicted to MBWA/Managing by Wandering Around. In touch. Always.)

Electronic. (Partners with the world 60/60/24/7/365 via electronic community building and entanglement of every sort. Crowdsourcing/crowd-doing power!)

Encompassing. (Relentlessly pursue diverse opinions— the more diversity the merrier! Diversity works!)

Emotion. (The alpha. The omega. The essence of leadership. The essence of sales. The essence of marketing. The essence. Period. Acknowledge it.)

Empathy. (Connect, connect, connect with others' realities and aspirations! Walk in the other person's shoes until the soles have holes!)

Experience. (Life is theater! Make every activity memorable! For example, aim for the Steve Jobs measure: "Insanely Great.")

Experimental. (Ready! Fire! Aim! Whoever Tries the Most Stuff Wins.)

Error-prone. (Fail faster, succeed sooner. If you try a lot of stuff, you will screw a lot of stuff up along the way. It's a necessary and applause-worthy part of the process.)

Evenhanded. (Fair to a fault! Honest as Abe!)

Expectations. (Michelangelo: "The greatest danger for most of us is not that our aim is too high and we miss it, but that it is too low and we reach it." Amen!)

Eudaimonia. (Pursue the highest of human moral purpose, the core of Aristotle's philosophy. Be of service. Always.)

EXCELLENCE. (The only standard!)

(Original source: Tom Peters Company poster.)

2.13 EXCELLENCE: ALWAYS

Excellence. Always.

If not excellence, what?
If not excellence now, when?

2.14 EXCELLENCE: ABOVE AND BEYOND

Excellence . . . can be obtained if you:
. . . care more than others think is wise;
. . . risk more than others think is safe;
. . . dream more than others think is practical;
. . . expect more than others think is possible.

—K. Sriram, posted at tompeters.com

3 CULTURE, THE SINE QUA NON

MY STORY

IT WAS WAR. TOTAL WAR. AND THAT'S TOTAL NONSENSE. THOUGH IT FELT LIKE THAT TO ME AT THE TIME.

It was 1977, and McKinsey's managing director, Ron Daniel, felt that his preeminent institution was under attack from the Boston Consulting Group in particular. McKinsey was beyond doubt pick of the litter as "counselors to top management." Some argued that McKinsey shaped American business and, increasingly, business around the world. But BCG was offering a well-formed body of concepts. McKinsey's stars were counselors to top management. BCG's stars were the idea people who prepared companies for tomorrow.

Daniel wanted to maintain the role of preeminent counselors but also wanted to get into the ideas arena fast. And, in fact,

McKinsey's intellectual horsepower *was* a match for BCG's. Daniel launched two big projects headed by senior power players out of the New York office—one on creating *winning strategies*, the other on *operations systems that maximized efficiency* in a client's businesses.

But Daniel also had a personal itch to scratch. He had noticed over the years that McKinsey provided sound advice to its clients, but far too often the grand plans failed the implementation test. Hence he decided to launch a low-power, mostly beneath the radar, third "ideas" project on *organizational effectiveness*. I was a junior-ish McKinsey non-partner with a good, albeit brief, track record in the "crazy" San Francisco office. Of particular interest to Daniel, I had recently received my Ph.D. from Stanford in organization effectiveness. Bottom line: To my surprise, the project landed on my desk, and I was assigned a guiding partner, Bob Waterman, who five years later became the coauthor of *In Search of Excellence*.

To launch the project, I was in effect given an unlimited travel budget to roam the world, particularly the academic world, in pursuit of the best and most progressive and provocative thinking on org effectiveness. My roaming took about six months, and my frequent flyer miles totaled in the tens of thousands. I did pretty much visit "everybody who mattered," including soon-to-be Nobel Laureate Herb Simon at Carnegie Mellon University.

Frankly, what I found mirrored the intellectual strains that had fueled my Ph.D. work. One of my mentors had been Jim March, who had come to Stanford from Carnegie Mellon and who had been Dr. Simon's principal partner for decades.

To make a long story short, my findings were greatly at odds with the McKinsey canon, as they didn't involve mathematical formulas or other quant tricks. I concluded that what makes an organization soar was derisively called by my McKinsey peers "the soft stuff"—for example, the nonlinear "people stuff." And I also discovered the importance of what is now called "corporate culture." That term did not exist in 1977. Its precursors were labeled "the informal organization," "management style," "the way we do things around here," and the like.

My presentations to McKinsey grandees were mostly met with indifference. However, I was building a network of renegades inside the firm, and those renegades were introducing me to their clients, who were intrigued by the concepts I had collected. The clients knew what McKinsey-ites considered secondary—the messy "implementation bit" was indeed the difference between winning and losing.

As I gained traction, McKinsey traditionalists fought back. Through my network, I managed to get an op-ed published in *The Wall Street Journal* that was all about the impact of corporate culture on business results and implicitly (pretty explicitly, to be honest) downgraded the role of strategy. I was told that the head of the New York office actually went to Daniel in an effort to get me fired over my heretical eight hundred words. But Daniel remained steadfast; in fact, such controversy and publicity around "McKinsey ideas" was just what he had been looking for.

Time passed, and a McKinsey German office renegade, Herb Henzler, got funds from his client, Siemens, to sponsor another 'round-the-world trip. This one focused on corporations, not academic institutions, and the goal was to unearth the secrets of the world's top companies. The findings were published internally in 1979, and the lead role went to that "soft stuff," in particular corporate culture.

The hard-soft war continued to rage, and, frankly, about half of McKinsey was outwardly distressed by the publication of *In Search of Excellence* in October of 1982. The good news for the resisters was that the publisher had low expectations, and the first print run was a meager five thousand. The bad news for the resisters was that a year later, that publisher journeyed to Palo Alto to host Bob Waterman and me at a party commemorating the sale of the book's one millionth copy.

The "soft guys" had prevailed—or at least gained a significant toehold. And the likes of "corporate culture" had made its way into the big leagues of business ideas. (The transition was slow, but some say that at modern-day McKinsey, a large share, maybe even half, of total revenue is at least indirectly tied to what's called the "Organization Effectiveness Practice" and its offspring.)

THE CULTURE NARRATIVE

3.1

3.1.1
CULTURE *IS* THE GAME

No one at McKinsey was more dismissive of the "soft stuff" I was championing than senior partner Lou Gerstner. Lou was tougher than tough as nails, outspoken, and a strategist's strategist: "Get the strategy right and you're three-quarters of the way down the road" was the implicit message. He eventually left McKinsey and went on to top jobs at American Express and then became CEO of RJR Nabisco. But there was another chapter to go: Big Blue.

IBM, in the '70s and '80s, was *the* iconic American company. As the '80s wound down, the company became flabby, missed many opportunities, and ended up in severe trouble.

In a last-gasp effort to return the firm to its glory, IBM's board called in Gerstner in 1993 to fix the mess. And fix it he did. At the end of his nine-year stint, IBM was once again riding high and well prepared for the years ahead.

Gerstner recounted his chapter of IBM history in his 2002 book, *Who Says Elephants Can't Dance?: Inside IBM's Historic Turnaround*. He reports at one point on what he called his premier "lesson learned":

> **If I could have chosen not to tackle the IBM culture head-on, I probably wouldn't have. My bias coming in was toward strategy, analysis, and measurement. In comparison, changing the attitude and behaviors of hundreds of thousands of people is very, very hard. Yet I came to see in my time at IBM that culture isn't just one aspect of the game—it *is* the game.**

Gerstner.
Culture.

It *is* the game.

Indeed it is. Throughout this book, the word *culture* will appear many times. I'll talk about a key notion, such as, in the initial innovation chapter, the importance of running a zillion rapid experiments in parallel. I'll write something like the following: "The idea of constant innovation as a by-product of trying stuff fast is far, far easier said than done. To make it work, one needs no less than a 'try-it culture' deeply imbedded in the company's psyche." This or that big idea is virtually meaningless and certainly not sustainable without a supporting/encompassing culture umbrella.

3.1.2
CULTURE MATTERS MOST

Affirmations:

1. Ed Schein, MIT professor, generally considered the founder of the culture movement:

"Culture eats strategy for breakfast."

2. *The Wall Street Journal*, 2013, interview:
   Reporter: *"What matters most to a company over time? Strategy or culture?"*
   Dominic Barton, Managing Director, McKinsey & Co.:

"Culture."

   (That's a long way from the McKinsey resistance to the culture notion as described in the chapter's opening vignette.)
3. Culture is the game, even when the game is football:
   Hall of Fame NFL coach Bill Walsh inherited a horrible San Francisco 49ers team in 1979. Though expectations

were sky high, in his first year there was no improvement in the won and loss record. (Year before Walsh arrived: two wins, fourteen losses. Walsh's first year: two wins, fourteen losses.)

Why no instant turnaround? Walsh reports in his book *The Score Takes Care of Itself* that he spent that first year working on *culture*—yes, on a football team!

He explained:

"The culture precedes positive results. It doesn't get tacked on as an afterthought on your way to the victory stand."

During that first year, Coach Walsh reports that he worked on establishing an ethos of professionalism, decorum, support for one's teammates, and the like. The first year's result was that two wins, fourteen losses record, but a scant two years later, in 1982, the 49ers won the Super Bowl with a record of seventeen wins, two losses.

3.2 A CEO'S LIFE: AN ENDURING OBSESSION WITH CULTURE

Coming out of the above is my uncompromising "CEO's First Commandment":

CEO Job #1 is setting—*and micro-nourishing, one day, one hour, one minute at a time*—an

effective people-truly-first, innovate-or-die, excellence-or-bust corporate culture.

The key words in my declaration are . . .

"one day, one hour, one minute at a time."

Culture is the chief's obsession or it's pretty much nothing at all.

Culture is shaped by the casual comment the boss makes to the receptionist as she walks through the door in the morning.

Culture is shaped by three casual comments—no more than thirty seconds each—that the boss makes as she walks the twenty-five yards from the receptionist's desk to her office.

Culture is shaped dramatically by the tone and quality and care put into the six e-mails the boss responds to in the fifteen minutes after she gets to her desk.

Culture is shaped by every twitch and blink and comment the boss makes at the morning meeting.

THE RULES:
CULTURE COMES FIRST.
CULTURE IS EXCEEDINGLY DIFFICULT TO
    CHANGE.
CULTURE CHANGE CANNOT BE/MUST NOT BE EVADED
    OR AVOIDED.
CULTURE MAINTENANCE IS ABOUT AS DIFFICULT AS
    CULTURE CHANGE.
CULTURE MAINTENANCE: ONE DAY / ONE HOUR / ONE
    MINUTE AT A TIME.

CULTURE CHANGE/MAINTENANCE MUST BECOME A
    CONSCIOUS/PERMANENT/PERSONAL AGENDA ITEM.
CULTURE CHANGE/MAINTENANCE IS MANIFEST IN "THE
    LITTLE THINGS" FAR MORE THAN IN THE BIG THINGS.
REPEAT; CULTURE CHANGE/MAINTENANCE:
ONE DAY/ONE HOUR/ONE MINUTE AT A TIME.
FOREVER.
AND EVER.
AMEN.

3.3 CULTURE IS A CLEAN SHOELACE

Mayo Rochester employee Mary Ann Morris, the adminis-
trator of General Service and the Office of Patient Affairs,
often tells a story about her early days with the organization. She was working in a laboratory—a job that required
her to wear a white uniform and white shoes—and after
a hectic morning getting her two small children to school,
she arrived at work to find her supervisor staring at her
shoes. The supervisor had noticed that the laces were dirty
where they threaded through the eyelets of Morris's shoes
and asked Morris to clean them. Offended, Morris said that
she worked in a laboratory, not with patients, so why should
it matter?

Her boss replied that Morris had contact with patients in
ways she didn't recognize—going out on the street wearing
her Mayo name tag, for instance, or passing by patients and
their families as she walked through the halls—and that
she couldn't represent Mayo Clinic with dirty shoelaces.

"Though I was initially offended, I realized over time [that] everything I do, down to my shoelaces, represents my commitment to our patients and visitors . . . I still use the dirty shoelace story to set the standard for the service level I aspire to for myself and my coworkers."

—Leonard Berry and Kent Seltman,
"Orchestrating the Clues of Quality,"
chapter 7, from *Management
Lessons from Mayo Clinic*

(Mayo is routinely voted the best health care provider in the United States. Elements of its distinctive "team medicine" practice [culture!] are described in chapter 1.)

3.4

3.4.1
CULTURE PLUS: "HARD IS SOFT. SOFT IS HARD."

It is only a slight exaggeration to say that you can summarize *In Search of Excellence* in six words:
"Hard is soft.
Soft is hard."

Hard **(numbers/plans)** *is soft*: **Plans are often fantasies, and numbers are readily manipulated. Case in point: "quants" and ratings-agency staffers cleverly packaged and evaluated "derivatives" of valueless mortgages, thus spurring the multi-trillion-dollar financial crash of 2007–2008++).**

Soft (people/relationships/culture) **is hard** (difficult to achieve and enduring only if incessantly worked at).

While I hardly dismiss the traditionally emphasized "hard stuff," I do insist that the "soft stuff" is the key to long-term success and the bedrock of excellence.

I am a certified numbers guy. I have no less than four "quant" degrees—two in engineering, two in business. The *Excellence* book coauthor, Bob Waterman, also had a quant's education: an engineering degree, a business degree.

In the opening story in chapter 1, I recounted my experience as a combat engineer in Vietnam. I arrived in country with civil engineering tools aplenty, but I was soon given a detachment to command in a rather unpleasant setting. Overnight, I discovered that 99 percent of my concerns were "people concerns" (so-called/mistakenly called "soft" concerns).

And I was totally unprepared for "soft-stuff leadership" in a setting where bad guys were shooting at us and the roads were intensively mined.

Long-term result from that harsh introduction to "managerial" life:

My life's work.
Hard is soft.
Soft is hard.

3.4.2
HARD IS SOFT/SOFT IS HARD: "THE MCKINSEY 7S MODEL"

The 7Ss:

> STRATEGY
> STRUCTURE
> SYSTEMS
> STYLE
> SKILLS
> STAFF
> SHARED VALUES

The (commonly emphasized) "hard Ss":

> STRATEGY
> STRUCTURE
> SYSTEMS

The (frequently ignored/undervalued) "soft Ss":

> STYLE ("the way we do things around here"/corporate "culture")
> SKILLS ("distinctive competency/competencies")
> STAFF (people-talent)
> SHARED VALUES (the bedrock of sustained superior performance)

The "McKinsey 7S Model" that Bob Waterman and I developed in 1979 with Tony Athos, Richard Pascale, and Julien Phillips has stood the test of time—thirty-nine years to date. McKinsey eventually accepted the 7Ss as near Holy Writ. The firm's managing director in the 1990s claimed the model remains *"the most useful framework for assessing organizational effectiveness."*

The idea, encompassed by the "hard is soft, soft is hard" notion and expanded via the full framework, is that there are soft Ss as well as hard Ss that must be considered and managed to maximize organization well-being and competitive strength. And, historically, those soft Ss have sat in the back row—if they were invited at all.

The real trick is not ceding the front row to the soft Ss; it is balance—equal attention to all the elements. In fact, the magic on top of the magic is achieving sustainable success by getting the balance among the Ss right according to the needs of the times. And that requires a master conductor with perfect pitch. Ninety years ago, the fabled General Motors chief Alfred Sloan (the iconic CEO of the times) said his key to effectiveness was constantly rejiggering the balance between centralization (hard: firm hand on the tiller) and decentralization (soft: allowing a hundred flowers to bloom). At times, he said, you needed tight controls, and at other times, the division general managers (Chevrolet, Cadillac, etc.) needed to be given free rein. So, too, with implementing a 7S approach.

3.4.3
NOTE ON "HARD STUFF" AND NUMBERS/METRICS IN PARTICULAR

I am not averse to or an enemy of "hard stuff." Take numbers. For better or for worse, I think and dream numerically. The point here is *not* to dismiss numbers. It *is* that numbers should not be the default tail that wags the dog.

Numbers are abstractions.

Numbers are derivative of real action.

"Soft" relationships, on the other hand, bleed real blood.

Numbers matter.

A lot.

But "business by the numbers" is a loser's delusion.

(Yes, even in the age of Big Data and the like.)

Few have said all this better than pollster Daniel Yankelovich, quoted in Jack Bogle's book *Enough*, on the limitations of analytic models:

The first step is to measure what can easily be measured.

This is okay as far as it goes.

The second step is to disregard that which cannot be measured, or give it an arbitrary quantitative value.

This is artificial and misleading.

The third step is to presume that what cannot be measured is not very important.

This is blindness.

The fourth step is to say what cannot be measured does not really exist.

This is suicide.

(Amen.)

3.4.4

THE SOFT EDGE: LINING THE PATH TO SUSTAINED SUCCESS—IN SILICON VALLEY, TOO

Forbes publisher and Silicon Valley stalwart Rich Karlgaard has long been a keen observer of the forces reshaping the technology powerhouses that now drive so much of the economy. He encompassed his assessment of the factors determining success and failure in his 2014 book, *The Soft Edge: Where Great Companies Find Lasting Success.* The heart of Karlgaard's argument:

> I believe the business world is at a crossroads, where hard-edge people are dominating the narrative and discussion. . . . The battle for money and attention boiling inside most companies and among most managers is that between the hard and soft edges. . . .
> Far too many companies invest too little time and money in their soft-edge excellence. . . . This mistake has three main reasons:
>
> - The hard edge is easier to quantify. . . .
> - Successful hard-edge investment provides a faster ROI. . . .
> - CEOs, CFOs, COOs, boards of directors, and shareholders speak the language of finance. . . .
>
> Let me make the case for investing time and money in your company's soft edge.

- Soft-edge strength . . . leads to greater brand recognition, higher profit margins . . . [It] is the ticket out of Commodityville.
- Companies strong in the soft edge are better prepared to survive a big strategic mistake or cataclysmic disruption . . .
- Hard-edge strength is absolutely necessary to stay alive and compete, but it provides a fleeting advantage.

A rather imposing list of benefits, eh? With all due respect to *In Search of Excellence*, I think Karlgaard's hard-soft assessment here is by far the best I've come across.

To give you a flavor of how Karlgaard fleshed out his argument, consider the major "soft" section titles from *The Soft Edge*:

- Trust
- Teams
- Taste
- Smarts
- Story

The book's examples range far and wide, well beyond high tech and Silicon Valley. Nonetheless, much of the power of the book for me comes from its Silicon Valley roots. Think Silicon Valley and the words that come to mind are *engineering, coding, software, algorithms, the cloud,* and *big data*—that is, the hardest of the "hard stuff." Yet Karlgaard convincingly argues that the winners—even, or maybe especially, in the Valley—are those who are most effective at assimilating the other side of the coin; that "soft stuff" as it were.

It is a powerful message; the book, incidentally, gets my vote as top business book of the decade to date. God alone knows how many copies I've given away or how many casualties I have caused by whacking people over the head with the hardcover version.

3.4.5
THE SOFT EDGE: LIBERAL ARTS THINKING COMES TO "THE VALLEY"

As illustration of the above, consider this unlikely cover story in *Forbes* in July 2015:

THE NEW GOLDEN TICKET: YOU DON'T HAVE TO CODE TO GET RICH. HOW LIBERAL ARTS GRADS ARE CONQUERING SILICON VALLEY.

Highlights:

Revenge of the Philosophy Majors: In Silicon Valley brilliant coding and engineering is a given. The real value added, increasingly, comes from the people who can sell and humanize. Which is why tech startups suddenly crave liberal arts majors.

[It's] one of the most glistening of tech's ten-digit "unicorn" startups, boasting 1.1 million users and a private market valuation of $2.8 billion. If you've used Slack's team-based messaging software, you know that one of its catchiest innovations is Slackbot, a helpful little avatar that pops up periodically to provide tips so jaunty that it seems human.

Such creativity can't be programmed. Instead, much of it is minted by one of Slack's 180 employees, Anna Pickard, the 38-year-old editorial director. She earned a theater degree from

Britain's Manchester Metropolitan University before discovering that she hated the constant snubs of auditions that didn't work out. After winning acclaim for her blogging, videogame writing and cat impersonations, she found her way into tech, where she cooks up zany replies to users who type in "I love you, Slackbot." It's her mission, Pickard explains, "to provide users with extra bits of surprise and delight." The pay is good; the stock options, even better.

One cover story is not a trend. On the other hand, it *does* suggest a growing awareness of "soft is hard" and the importance of "the soft edge" in an unlikely locale.

3.4.6
THE SOFT STUFF: BENEATH THEM?

In *The Advantage: Why Organizational Health Trumps Everything Else in Business*, author Patrick Lencioni recounts a revealing incident:

As I sat there at the conference listening to one presentation after another highlighting the remarkable and unorthodox activities [people-first dogma, leadership style, communal culture, etc.] that have made this organization so healthy, I leaned over and asked the CEO a semirhetorical question: "Why in the world don't your competitors do any of this?"

After a few seconds, he whispered, almost sadly, *"You know, I honestly believe they think it's beneath them."*

Wow.

And it surely squares with my decades of enterprise observation.

3.4.7
FINAL HARD/SOFT THOUGHT: "SECURITY" THROUGH THE "SOFT STUFF"?

The "tech tsunami" and the possible (probable?) "jobs apocalypse" that most likely will accompany it:

How does one fight back?
Or, far better yet, get ahead of the curve?

In my considered opinion, the best avenue, maybe the *only* effective avenue, is likely through emphasizing the "soft stuff" (e.g., culture, people, obsessive listening, innovation via "most failures wins," differentiation through "insanely great" design) and always an abiding commitment to, one hour at a time five minutes at a time, no less than EXCELLENCE.

There are certainly no guarantees.

There *are* promising paths worth exploring.

And there are exemplars to inspire us.

4 THE TRAILBLAZERS, SMALL- AND MEDIUM-SIZE ENTERPRISES

MY STORY

A *SEA ANCHOR* IS ALSO KNOWN AS A DRIFT ANCHOR, DRIFT SOCK, PARA-ANCHOR, OR BOAT BRAKE AND IS A DEVICE USED TO STABILIZE A BOAT IN HEAVY WEATHER. RATHER THAN TETHERING THE BOAT TO THE SEA FLOOR, THE SEA ANCHOR INCREASES THE DRAG THROUGH THE WATER AND THUS ACTS AS A BRAKE. IT CAN ALSO BE ATTACHED TO THE STERN OF A VESSEL, PREVENTING THE SHIP FROM TURNING BROADSIDE TO THE WAVES.

My wife and I typically spend North America's winter months on the other end of the globe in New Zealand, at the "Top of the South" (as in South Island). We have a small cottage by the Tasman Sea.

About twenty-five miles away is the tiny town of Motueka.

On the main street in Motueka, you will find a nondescript door leading to the operations office and factory of W. A. Coppins, which by most accounts is the global leader in designing and building sea anchors and related products.

With roots going back to textile design and production in 1896, today Coppins thrives on what the company's chief calls "wicked problems." Its products range from light recreational gear to monster systems for premier clients such as the United States Navy and the government of Norway.

I admit it. I'm in love with W. A. Coppins (and others of its ilk). Coppins et al. are "category killers," to use the retail term, that through unbridled imagination and excellence dominate a niche market, often globally, often from out-of-the-way places like Motueka.

Companies like W. A. Coppins and somewhat larger firms, which come under the heading of SMEs/small- and medium-sized enterprises, are the "secret backbone," as one wag put it, of every economy, whether Kiwi (GDP approximately $200 billion) or American (GDP of $17 trillion); backbone as in (1) chief source of innovation and (2) chief source of employment and job creation, especially important in the face of the technology upheaval we are facing.

In 2014, I gave a keynote speech to the premier annual business-government conference in New Zealand. I ruffled more than a few feathers when I said that the Kiwis need to birth and nurture in any way possible their Coppinses, rather than overly depend, as they traditionally have, on volatile commodities. (Powdered milk for baby formula for the Chinese market is the country's export mainstay these days—talk about precarious; one spoiled shipload and watch national export dollars take the deepest dive.) As I said, feathers were ruffled, which was my unabashed goal.

Oh my, I do indeed love those global-niche dominating Mighty Magicians of Motueka—W. A. Coppins.

Bravo!

A hundred times over, BRAVO!

(Coppins, not so incidentally, is supported by two Mighty Magician partners. Its sea-anchor product base is a form of nylon, Dyneema, developed and produced by specialist DSM Netherlands; and Coppins relies upon custom-produced fabric from another modest-size specialist—W. Wiggins of neighboring Wellington. Such combinations of small superstars are not uncommon and support the notion that national success is boosted enormously by a dynamic, self-reinforcing SME ecosystem.)

The Coppinses are everywhere, though you'd not know it from the monster-firm-obsessed "business guru literature" (I do not deny my own guilt) or business school curricula. My goal in this chapter is three-fold: First, to make it clear, in New Zealand and Germany and the United States and elsewhere, that winners like W. A. Coppins deserve our standing ovation and strong private and public support for their economic contributions to their country and their communities and especially for the millions upon millions of good jobs they create and maintain. Second, to also make it clear that there are stellar role models in every nook and cranny in the economy; sometimes it seems as though the likes of Silicon Valley code kings and app creators are grabbing all our attention, when in fact we should be searching for sea anchor kings who groove on "wicked problems." Third, that the Coppinses and their ilk are where you should be looking for the purist manifestations of business excellence, offering lessons to learn by the bushel.

So let's up (sea) anchor and look at the bigger story . . .

THE SME NARRATIVE

4.1 UNLIKELY SUPERSTARS: COPPINS++

I do love sea anchor business excellence.

Where shall we look next?

From underwater to under-house?

4.1.1
THE DRY BASEMENT KINGS: BASEMENT SYSTEMS INC./"ALL THINGS BASEMENTY"

Basement Systems Inc. of Seymour, Connecticut, is primarily in the business of getting mold and dampness out of basements. Your home's once foul and perhaps poisonous but now rejuvenated lower reaches become fit for storage or use as a family room or extra bedroom—that is, effectively adding a room to your house. (No small thing, eh?)

"Basement improvement."

What a dreary business?

Not to Larry Janesky!

For Larry J. and his spirited crew, basements rock!

Among many other things, Janesky codified his activities ("all things basementy") and the value thereof in his book *Dry Base-*

ment Science—which sold over one hundred thousand copies. He also holds more than twenty-five patents.

Started in 1986, the fast-growing company has at least four hundred dealers in six countries and revenue exceeds $100 million.

Basement Systems is also a consistent prize winner (local, state, national) in categories such as "Best Places to Work," "Best Small Business," and "Entrepreneur of the Year." The company is a paragon on just about any dimension you can name.

4.1.2
HOW ABOUT THE GARAGE? 1111 LINCOLN ROAD

In his superb book *Simply Brilliant: How Great Organizations Do Ordinary Things in Extraordinary Ways!*, Bill Taylor takes us, among other places, to Miami Beach, and more specifically . . .

1111 Lincoln Road

That address has become a Miami Beach landmark. For example, LeBron James, then with the Miami Heat and arguably the world's best basketball player, introduced his eleventh Nike shoe, celebrated with hoopla of the first order, at 1111 Lincoln Road.

Just what is this special address?

A three hundred–car parking garage!

Developer Robert Wennett wanted to "reintroduce the original 1920 vision of Lincoln Road." Among many other things, that meant having a makeover designed by the world-renowned

Swiss architects Herzog & de Meuron. The "product" amounted to, per one member of the press, "carcitecture," an "unimaginable marriage of high-end architecture and car storage."

1111 Lincoln features, among many other things, public art and a grand staircase (joggers by the score work out there every morning; many then move on to in-garage yoga classes). Wennett calls it a "curated space which provides an experience, telling a story."

Wennett himself lives in a penthouse at the top of the garage.

Is this over the top? Of course. But it is also a very profitable venture, a community changer, and a peerless act of imagination!

(*Simply Brilliant* features a bushel or two of such inspiring examples.)

4.1.3
JIM'S GROUP: AUSTRALIA'S STAR AT THINGS CUSTOMERS DON'T WANT TO DO THEMSELVES

Jim Penman started Jim's Mowing in 1984 (he was getting a Ph.D. in cross-cultural anthropology, and he paid his rent via mowing lawns on the side). By 2016, his one-man, one-mower firm had grown to Jim's Group, with **3,600 franchisees** in Australia, New Zealand, the United Kingdom, and Canada. His avowed bread and butter, as the section title suggests: "Things that customers don't want to do themselves."

Category killers, a sampler:

Jim's Mowing Canada
Jim's Mowing UK

Jim's Antennas

Jim's Bookkeeping

Jim's Building Maintenance

Jim's Carpet Cleaning

Jim's Car Cleaning

Jim's Computer Services

Jim's Dog Wash

Jim's Driving School

Jim's Fencing

Jim's Floors

Jim's Painting

Jim's Paving

Jim's Pergolas

Jim's Pool Care

Jim's Pressure Cleaning

Jim's Roofing

Jim's Security Doors

Jim's Trees

Jim's Window Cleaning

Jim's Windscreens

And so on.

(Like Larry Janesky, with *Dry Basement Science*, Jim Penman recounted his journey in print with *What Will They Franchise Next?* and *Every Customer a Raving Fan*.)

Coppins, Basement Systems Inc., 1111 Lincoln Road, and Jim's Group are illustrative of the best of the all-important SME/ small- and medium-sized enterprise sector. And the best where you'd least expect it—a long way from Palo Alto.

No, you'd never know about SME economic dominance from reading guru literature or checking out a typical business school course list. The gurus, the business schools, and the national press focus on the big guys almost exclusively. That's a bad idea. First, because there are so many great SMEs in so many fascinating places doing fascinating things we can learn from. Second, and equally important, it is not clear how much those vaunted big guys have to teach us. Frankly, their long-term performance is questionable, and that's an understatement.

4.2 LET'S BACK UP AND RESTART THIS CHAPTER'S STORY WITH A BRIEF ASSESSMENT OF THE (WOBBLY) BIG GUYS

What follows amounts to a solid case but is hardly the stuff of an Oxford economics dissertation. There are superb giant firms; for heaven's sake, that was the whole point of my first book, *In Search of Excellence*. And we can learn from them. (But the "excellence edge" is devilishly hard to maintain. Overall, "our" companies have done surprisingly well in financial terms, but a significant share of the *Search* superstars have lost much of their sparkle in the thirty-six years since the book was published.)

In the end, the giants' contribution to the economy is grossly exaggerated, especially when it comes to employment, job creation, and innovation. Moreover, the big guys' long-term performance as a whole stinks. And typical efforts to make a comeback via, say, mergers and acquisitions (M&A) fail miserably; in fact, the M&A efforts border on being laughable—though not to the hundreds of thousands of workers tossed out on the street when Mr. Big tries to justify the outrageous price he paid for an acquisition by slashing costs (invariably including R&D) and decimating payrolls.

Hence below you will simply find a small sample of evidence that adds up to a big blemish on the biggies' records:

> **I don't believe in economies of scale. You don't get better by being bigger. You get worse.**
> —Dick Kovacevich, retired CEO, Wells Fargo

Supporting the substance of the quote, Wells's growth-for-growth's sake strategy has in recent times backfired badly (e.g., pushing too hard for revenue growth has led to egregious behavior toward its customers).

> **Mr. Foster and his McKinsey colleagues collected detailed performance data stretching back 40 years for 1,000 [large/public] U.S. companies. They found that NONE of the long-term survivors managed to outperform the market. Worse, the longer companies had been in the database, the worse they did.**   —*Financial Times*

(Reread: That's *zero* for one thousand. A rather poor batting average, eh?)

> **I am often asked by would-be entrepreneurs seeking escape from life within huge corporate structures: "How do I build a small firm for myself?"**

The answer seems obvious: Buy a very large one and just wait.

—Paul Ormerod, economist,
*Why Most Things Fail: Evolution,
Extinction and Economics*

(Funny. Or is it?)

Multinational companies, the agents behind global integration, were already in retreat well before the populist revolts of 2016. Their financial performance has slipped so that they are no longer outstripping local firms. Many seem to have exhausted their ability to cut costs and taxes and to out-think their local competitors. . . . Central to the rise of the global firm was its claim to be a superior moneymaking machine. That claim lies in tatters.

—*The Economist*, January 28, 2017, cover story,
"The Multinational Company Is in Trouble"

Almost every personal friend I have in the world works on Wall Street. You can buy and sell the same company six times and everybody makes money, but I'm not sure we're actually innovating.

—Jeff Immelt, former CEO, GE

(Mr. Immelt's not sure, but I am; the innovation record of this sold-and-resold crowd is, to be kind, less than sterling. One senior Wall Street observer of the scene calls the wretched process by its true name: buy and cut.)

To Mr. Immelt's point:

> **When recently asked to name just one big merger that had lived up to expectations, Leon Cooperman, former cochairman of Goldman Sachs's investment policy committee, answered, "I'm sure there are success stories out there, but at this moment I draw a blank."** —Mark Sirower, *The Synergy Trap*

(Whoops. Another *zero*.)

> **Not a single company that qualified as having made a sustained transformation ignited its leap with a big acquisition or merger. Moreover, comparison companies—those that failed to make a leap or, if they did, failed to sustain it—often tried to make themselves great with a big acquisition or merger. They failed to grasp the simple truth that while you can buy your way to growth, you cannot buy your way to greatness.**
>   —Jim Collins, *Time*

(The extensive research on large-scale mergers and acquisitions typically concludes that about 75 percent of the new combinations destroy value.)

I rest my case—certainly not the last word, but indeed a nontrivial sample of consistently damning evidence.

4.3

4.3.1
THE REAL STARS: MIDSIZE NICHE DOMINATORS!

Research shows that new, small companies create almost all the new private sector jobs—and are disproportionately innovative. *—The Future Is Small: Why AIM* [Alternative Investment Market] *Will Be the World's Best Market Beyond the Credit Boom*, by Gervais Williams, superstar fund manager, reported in the *Financial Times*

Most ("almost all"—see above) the jobs.

Most of the innovation.

(And, to repeat, limited attention—from policy makers or from me.)

4.3.2
BE THE BEST

George Whalin's book, *Retail Superstars: Inside the 25 Best Independent Stores in America*, chronicles twenty-five stellar acts of SME boldness and imagination.

I give *Retail Superstars*, as inspiration, to accountants and HR directors, not just small businesspeople; I've given away dozens and dozens of copies.

Peerless examples of imagination at work!

Big wins from small-ish folks over the biggest of the big guys!

It can be done!

In addition to being attracted by the imagination component,

I give the books away for a second reason—namely, Whalin's stellar one-liner:

"Be the best. It's the only market that's not crowded."

If ever there could be a condensed version of the SME credo, that's it.

(The Grateful Dead's late Jerry Garcia went even further than Whalin: "You do not merely want to be the best of the best. You want to be considered the only ones who do what you do.")

4.3.2.1
AMERICA'S BEST RESTROOM!

Consider **JUNGLE JIM'S INTERNATIONAL MARKET** in Fairfield, Ohio. Customers come from near, far, and *very* far to experience what the boss calls **"shoppertainment."**

Start with the food itself: Try a selection of **1,600** cheeses, **1,400** hot sauces, **12,000** wines from $8 to $8,000 per bottle. But in a way, the food is the least of it. The late Mr. Whalin went on to report:

Jungle's creations literally jam-pack the store with visual surprises. In addition to the oasis filled with animals outside and the race car above the entrance, a seven-foot-high mechanized lion entertains shoppers by singing Elvis Presley's "Jailhouse Rock." The Sherwood Forest display in English Foods comes complete with a talking Robin Hood. An antique Boar's Head truck hangs above the Deli. A full-size

rickshaw sits in Chinese Foods. . . . Other delights include an Amish horse-drawn buggy in Meats and Coney Island bumper cars filled with sweets in the Candy Department.

The props can also be a bit bizarre. Two men's and women's Porta Potties situated in the front area of the store look as though they belong on a construction site rather than in a food store. But they are false fronts, and once through the doors, customers find themselves in beautifully appointed restrooms. These creative facilities were recognized in 2007 as "America's Best Restroom" in the sixth annual competition sponsored by Cintas Corporation, a supplier of restroom cleaning and hygiene products.

I am particularly taken with "America's Best Restroom."

There are many honors a business could get, including, say, a Malcolm Baldrige National Quality Award (MBNQA), sometimes presented on the White House lawn by the president. But if I were a business owner in the appropriate market, I'd far prefer America's Best Restroom to a romp on the White House lawn. It speaks to imagination and customer care in a way that simply cannot be topped.

FYI: Before leaving the topic of restrooms, consider this Texas highway billboard:

ONLY 262 MILES TO BUC-EE'S. YOU CAN HOLD IT.

Or this one:

RESTROOMS SO CLEAN, WE LEAVE MINTS ON THE URINALS.

Buc-ee's is a chain of Texas convenience stores/gas stations. The biggest, in New Braunfels and considered the largest convenience store in America at sixty-eight thousand square feet, includes one hundred twenty fueling positions, eighty-three toilets, thirty-one checkout registers, and much more. And, yes, the New Braunfels Buc-ee's won 2012's contest for **America's Best Restroom.** Gotta love it, eh? "Excellence in Braunfels" is one more giant reminder of SME imagination on parade with the strangest damn features in the strangest damn places.

(Why I love my job: *The day I drafted this, I unexpectedly received an e-mail from a Brazilian who'd attended a seminar of mine. The e-mail included four pictures of a glorious gas station restroom in Bauru, Brazil. The sender said he'd immediately thought of me and a lecture I gave in São Paulo when he happened upon it. Excellence in Bauru! Excellence in restrooms! Yes!*)

4.3.2.2

ANOTHER RETAIL SUPERSTAR: ABT ELECTRONICS— AN UNBRIDLED ACT OF IMAGINATION AND DIFFERENTIATION

Traditional electronics retailing is being killed by the Internet. But there are brick-and-mortar exceptions; here's another case study from Whalin's *Retail Superstars*.

Established in 1936, family-owned Abt Electronics is still going strong and is in fact continuing to grow and prosper in the insanely competitive Chicagoland market. Below, in shorthand form, are a few of the things that make Abt stand out:

- Campus is 350,000 square feet/37 acres
- $300 million in revenue
- Design Center (Classes on every damn thing, etc.)
- "Destination" (like IKEA): restaurant, atrium with spectacular flowers, 7,500 gallon aquarium, etc.
- In-house delivery teams (spiffy uniforms, etc.)
- Training in general/knowledge training
- Staff treated exceptionally well, financially and otherwise.
- "Yes." Period—to the nuttiest customer requests: NO EXCUSES.
- "Over"-staffed!
- Merchandising (boats displaying marine electronics, cars with various systems, etc.)
- Web fanatics (encyclopedic information regarding almost all stuff sold, blog, live chat with live experts 24/7, etc.)
- Rating of services: far above Home Depot, Lowe's, and so on.

4.3.3
SMALL GIANTS: COMPANIES THAT CHOSE TO BE GREAT INSTEAD OF BIG

The section title is a book title from *Inc.* cofounder Bo Burlingham. He effectively wrote a companion piece to Whalin's *Retail Superstars*. Burlingham studied fourteen companies. Their markets were typically very specialized; for example, ECCO of Boise, Idaho, is "the leading manufacturer of backup alarms and amber warning lights for commercial vehicles." Reell Precision Manufacturing of Saint Paul, Minnesota, makes "motion control products, such as hinges used on the covers of laptop computers."

These top performers dominated their specialty markets. Burlingham reports that the fourteen shared four traits:

1. They cultivated exceptionally intimate relationships with customers and suppliers, based on personal contact, one-on-one interaction, and mutual commitment to delivering on promises.
2. Each company had an extraordinarily intimate relationship with the local city, town, or county in which it did business—a relationship that went well beyond the usual concept of giving back.
3. The companies had what struck me as unusually intimate workplaces.
4. I noticed the passion that the leaders brought to what the company did. They loved the subject matter, whether it be music, safety lighting, food, special effects, constant torque hinges, beer, records storage, construction, dining, or fashion.

Four powerful success traits available to one and all. The list is at once mundane and inspiring and a winning marketplace formula and eerily consistent with George Whalin's findings. Let me single out the last point—the passion. That's near the top of the list of MIA among the typically bedraggled giants—not fair; there typically *is* a passion for short-term results but little desire to bag that America's Best Restroom trophy.

4.3.4

HIDDEN CHAMPIONS OF THE TWENTY-FIRST CENTURY: SUCCESS STRATEGIES OF UNKNOWN WORLD MARKET LEADERS

In *Hidden Champions*, Hermann Simon, generally considered Germany's #1 management thinker, has given us another SME masterpiece. I carry it around with me—the hardback edition—and bang it loudly on podiums, growling, **"YES, YOU CAN."**

ODDBALL PLACES.
ODDBALL AND OFTEN "BORING" BUSINESSES.
SUPERDUPERSTARS.
REPEAT: COLLECTIVELY THE BACKBONE OF ALL NATIONAL ECONOMIES.

Here are a few of Simon's "hidden champions" (criteria for inclusion: at least global top three in their market, less than $4 billion in revenue):

Baader (Iceland; 80 percent world market share, fish-processing systems)

Gallagher (New Zealand; electric fences)

WET (Germany; heated car seat tech, 50 percent world market share)

Gerriets (Germany; theater curtains and stage equipment)

Electro-Nite (Belgium; sensors for the steel industry)

Essel Propack (India; toothpaste tubes)

SGS (Switzerland; product auditing and certification)

DELO (Germany; specialty adhesives)

Amorim (Portugal; cork products)

EOS (Germany; laser sintering)

Omicron (Germany; tunnel-grid microscopy)

Dickson Constant (France; technical textiles)

O. C. Tanner (United States; employee recognition systems)

Hoeganaes (United States; powder metallurgy supplies)

4.3.5
THE MITTELSTAND

Agile creatures darting between the legs of the multinational monsters. —*Bloomberg Businessweek* on the effectiveness of German **MITTELSTAND** companies

Midsize, niche-dominating firms—Mittelstanders—are unequivocally responsible for Germany's stunning, sustaining, peerless export record. For years, Germany ranked #1 in exports ahead of the United States, Japan, and China. Recently, China has taken over the top spot on the list.

4.4

4.4.1
AXIOM: BETTER BEFORE CHEAPER

During a five-year research effort, Deloitte senior partners Michael Raynor and Mumtaz Ahmed mined a database of over twenty-five thousand companies from hundreds of industries, stretching back forty-five years. They uncovered 344 firms whose performance qualified as statistically "exceptional." Finally, following more analytic winnowing, the set was reduced to twenty-seven firms whose long-term strategies were examined in excruciating detail. Those surviving this hyperintense scrutiny included Linear Technology, Thomas & Betts, Weis Markets, and Heartland Express. The research became the basis for the masterful book *The Three Rules: How Exceptional Companies Think*.

Dozens of plausible hypotheses regarding superior performance were tested, and the winners—the three (and *only* three) rules—that emerged were:

1. BETTER BEFORE CHEAPER.
2. REVENUE BEFORE COST.
3. THERE ARE NO OTHER RULES.

This may sound straightforward and obvious. It is not. Those who stick to these dictums through hell and high water are, the *Three Rules* research underscores, rare indeed—see above, twenty-seven out of twenty-five thousand!

4.4.2
AXIOM: VALUE BEFORE SHORT-TERM EARNINGS

Strikingly similar conclusions were reached by *Fortune*'s premier management expert, Geoff Colvin. In a feature article titled "The Economy Is Scary, but Smart Companies Can Dominate," Colvin offers these findings from the superior performers:

1. THEY MANAGE FOR LONG-TERM VALUE, NOT FOR SHORT-TERM EARNINGS.
2. THEY GET RADICALLY CUSTOMER-CENTRIC.
3. THEY KEEP DEVELOPING HUMAN CAPITAL.

Bingo.

Bingo.

Bingo.

4.4.3
AXIOM: COST CUTTING IS A DEATH SPIRAL—OUR WHOLE STORY IS GROWING REVENUE

Take three: Recall from the introduction the tale of two million dog biscuits—that is, the Commerce Bank/Metro Bank/Vernon Hill story. Get 'em into the branches, keep the branches open, give 'em love, turn 'em into fans, sell Commerce Bank for $8.6 billion to TD Bank, then take the show to the United Kingdom with Metro Bank—and in short order grab one million accounts away from the established banks.

The guiding philosophy, wholly consistent with the first two takes above:

1. "ARE YOU GOING TO COST CUT YOUR WAY TO PROSPERITY? OR ARE YOU GOING TO SPEND YOUR WAY TO PROSPERITY?"
2. "OVERINVEST IN OUR PEOPLE, OVERINVEST IN OUR FACILITIES."
3. "COST CUTTING IS A DEATH SPIRAL. OUR WHOLE STORY IS GROWING REVENUE."

SME dogma: Take #1 = Take #2 = Take #3.

Top-line priority. Product and service excellence. And invest in people.

4.4.4
AXIOM: THERE NEED BE NO SUCH THING AS A COMMODITY

David Lefkovitz, of LEFKO Renovations in Atlanta, avoids standard pitch letters. Instead, when he starts a home-remodeling project, he writes to neighbors, saying he wants to avoid inconveniencing them. He invites them to call him personally with any complaints. Many save his letters and, impressed by his courtesy, hire him later.

—Verne Harnish, *Fortune*

I hate the word *commodity*, as in, "This is a commodity market; you sell on cost, or else." As I see it and, above, as David Lefkovitz of LEFKO Renovations sees it, *commodity* is a state of mind, a loser's state of mind. *Anything* can be significantly (dramatically?) differentiated. The opportunity for discernable excellence is ubiquitous.

For example:

The local plumber or electrician does not provide a "commodity service" . . .

- *if* he or she knows the job
- *if* he or she is learning new tricks all the time
- *if* he or she has a good disposition
- *if* he or she shows up on time

- *if* he or she is neatly dressed
- *if* he or she has a spiffy truck
- *if* he or she fixes the problem in an elegant and timely fashion and clearly explains what was done and why it was done this way or that
- *if* he or she cleans up so that after the fact the client could "eat off the jobsite floor"
- *if* he or she volunteers to do a few tiny tasks outside the one at hand—gratis
- *if* he or she calls ("call" = phone, not e-mail) twenty-four hours later to make sure all is well
- *if,* perhaps, he or she creates a blog with occasional posts featuring practical tips for his or her clientele; for example, a tiny Virginia swimming pool company became a literal "best in the world" following such a social media strategy
- *if* . . .

He or she ain't a commodity!

I call such de-commoditization and relentless pursuit of EXCELLENCE . . . DWPF—Distinction Worth Paying For!

(*I had an out-and-out tiff in the course of a late 2016 speech. It was to a group of franchisees who were complaining bitterly that their harrowing situation* [new competitors, new technology, new regulations] *forced them to pay low wages, which in turn often led to outbreaks of shabby work and poor customer service.*

I acknowledge that I went a little off the rails chastising them, summoning in particular the spirit of George Whalin and Vernon Hill and Larry Janesky and Jim Penman and David Lefkovitz. I said I thought their avowed goal should be to pay the highest wages in the industry and to enable that by providing a "be the best," "only ones who do what we do" service worthy of their charging a significantly above-market price.

There was substantial pushback, though the [my] day was saved when perhaps their most successful, and quite large, franchisee rose [literally] to my defense and insisted that what I'd said was "dead on" and "needed saying.")

4.4.5
MY ONE MILLION JOBS SME DREAM

My mind returned to that hypothetical plumber/electrician not too long ago. On my way to pick up plans from a local engineering firm for a septic system repair, I was driving through a suburban area about fifty miles south of Boston. At one point, I passed a modest-size quadrangle with shops and offices. The roadside sign included:

- Quilt shop
- Wedding cake provider
- Swimming pool sales, service, and installation company
- Tailor offering alterations
- Medical billing service
- Solo lawyer
- Fitness center
- Etc.

There are thousands upon thousands of such setups around the country; fact is, they employ many millions of us. And another fact is that each and every one has the opportunity to be no less than a local *superstar*. No, not a jillion-dollar "unicorn," but to be like that hypothetical plumber/electrician or the real David Lefkovitz cited above. To be special. Very special. To be the best. To be an employer of choice, too—not hiring dozens, but with sustained stellar performance and growing reputation, increasing staff size from, say, three to five or six or even nine. And the jobs added would be damn good jobs. Probably not terribly high-paying jobs, but moderate-paying jobs at a great company; the three or five or six or nine employees of this little "be the best" outfit would ingest a bushel of good habits and pick up precious hard and soft skills that would increase their employability quotient and, thus, serve them well in the years, even decades, to come.

Despite at first blush what appear to be ordinary-sounding services, none of these operations needs to be a commodity. Special/Excellent/"Wow!"/"Only Ones (in the region) Who Do What We Do" is not an opportunity open to a chosen few! These differentiating attributes are available to anyone with a vivid imagination, a sterling work ethic, a passion for improvement, a caring attitude, and an unwavering pursuit of excellence.

Oddly enough, after picking up my septic plans, I went on to get a haircut. I was a bit early and sat down to wait. As fate would have it, there was a small framed motto on the magazine table next to me: *When you support small business, you support a dream.* What a fitting end to my wee local journey.

Dream on!
Excellence or bust!
Be the best!
An employer of choice!
Dream big/be the best/universal excellence/program one

million (good!) new jobs: One million small businesses (less than, say, ten employees) commit in 2018 to providing their customers with a level of Excellence and "Wow" such that each of said businesses will prosper to the point of needing to hire one new employee, who in turn they will train in Excellence/"Wow" to the extent that the new employee's future job prospects are exponentially improved.

BOTTOM LINE REGARDING MY "DREAM ONE MILLION": FROM INDIVIDUAL TO COMMUNITY TO NATION, EVERYONE WINS. BIG-TIME.

(I am going a bit batty on this topic. Well, perhaps more than a bit. Whenever I drive or walk past a small business, I start imagining the additional services they could offer, the infinite number of ways in which they could stand out, what excellence would look like in their context. THERE REALLY ARE NO LIMITS TO THIS SORT OF THINKING. Call it "Tom's SME nirvana." WHY NOT?)

4.5 HOPE = SMES

We are in no danger of running out of new combinations to try. Even if technology froze today, we have more possible ways of configuring the different applications, machines, tasks, and distribution channels to create new processes and products than we could ever exhaust.

—Erik Brynjolfsson and Andrew McAfee, *Race Against the Machine: How the Digital Revolution Is Accelerating Innovation, Driving Productivity, and Irreversibly Transforming Employment and the Economy*

If there is hope of weathering the coming tech tsunami—and Brynjolfsson and McAfee (and I) think there is hope—it will not come from the sputtering behemoths but from entrepreneurs: the likes of Coppins, Jungle Jim's, Basement Systems, Abt Electronics, Burlingham's "small giants," Taylor's "brilliant" firms, and the Mittelstanders of Germany or any other nation.

SECTION III
PEOPLE

5 ONE MORE (DAMN) TIME: PUTTING PEOPLE FIRST

MY STORY

PAT CARRIGAN WAS STANDING WHEN I ENTERED HER BAY CITY, MICHIGAN, OFFICE IN EARLY 1988.

Not as a demonstration of good manners but because she didn't want to start off with formalities across a desk. If we were here to talk about her plant, then we needed in Moment #1 to get out on the shop floor.

(I was visiting to shoot a segment on her for a PBS special subsequently titled "The Leadership Alliance.")

Pat was the first woman to run a General Motors plant (Lakewood, Georgia), but, after performing a miracle there (turning war with the UAW into a wildly productive peace—among other things, several thousand jobs lost in a shutdown were resurrected), she had been moved to Bay City to captain a struggling GM power train operation.

Pat and I and my director headed out on the floor. There was no camera running (we were merely getting a feel for the place) and no execs or exec assistants in tow. I don't want to deify Pat, but that next hour or so was a marvel of extraordinary ordinariness. I honest-to-God believe she knew the names of every one of her one thousand–plus employees, and she seemed to know a little something about each one. On several occasions, as if we weren't there, she'd ask them about something they were doing and always ended with, "Don't forget our Golden Rule: If there's anything I can do to help, it's your responsibility to ask, and my door is always open." (This, we were told by several people, was routine, not a made-for-TV line; and that the door *was* always open.)

Pat ended our little tour by dropping us off at the office of the plant's UAW boss. They exchanged some social chitchat and talked about a couple of small items on their mutual agenda. Pat reported on a meeting with her GM higher-ups the day before, rolling her eyes a couple of times about some hurdles she'd run into; they both laughed. She closed with that apparently characteristic, "LemmeknowifIcanhelp."

When Pat left, we sat down and the UAW chief told us a half-hour tale of the "before-after" Pat story. One item sticks in my mind. I'll do my best, though I acknowledge that my quotes are a bit short of 100 percent accurate:

"Pat had just arrived at midday, and maybe an hour afterward there's a knock on my door, and this woman says, 'I'm Pat Carrigan. Can I come in and say hello?'"

So far so good. But you may have trouble believing the next bit.

He continued, "Tom, I'd been the union guy in charge here for a decade. It was the first time the plant manager had ever come to *my* office door and knocked and asked permission to enter in ten years. Previously, when anything came up, I was summoned to the office for meetings." He must have said "first time" about three times. Later, with camera rolling, he uttered my favorite line in the subsequent PBS show, "Pat Carrigan ain't got a phony bone in her body."

(On the "first time" point, we did a shoot with a half dozen line workers at shift-change time one morning. The seniority was uniformly high; the six collectively represented one hundred–plus years of plant experience. To my utter astonishment [which you can see on my face on the screen], they said—and I made each one repeat it on camera—that they had never met a plant manager in *their* workspace until Pat arrived. I also asked them if they'd had any priming for my interview. One said, "Yeah, [UAW boss mentioned before] told us, 'Pat says no bullshit; tell these guys [me and my director] the truth, warts and all—no "pretty pretty" stuff.'")

So this chapter is about putting people (REALLY) first, beyond the slogans. The intellectual content in the chapter does not require an advanced degree to understand. It could consist of 25 or 125 stories about Pat Carrigan–like people, who achieved stunning results by remembering names, wandering the floor, asking, "How can I help?" and listening ten times more than talking.

If my story were complicated, then my blood pressure would be much lower. If there were a convoluted formula, then you could excuse people for getting it wrong. But it's by and large not complicated. Hence, there is ZERO (repeat, ZERO) excuse for not getting it right. Accordingly, my private name for this chapter is "The Batshit

Chapter." I go batshit over bosses who don't ask, "How can I help?" I go batshit over bosses who are not maniacal about training, training, and more training. So, alas, I go batshit a lot, and I have without letup for the last thirty-five years.

Have a look at what follows, then tell me what's so hard about it. (I'm not very religious, but there is a "religious" benefit in all this. If you help people, you'll also feel better about yourself and your short visit here on earth. Hey, I'm writing this on a Sunday, hence my micro-sermon.)

(Two other Pat Carrigan notes: After her retirement from GM, the Michigan legislature passed a joint resolution honoring her work. Secondly, let me make it clear my Carrigan TV segment was not a whitewash; my director had been Mike Wallace's director at CBS's *60 Minutes*, and he was no pussycat and could detect bullshit from a hundred miles away. I observed his BS detector at work on several occasions.)

THE PEOPLE NARRATIVE

5.1 PEOPLE REALLY FIRST: THIRTEEN SUCCINCT TAKES

NOT ROCKET SCIENCE

It's the people who do the work.
It's the people who make the customer connection scintillating or sour.
It's the people who generate the growth and profit.
It's the people that matter—as individuals as much or more than as service providers.

5.1.1
BRAND = TALENT

This is news?

Not for the Metropolitan Opera.
Not for the MIT Media Lab.
Not for the Golden State Warriors.

But, alas, so it appears to be for many in business.

Which is why, at age seventy-five, I'm writing this book and still madly traveling around the world pontificating on the obvious instead of snoozing in the front porch rocker.

So I have an image. The famous pro football coach sends me an e-mail, asks me to consult on the effectiveness of his organization. I agree and name an outrageous sum. He agrees. I do my review, which takes about a month.

Time to report. I go into the famous coach's office, and we exchange pleasantries. Then I assume a stern face and begin, "Coach, I think your players are your most important asset." At that point, he picks up a heavy trophy sitting on his desk and throws it at me, and I run like hell.

I contend that I would have had a different reception in the average corporate office. My observation would have been viewed as astute, and I would have been praised for my work and the check would have arrived in the next mail.

Of course I exaggerate. But I don't think I exaggerate all that much.

5.1.2
"PEOPLE BEFORE STRATEGY"

Source: Title, lead article, *Harvard Business Review*. July–August 2015, by Ram Charan, Dominic Barton (Managing Director, McKinsey), and Dennis Carey

Ah, even McKinsey, the strategy-quant headquarters, has apparently come around to "People first."

Hallelujah.

5.1.3
"YOU HAVE TO TREAT YOUR EMPLOYEES LIKE CUSTOMERS"

Courtesy of Herb Kelleher, Southwest Airlines founder and former CEO, upon being asked his #1 "secret to success."

Over the years, I've spent a substantial amount of time with Kelleher. This is not some sort of marketing slogan. It is gospel—in an industry, the airlines, where time and again over the last twenty-five years employees have faced cuts and cuts and then more cuts as competition heated up and then boiled over.

FYI: When Kelleher retired, Southwest's unionized pilots took out and paid for full-page newspaper ads thanking him for his thirty-five years of inspired leadership.

5.1.4
"IF YOU WANT STAFF TO GIVE GREAT SERVICE, GIVE GREAT SERVICE TO STAFF"

Per Ari Weinzweig, Zingerman's (superfood emporium), from Bo Burlingham's book, *Small Giants: Companies That Choose to Be Great Instead of Big*

Read this quote a couple of times. You (boss) are in the service business—that is, it's your Job #1 to serve your employees more or less full-time.

Another successful entrepreneur put it this way: "When I hire someone, that's when I go to work for them."

Do not think of these section headers as "clever lines." Please consider them to be what in fact they are—profound truths. So does (will/did) your day today reflect the priority implied by these quotes? Please don't generalize; be precise.

5.1.5
"WHAT EMPLOYEES EXPERIENCE, CUSTOMERS WILL EXPERIENCE. THE BEST MARKETING IS HAPPY, ENGAGED EMPLOYEES. YOUR CUSTOMERS WILL NEVER BE ANY HAPPIER THAN YOUR EMPLOYEES."

From successful entrepreneur and service guru John DiJulius, in his book *The Customer Service Revolution: Overthrow Conventional Business, Inspire Employees, and Change the World*

SO TRUE.

This is such a lovely, parsimonious use of words!

Again: please don't speed through. Instead: pause. Reflect. (And perhaps post it on the wall behind your desk as a constant reminder.) (FYI redux: not rocket science.)

5.1.6
"WE ARE LADIES AND GENTLEMEN SERVING LADIES AND GENTLEMEN"

From the Ritz-Carlton Credo. (The company is routinely voted one of the best companies to work for in America.)

In the hotel business, members of frontline staff have historically been treated more like cannon fodder than "ladies and gentlemen"— this mark of respect, certified as a written core belief, is a very big deal. And, in my experience, very much "for real."

EMPLOYEES AS "LADIES AND GENTLEMEN." LOVE IT!

5.1.7
"BUSINESS HAS TO GIVE PEOPLE ENRICHING, REWARDING LIVES OR IT'S SIMPLY NOT WORTH DOING."

From Richard Branson: In my translation, Branson is effectively saying that no matter how cool or irresistible or profitable your product or service may be, the great game of business is *not* to be played unless your employees are the ultimate winners.

Remember these words: **"NOT. WORTH. DOING."**

Take note, and yes, I re-repeat myself: This quote is in no way "soft." Simply put, helping your employees achieve a worthwhile future turns out to be the most profitable way to run a company. Period.

5.1.8
FROM RALPH NADER: "I START WITH THE PREMISE THAT THE FUNCTION OF LEADERSHIP IS TO PRODUCE MORE LEADERS, NOT MORE FOLLOWERS."

Why, oh, why, oh, why do so few understand this one? (I know, I say this a lot, particularly in this chapter.) When I wrote *The Brand You 50* in 1999, so many bosses said that the idea of, say, twenty-five frisky Brand Yous running around was tantamount to anarchy.

I disagreed vociferously and argued that in our brave new world, survival depends on each of our 25—or 2 or 250—employees being personal growth fanatics with an entrepreneurial bent. Only by following that path do the workers and the organization have a chance of adapting and surviving, let alone thriving.

We want, for the sake of survival . . . **leaders all!**

Mr. Nader pegged it!

5.1.9
NOW PLEASE CONSIDER ADDING "HOSTMANSHIP"— LEADER AS HOST TO HER EMPLOYEES

The path to a hostmanship culture paradoxically does not go through the guest. . . . True hostmanship leaders focus first on their employees.

We went through the hotel [immediately upon acquiring it] and made a . . . "consideration renovation." Instead of redoing bathrooms, dining rooms, and guest rooms, we gave employees new uniforms, bought flowers and fruit, and changed colors. Our focus was totally on the staff. They were the ones we wanted to make happy. We wanted them to wake up every morning excited about a new day at work.

—Jan Gunnarsson and Olle Blohm,
Hostmanship: The Art of Making People Feel Welcome

(Gunnarsson and Blohm are management gurus *and* own a hotel; this ain't theory.)

Consideration renovation—a lovely term. PONDER IT.

The authors continue: **"Would you prefer to stay at a hotel where the staff love their work or where management has made customers its highest priority?"**

At first blush, that may sound odd. But we often see a mission statement that puts the customer first and pays but lip service to the employees who serve that customer. How often is this the case? Alas, I'd say with confidence more often than not. The reverse—the logic presented here—is well worth reflecting upon.

Which is to say, it's right on the money!

5.1.10
STRETCH YOUR IMAGINATION: MANAGER AS "DREAM MANAGER"

An organization can only become the-best-version-of-itself to the extent that the people who drive that organization are

striving to become better-versions-of-themselves. . . . Our employees are our first customers, and our most influential customers.   —Matthew Kelly, *The Dream Manager*

"Become better-versions-of-themselves": Every employee, Kelly asserts, has a dream related to his or her current job and, most likely, more generally regarding his or her future. For example, consider the hotel housekeeper, a single mom with two kids and two jobs who would dearly love to work toward a junior college certificate or degree or something similar that would help her imagine a future with options unrelated to mops, rags, and vacuum cleaners.

Focusing on helping employees attain those on- *or* off-the-job dreams—hence, the boss as "dream manager"—is simply an extraordinarily effective way to create an environment where employees strive to improve themselves more or less each and every day and in the process almost invariably serve each other, and the client, with verve.

(And, I'd add, it is also the decent thing to do in a world where the only possibility of continued employability is growth.)

The Dream Manager, presented in parable form (normally not my cup of tea), is in fact directly based on an extremely successful industrial cleaning services company that preferred not to be identified. I was fortunate to meet the publicity-shy CEO. She's the real thing.

Thanks to Matthew Kelly, each time I now come in contact with, say, a frontline hotel employee, I wonder if she or he is lucky enough to have a dream manager.

(As usual, and it must be regularly repeated, the key to implementing some version of the dream manager approach is corporate culture. The leadership team must be unanimously disposed toward helpfulness, must genuinely be engaged with abetting large-scale dream fulfillment. Otherwise, the idea will be a flop and quite likely do harm; the harm of promises unfulfilled.)

5.1.11
STAFF FIRST: A HEALTH CARE REVOLUTION?

Nobody comes home after a surgery saying, "Man, that was the best suturing I've ever seen!" or, "Sweet, they took out the correct kidney!" Instead, we talk about the people who took care of us, the ones who coordinated the whole procedure—everyone from the receptionist to the nurses to the surgeon. And we don't just tell stories around the dinner table. We share our experiences through conversations with friends and colleagues and via social media sites like Facebook and Twitter.

—Paul Spiegelman and Britt Berrett, *Patients Come Second: Leading Change By Changing the Way You Lead*

Health care is our biggest industry by far and surely the most complex. Patients are increasingly treated like cattle. For example, docs are saddled with ridiculous quotas on patients to be seen per day, which frequently results in a perfunctory visit that in turn leads to diagnoses that all too frequently miss the mark. Then there's the technology that effectively requires a nurse to spend her bedside time entering data into a tablet—hence, and numerous studies confirm this, she rarely even makes eye contact, which is all too important to healing, with the patient.

The point here is that the harried hospital staffer cannot give the patient memorable (or compassionate or *safe!*) care until the hospital focuses on dealing with the constraints that keep the staffer from doing so. Following something like the "hostmanship" vignette above, the wise boss might start with an employee-focused "consideration renovation." Only after that can we rightfully expect the quality of customer (patient) care to soar.

Happy (or at least less unhappy) employee = Better in-patient care and, which has been repeatedly demonstrated, significantly better patient outcomes.

In summary, first things first. And in this case, the story told in *Patients Come Second*, that first thing is to enable and encourage hospital employees to do what caused so many of them to go into the trade in the first place—that is, to give emotionally supportive assistance to the bedridden, usually fearful, and typically overwhelmed patient.

Pause for a moment—or two or three or four.
Or five or ten.

Carefully reread each of the lead quotes in this section and reflect on the precise wording:

- Business is not worth doing if you don't enhance the lives of your employees. From an unimpeachable source, Richard Branson, who has tackled and mastered the toughest industries. NOT WORTH DOING. If it ain't great for the workforce, fuggeddabout it.
- And Southwest Airlines founder Herb Kelleher chimes in.

Asked his secret to success, he, like Conrad Hilton in the leadoff to this book, uttered but a single sentence: the Southwest employee is "Customer #1."

- Super deli man Ari Weinzweig, a star of the book *Small Giants*, says his role is to "give great service" to his staff.
- John DiJulius tells us that our paying customers will never be any happier than the employees who serve them.
- And: Employees-first "consideration renovation"
- And: "Dream managers" who help employees achieve life goals, often independent of the firm
- Etc.

Action: I'd ask that you think back in some detail on the last twenty-four hours.

How do you (and your organization) measure up (specifics, please) on these formulations from business Hall of Famers?

PLEASE: These are NOT meant to be "cool quotes." These are hard-nosed, profit-maximizing, practical approaches in enterprises large and small in tougher-than-tough industries that can be . . .

OPERATIONALIZED.
Starting NOW.

5.1.12
MY SUMMARY OF ALL THIS

> **EXCELLENT customer experiences depend ENTIRELY on EXCELLENT employee experiences!**
>
> **If you want to "WOW!" your customers, FIRST you must WOW those who WOW the customers!**

5.2

5.2.1
A BRIEF NOTE ON "PEOPLE (REALLY) FIRST" LEADERSHIP: LES GETS RELIGION

I got as excited about developing people [as I had been about identifying fashion trends].
                    —Les Wexner, founder/CEO, the Limited Brands

Founder/CEO Les Wexner's Limited Brands/now L Brands saga almost merits the term *peerless*. In addition to his revolutionary impact on affordable fashion retailing, he put together a long-term financial success record that *Bloomberg Businessweek* assessed, among other things, as better than that of Jack Welch during his storied time at GE's helm.

In the *Bloomberg Businessweek* article, Wexner responded to a query about the source of his long-term success with the quote above. He reported that as time went on, he realized expanding his enterprise and keeping it fresh was entirely dependent upon creating a peerless team, from the young saleswoman on the floor to his portfolio of executives.

In fact, that is the subtext of virtually all the quotes above. I am fortunate enough to have gotten to know most of the execs who are quoted, including Wexner. Their passion for putting people at the top of the agenda, today and over the long term, unmistakably stands out.

5.2.2
PEOPLE (REALLY) FIRST: WHAT IS THE MOMENT-TO-MOMENT TRANSLATION OF "PUTTING PEOPLE FIRST"?

The following is an exchange that occurred at a break in a seminar a while back:

"So, Tom, the core of your practice is 'people first.' But what does that really mean? How does that translate into my day's work?"

I paused for quite a while before answering, several responses churning through my head. And then something almost literally clicked. I recalled a conversation from some years ago with an exceptionally successful Nordstrom regional manager. We were talking about this and that, and then, and I don't know what triggered it, she said, almost wistfully, and my memory is quite vivid:

What I do today is important to the company, but it will never match the joy of having my own store as I did for almost five years. There were always a dozen problems to solve, but when I was stuck or frustrated or just plain weary, I knew exactly what to do.

I'd get up from my desk and wander through the store. I'd chat up an employee for thirty seconds, or sometimes five minutes. I'd probably meander all told about a half hour. Corny as it probably sounds, just being in their presence was a genuine high. We were truly a team, and we cared about each other. They were in fact my personal community.

I don't want to sound melodramatic, but when I got back to my desk after that thirty minutes or so roaming the store, my head would be clear, and usually I saw the "problem" that had befuddled me transform itself into an opportunity to do something positive. Now that I'm an "executive," I'll never have that thrill again.

That, dear colleagues, is a "people person"!

5.3 PEOPLE (REALLY) FIRST: THE FULLY ENGAGED "SOCIAL EMPLOYEE" EMPOWERED BY AI

To some, "people first" might seem like an anachronism, as artificial intelligence continues its hell-bent drive toward job restructuring and, often, destruction. But there is a sound argument that says precisely the opposite is the case; "people (really) first" will in fact be a survivor's trait. It can, and more likely will, be more important than ever. Moreover, there is a case for AI-as-ally rather than destroyer—that is, fully empowered employees interacting to use AI to create novel, highly differentiated customer experiences.

For example, in their pioneering book, *The Social Employee*, Cheryl Burgess and Mark Burgess describe a world in which every employee, augmented (rather than deconstructed) by the new technology, adds significant and distinct value as he or she potentially becomes no less than an innovating customer-contact star.*

Among giant firms, IBM has been a leader of the pack in pursuing this strategy of radically enhanced "all hands," technology-powered engagement. The emerging theory, in the words of Ethan McCarty, former IBM director of enterprise social strategy, goes something like this:

Picture a ball and a bag of marbles side by side. The two items might have the same volume—that is, if you dropped them into a bucket, they would displace the same amount of water. The difference, however, lies in the surface area.

A bag of marbles is comprised of several individual pieces, and the combined surface area of all the marbles far outstrips (if the bag is sizeable, by orders of magnitude) the surface area of a single ball.

The expanded surface area within the bag of marbles represents a social brand's increased diversity. The surfaces of each of the marbles connect and interact with each other in unique ways, offering customers and employees alike a variety of paths toward a myriad of solutions. If none of the paths prove to be suitable, social employees can carve out new paths on their own.

---

* The distinction is often made in terms of AI (artificial intelligence) and IA (intelligence augmented). The Burgesses examine and effectively make the case for IA.

I think this image is exceptionally powerful. In simple terms, a world of 100 percent engaged employees exploiting, rather than being exploited by, AI can bring exceptional innovative potential to their tasks, compared with the narrow-gauged version of "empowered" that prevails in the relatively static organizational models that are still the norm.

While the bag-of-marbles image is compelling, the challenge of the doing is monumental and is effectively addressed by the Burgesses in *The Social Employee*. Suffice it to say that every aspect of the enterprise must be transformed—hiring, training and development, execution and control mechanisms, and, above all, the establishment of a corporate culture that supports a radically new approach to organizing and wholesale employee growth.

5.4 PEOPLE FIRST: HIRING

In short, hiring is the most important aspect of business and yet remains woefully misunderstood.
> —*The Wall Street Journal*, review of
> *Who: The A Method for Hiring*,
> Geoff Smart and Randy Street

Reread.

Strong statement.

Correct statement.

Action item of the first order.

And:

Development can help great people be even better—but if I had a dollar to spend, I'd spend 70 cents getting the right person in the door. —Paul Russell, director, leadership and development, Google

So, how do you rate your hiring skills? Can you—think long and hard and honestly on this—call yourself a true "hiring professional"? Are you an assiduous student of all that goes into effective hiring? For one thing, how many books on hiring per se have you read? Have you ever taken a course exclusively focused on hiring? If, as stated above, hiring is the "most important aspect of business" and business is what you do, then "hiring excellence" deserves at least the same attention that would go into becoming a first-rate mechanical engineer or biochemist. Right?

5.4.1
HIRING: ATTRIBUTES THAT MAKE ALL THE DIFFERENCE (AND THAT TOO OFTEN GET SHORT SHRIFT)

To create cultures for tomorrow that can deliver startling innovations on a regular basis and distinct, emotionally fulfilling customer experiences, one needs to emphasize far more than technical skills, more than even *superb* technical skills in the hiring process.

5.4.1.1

LISTENING, CARING, SMILING, SAYING "THANK YOU," BEING WARM

Take Southwest Airlines. It remains a low-price airline with a high-value "people culture" that delivers top-rated customer service and experiences. It begins, from pilots and mechanics to flight attendants, with a distinctive hiring approach.

Per former Southwest president Colleen Barrett:

We look for . . . listening, caring, smiling, saying "Thank you," being warm.

Is Barrett's list for public consumption? Or is it real?

An example: I'm about to board a Southwest flight from Albany, New York, to Baltimore. The plane is ready for boarding. As is typical, three or four wheelchairs are lined up at the gate. The crew makes their appearance, obviously rushing from a flight that arrived late, and heads for the jetway. The pilot stops, turns to the older woman in the first wheelchair in the line, and says, *"May I help you down the jetway?"*

She says, "Thank you, yes."

Off she goes with the pilot conveying her to the aircraft.

I've chalked up about ten thousand flight legs, yet this experience was a first. (I actually think I gasped; airlines are frequently entry #1 on the "customer unfriendly" lists.)

I contend that the pilot's courtesy—and courtesy while under pressure to boot—was no accident, that in fact it was a direct by-product of "We look for listening, caring, smiling, saying 'Thank you,' being warm."

5.4.1.2
NICE

When we talk about "soft" traits, one would hardly expect the conversation to turn to a pharmaceutical company. Well, let me introduce you to Peter Miller, CEO of pharma's OptiNose.

> **The ultimate filter we use [in the hiring process] is that we only hire nice people. . . . When we finish assessing skills, we do something called "running the gauntlet." We have them interact with fifteen or twenty people, and every one of them has what I call a "blackball vote," which means they can say if we should not hire that person.**

Miller continues,

> **I believe in culture so strongly and that one bad apple can spoil the bunch. There are enough really talented people out there who are nice; you don't really need to put up with people who act like jerks.**

Nice!

Pharmaceuticals!

Yes!

(Along this same line, a friend reports on an extremely successful New Zealand company in a very competitive environment within the entertainment industry. The founder's chief hiring criterion: **"No shitheads."** I'll second that!)

5.4.1.3
EMPATHY

This is courtesy of Stewart Butterfield, cofounder/CEO of Slack and founder of Flickr:

> **When we talk about the qualities we want in people, empathy is a big one. If you can empathize with people, then you can do a good job. If you have no ability to empathize, then it's difficult to give people feedback, and it is difficult to help people improve. Everything becomes harder.**
>
> **One way that empathy manifests itself is courtesy. . . . It's not just a veneer of politeness, but actually trying to anticipate someone else's needs and meeting them in advance.**

5.4.1.4
BETTER PEOPLE/CHARACTER

Let's head for the football field. Surely the quality of the physical skills wins out? Not according to coaching legend Bo Schembechler:

> **I can't tell you how many times we passed up hotshots for guys we thought were better people, and watched our guys do a lot better than the big names, not just in the classroom, but on the field—and naturally, after they graduated, too. Again and again, the blue chips faded out, and**

our little up-and-comers clawed their way to all-conference and All-America teams.

(The legendary basketball coach John Wooden's parallel version of this was **"Ability may get you to the top, it takes character to keep you there."**)

CHARACTER:
THEO GETS RELIGION; 108-YEAR DROUGHT COMES TO AN END

In mid-2017, *Fortune* magazine featured "World's 50 Greatest Leaders." Astoundingly, Theo Epstein, the general manager who took the Chicago Cubs to their first World Series triumph in 108 years, topped the list.

The story revolved around a single word: **CHARACTER**.

Against long odds, Epstein had taken the Boston Red Sox to the top of the heap thanks, significantly, to hiring decisions based on advanced statistical analysis ("analytics"). But then the team effectively fell apart, due mostly to internal dissension. And Mr. Epstein moved on to the Cubs. And, it turns out, he discovered . . . character.

Fortune reports:

> **Character and chemistry were strengths that a "quant" approach couldn't capture, and in 2011, in what turned out to be Epstein's final season in Boston, their absence was painfully clear as the team underwent a late-season collapse. The more the team lost, the more it broke apart from within. . . .**

> **Once he'd joined the Cubs, Epstein gave his scouts very specific marching orders. . . . They were to dig into a player's makeup by talking to just about anybody who knew him: parents, guidance counselors, teammates, girlfriends, siblings. . . . Cubs scouting reports would never look the same again.**

Epstein went way beyond the stats and hired, effectively, for character.

The Cubs in 2016 ended a 108-year championship drought.

(Could the story be that simple? Of course not! On the other hand, the central theme, according to those I've talked with, is accurate, which makes enormous sense to me.)

5.4.1.5
CURIOSITY

Going to a slightly different compass point, there's another attribute that takes on special meaning in these upside down times.

For a *Vanity Fair* interview, Michael Bloomberg was asked to provide his "most significant trait." He gave a one-word reply:

CURIOSITY.

In Workplace 2018, *I insist that curiosity should be a "must-have" for 100% of jobs.* Curiosity could legitimately be called the #1 way in which we individually and collectively differentiate ourselves in the Age of Automation.

Some argue—including many who are among converts to

"algorithmic hiring"—that there are jobs where keeping one's nose to the grindstone full-time is imperative. And I am not arguing that there are not degrees of curiosity; what we might desire in a research scientist is not what we might seek in a call-center employee or hotel housekeeper.

Nonetheless, I will go to the mat when it comes to voting, in any job slot, for those who are inclined to regularly ask, "Why?" or "Why not?"

Consider a hotel housekeeping team: Our algorithmic hiring friends may well be able to deliver in the short-term a 6 percent increase in productivity from their hiring practices based on "Big Data" correlations. But over the long term, I'll bet a pretty penny that *my* "smiling," "nice," "empathetic," "curious" housekeeping team, working in a hotel where "ladies and gentlemen serve ladies and gentlemen," will win out over the algorithmically hired gang very decisively.

Wanna bet?

5.4.1.6
BOTTOM LINE

Be *explicit*. Use *these* words—**damn it!**—not HR gobbledygook equivalents:

- LISTENING
- CARING
- SMILING
- SAYING "THANK YOU"

- BEING WARM
- NICE
- EMPATHY
- BETTER PEOPLE
- CHARACTER
- CURIOSITY
- NO JERKS
- NO SHITHEADS

I cannot think of any position in any company of any size where these twelve characteristics would not pay off.

Can you?

I repeat:

BE EXPLICIT.
USE THESE EXACT WORDS.

I cannot resist adding two more traits, though perhaps not for every job, courtesy of Jeffrey Rothfeder in *Driving Honda: Inside the World's Most Innovative Car Company*:

> **Asked for the single most important attribute that an ideal Honda applicant should have, Soichiro [Honda] noted that he preferred "people who had been in trouble." . . . He believed genius arose from idiosyncrasy, "Nonconformity is essential to an artist or an inventor," he told his workers.**

Hence my "for your consideration" addenda to the list above:

- PEOPLE WHO HAVE BEEN IN TROUBLE
- NONCONFORMITY

5.4.2

5.4.2.1
PEOPLE FIRST: THE MISSING 50 PERCENT/DON'T BYPASS THE QUIET ONES

Consider what was for me a life-changing book—namely, Susan Cain's remarkable *Quiet: The Power of Introverts in a World That Can't Stop Talking*.

Susan Cain claims—with fervor and a train car full of hard data—that we are idiots. Well, she doesn't do any such thing. But as I read the book, I felt like a complete idiot. By and large (well, almost without exception), employers gravitate, starting with the hiring process, toward the noisy ones. And that is a colossal mistake, essentially depriving ourselves of the services of the nearly half of the population of "the quiet ones" who tend to think before they open their mouths and in general bring to the table a different and invaluable approach to their work. (As to my idiocy, I get paid to be on top of all this, and in fact I have been missing the boat by a jillion nautical miles.)

From *Quiet*:

1. The Very Questionable Extrovert Ideal: "The Extrovert Ideal has been documented in many studies. . . . Talkative people, for example, are rated as smarter, better looking, more interesting, and more desirable as friends. Velocity of speech counts as well as volume: we rank fast talkers as more competent and likeable than slow

ones. . . . But we make a grave mistake to embrace the Extrovert Ideal so unthinkingly."

2. Conversational Pairings/Experiment: "The introverts and extroverts participated about equally, giving the lie to the idea that introverts talk less. But the introvert pairs tended to focus on one or two serious subjects of conversation, while the extrovert pairs were lighter-hearted and surfaced wider-ranging topics."

3. Limits to Assertiveness: "Also, remember the dangers of the New Groupthink. If it's creativity you're after, ask your employees to solve problems alone before sharing their ideas. . . . Don't mistake assertiveness or eloquence for good ideas. If you have a proactive workforce (and I hope you do), remember that they may perform better under an introverted leader than under an extroverted or charismatic one."

4. Quiet Power: "So the next time you see a person with a composed face and a soft voice, remember that inside her mind she might be solving an equation, composing a sonnet, designing a hat. She might, that is, be deploying the power of quiet."

I plead guilty.

I've (mostly) fallen for the noisy ones.

I've associated noisy with "energetic," "enthusiastic," and all those other positive terms in the first quote above. What a bunch of nonsense on my part.

Damn it.

Thank you, Susan Cain.

Excuse the apparent hyperbole, but *Quiet* has changed my life, and its message has become a (bellowing, raging) staple of every presentation I give.

For God's sake, I've been blowing off practically half the population.

All hail the introverts!

Please read the book and perhaps join Ms. Cain's "Quiet Revolution" on the Web—www.quietrev.com.

Quiet is an unequivocal . . .

CALL TO (DIRECT) ACTION.
QUIET ROCKS.
QUIET PAYS.

YOU ARE NOW IN THE LOOP.
NO EXCUSES.

5.4.2.2
PEOPLE FIRST: THE "QUIET ONES" SAY "SAVE ME FROM THE BULLPEN"

Ms. Cain takes on another of my principal bugbears: the breathless promotion of open offices. I cannot do her case justice in this brief summary. But perhaps I can sow one or two seeds of doubt in what has become conventional wisdom.

Consider this powerful statement in *Quiet* from Apple cofounder Steve Wozniak:

Most inventors and engineers I have met are like me—they're shy and they live in their heads. . . . [They] work best alone and where they can control an invention's design. . . . I'm going to give you some advice that might be hard to take: **Work alone**. You're going to be best able to design revolutionary products and features.

More from *Quiet*:

Open-plan workers are more likely to suffer from high blood pressure and elevated stress levels and get the flu; they argue more with their colleagues. . . . Introverts seem to know these things intuitively and resist being herded together.

Also from *Quiet*, video-game design company Backbone Entertainment's creative director:

We switched over to cubicles [from a "warehouse" format] and were worried about it. You'd think in a creative environment people would hate that. But it turns out they prefer having nooks and crannies they can hide away in and be away from everybody.

Three quotes doth not a case make. But they do, I hope, raise questions.

Disclaimer: Ignore me on this topic if you wish. I ADMIT TO DESPISING THE VERY MENTION OF "OPEN OFFICES." I WOULD SOONER DIE THAN WORK IN AN OPEN

OFFICE (uh, maybe that's a bit extreme—but, then again, maybe not).

David Burkus titled one chapter in his superb book *Under New Management* "Close Open Offices."

Works for me.

5.5 PEOPLE FIRST: GETTING (REALLY) SERIOUS ABOUT EVALUATION

Evaluating People Effectively = #1 Differentiator

After superb results during his first decade as CEO, Jack Welch finally convinced Wall Street that GE was more than an unclassifiable (ragtag) "conglomerate." He said that a large part of the GE difference was a unique capability to developing great leader-managers. The results of his people development success, he said, were worth tens of billions of dollars in market capitalization.

The market agreed.

And at the center of that management development excellence was unique attention to and skill at . . . EVALUATION. McKinsey's Ed Michaels gave a flavor of the GE process in *The War for Talent*:

> **In most companies, the Talent Review Process is a farce. At GE, Jack Welch and his two top HR people visited each division for a day. They reviewed the top 20 to 50 people by name. They talked about Talent Pool strengthening issues. The Talent Review Process is a contact sport at**

GE; it has the intensity and the importance of the budget process at most companies.

Interestingly, Welch's successor, Jeff Immelt (who was no Welch clone), also said that the evaluation process is contributor #1 to the company's success.

Powerful, eh?

(And, alas, I agree with Michaels that most review processes are spineless and do not focus on the overall quality of the talent pool. Which is not to say that GE always got it right. Some practices, for example, encompassed unvarnished verbal brutality; Immelt made a great number of long-overdue changes in that regard. But the intensity, seriousness, and strategic importance of the process remains undiminished.)

SOME THOUGHTS ON EVALUATIONS

- Do football coaches or theater directors use a standard HR evaluation form to assess their players or actors? Stupid question, eh? The whole point in these instances is to build on the differences and cherish the peculiarities; "same-same" templates should be avoided at all costs.
- Does the CEO use a standard evaluation form for her VPs? If not, then why use one for frontline employees? Standardized evaluation forms are as wrongheaded for assessing the ten baristas at a Starbucks shop as for assessing Starbucks' ten top vice presidents. I am dead serious about this. Again, see above; the idea is to create

an interesting team that provides memorable customer experiences. Interesting differences in personality are as important as similarities on dimensions such as, say, demonstrated punctuality.

- Each of your, say, eight direct reports has an utterly unique professional trajectory. How could a standardized evaluation form serve any useful purpose?

- Effective evaluations emerge from a series of loosely structured, continuing conversations, not from filling out a form once every six months or year.

- Boss: Does it take you at least a day to prepare for a one-hour evaluation meeting? If not, you are not very serious about the meeting or the employee being evaluated.

- Boss: If you are not exhausted after an evaluation conversation, then it wasn't a serious conversation.

- I am not keen on formal programs that identify high-potential employees. As a manager, I will treat all team members as possible high potentials! ("Hi-po" programs have a history of demotivating the "other 95 percent.")

- I have no problem with a shared checklist to guide the evaluation conversation. But the "off list" discussion will by far be the most important element of the exchange.

- Central to an evaluation conversation are company values and culture. How—be very explicit—does the person being evaluated adhere to and inject energy into the company culture and values?

- Topic #1 for a boss of bosses: What is her/his "leadership development" track record? (This should be examined before the session in *exacting* detail.)

Message #1: People are NOT "standardized." Their evaluations should NOT be standardized. EVER.

(Damn it!)

Wrap up: Can you honestly call yourself an **"EVALUATION PRO"**?

If not, how do you become one?

Study.
Practice.
Coaching.
Feedback.

BOSS: THIS IS WHAT THE HELL YOU DO FOR A LIVING! MASTERY IS EXTREMELY DIFFICULT. EXCELLENCE IN EVALUATION, I SUGGEST, IS AS COMPLEX AS EXCELLENCE IN NEUROSURGERY. THERE IS NOT A HINT OF EXAGGERATION IN THAT STATEMENT.

(Recap: Leadership may involve vision, authenticity, and so on. But in the main—and the source of managers'/leaders' highest impact—is "stuff"—that is, discrete tasks such as hiring and evaluating. And, frankly, very few managers/leaders merit the word *pro* when it comes to these discrete tasks that are the real meat and potatoes of their job.)

5.6 "BIG DATA." HR GENIUS? HR MADNESS? HR'S FUTURE?

From Leerom Segal, Aaron Goldstein, Jay Goldman, and Rahaf Harfoush, *The Decoded Company: Know Your Talent Better Than You Know Your Customers*:

DPSS/DATA-POWERED SIXTH SENSE
(Radical insights into what makes your people work)

A Decoded Company with the right systems in place can collect all of the required data to provide organizational proprioception ["digital body language"] from your people, giving them that background sense of what neighboring departments and teams are doing, as well as that of the efforts of their team members. We think of this as eliminating blind spots.

To me, the excerpt above reads word-for-word like a passage from George Orwell's *1984*. At the very least, it amounts to playing (key word: *playing*) with fire. Or in this instance, playing with people.

In short order, Artificial Intelligence and Big Data have plunged headlong and at flank speed into the world of human resources. While there is doubtless much of value, there are also extraordinary downsides or at least potential downsides. From the above: "as well as that of the efforts of their team members." AI, per an idea such as this, will have the power to monitor virtually every breath and grimace and grin you make and compare the results to that of your teammates. While I can possibly imagine some increase in ability to coordinate some activities, what stands out to me, among other things, is what feels like a perfect tool for crushing individuality and creativity at precisely the wrong moment—that is, a moment where creativity is becoming Key #1 to differentiation and job retention.

As to my comment about *playing* being the key word, most of the HR software is, in my opinion, less than adequately tested. To be sure, it's been carefully vetted by its producers, but the mid- to long-term impact on the likes of creativity and the human spirit in general is simply unknown.

I will only offer one scenario concerning the intrusiveness that awaits us. It comes courtesy of Eric Siegel's *Predictive Analytics: The Power to Predict Who Will Click, Buy, Lie, or Die*:

> **Flash forward to dystopia. You work in a chic cubicle, sucking chicken-flavored sustenance from a tube. You're furiously maneuvering with a joystick. . . . Your boss stops by and gives you a look. *"We need to talk about your loyalty to this company."* The organization you work for has deduced that you might be planning to quit. [The AI/Big Data model] predicts your plans and intentions, possibly before you have even conceived them.**

In short, the AI algorithm, based upon information of God knows what flavor from God knows how many organizations, has perhaps discerned from a careful analysis of every keystroke you've made (each stored in an electronic corporate Big Data cloud vault) that your choice of phraseology in e-mails and instant messages is consistent with phraseology used by people who have quit their jobs. Yes, the infinite correlations among big data collected from some enormous planetary population knows what you are thinking, as Mr. Siegal says, perhaps before you do. (Telltales are not primarily obvious, like the use of the word *headhunter*. It's typically more subtle, such as an increase in using the phrase *bureaucratic bullshit* or a jump in the percentage of times you go out to lunch rather than stay in.)

This is no fantasy. Siegal's example is derived from a Hewlett-Packard "flight risk" model developed by the company's HR unit.

In summary: Some very wise souls insist that we are entering a brave new future of AI-determined organization and work structuring. I have no doubt that tools such as DPSS or the HP flight risk algorithm may contribute to, say, a rapid short-term productivity increase. But I unequivocally draw the line at the notion that effective organizing and staffing for tomorrow is destined to be "algorithmically optimized," to use a term that appeared in a McKinsey article.

For one [B-I-G] thing, the primary defenses against AI-driven job destruction are widespread, relatively unconstrained creativity and novel organizational arrangements designed to produce products and services that will stand out in an automated world. I unequivocally believe that such creativity is antithetical to algorithmic optimization of human affairs.

The game is on!
The stakes are ludicrously high for organizations and individuals!
And too many of us are asleep at the switch—in particular, thoughtlessly purchasing and implementing powerful, minimally tested tools!

(If I were able to issue a single command on this topic, it would be to beg you to read carefully Cathy O'Neil's extraordinary book *Weapons of Math Destruction: How Big Data Increases Inequality and Threatens Democracy*. The title suggests oceanic issues accompanying the untrammeled use of big data—inequality and democracy—and Dr. O'Neil, who is a math Ph.D. from Harvard, delivers chilling evidence to support her concerns. Included in the book are two brilliant chapters on HR software. They contain example piled upon example of the unintended consequences of the promiscuous use of big data in HR settings. Perhaps the most important point is that these tools mess with us and are effectively untested on dimensions that matter to long-term business success or failure and to the way we treat our fellow human beings.)

5.7 PEOPLE FIRST: PROMOTING IS A LIFE-OR-DEATH MATTER

Promotions are **life and death decisions.**
—Peter Drucker, *The Practice of Management*

Drucker says "life and death" decisions. The sentiment is hard to argue with. As I see it, a leader at any given level makes on average two key promotion decisions every year. If she is in a job for five years, say, that adds up to ten promotion decisions. In short, and at the end of the day, those ten promotion decisions *are* her principal legacy!

Do most leaders take promotion decisions seriously?

Absolutely!

But the question is, do they take them seriously enough?

In general, in perhaps nine cases out of ten, I'd say no.

For example, as I see it, a promotion decision is a close kin to an acquisition decision. You (chief, deciding on who gets promoted) are effectively going to anoint someone or someone else with the wholesale responsibility ("ownership") for the future performance of a vital segment of the organization. He or she, regardless of the formal language on the organization chart, will in effect be the CEO of:

XYZ Division
Training Department
Customer Service
Etc.

You'd spend months on an acquisition decision of even a tiny company. And I believe a promotion that turns a company (or division or department) over to Ms. X or Mr. Y should get more or less the same degree of attention.

CONSIDERATIONS

Promotion Key #1: Obviously—I wish it were so in practice—the #1 consideration in the promotion is demonstrated people development skills.

Be very thorough, systematic, and precise in assessing these skills (e.g., interview, in particular, "graduates," people in the candidate's charge who have moved on, one hopes, to greater things); how well did Ms. X prepare her for the next job or promotion?

Promotion Key #2: The second primary consideration is the work culture that Mr. Y has established in his current assignment. In particular, has it been an energetic, civil, innovative, execution-focused environment?

Promotion Key #3: In "crazy 2018," promotions are arguably more important than ever. One interesting take on this comes from risk-management professional David Rothkopf:

Character is more crucial now than ever, because [in times of great uncertainty] past performance is no indicator of future performance. Experience falls away and all you're left with is character.

Summary:

"Life and death" decisions
Two per year = Legacy
#1, #2, #3 = People development, culture, character

READ! STUDY!
Profit Through Putting People First
Business Book Club

Business by and large has a lousy rep, and management books by and large focus on things that are broken and how to fix them. Yet there is also a robust body of "good news by putting people (really) first" books, like the informal list below. How about a yearlong "Profit Through Putting People First Business Book Club" for you and/or your leadership team?

Nice Companies Finish First: Why Cutthroat Management Is Over—and Collaboration Is In by Peter Shankman with Karen Kelly

Uncontainable: How Passion, Commitment, and Conscious Capitalism Built a Business Where Everyone Thrives by Kip Tindell

Conscious Capitalism: Liberating the Heroic Spirit of Business by John Mackey and Raj Sisodia

Firms of Endearment: How World-Class Companies Profit from Passion and Purpose by Raj Sisodia, Jag Sheth, and David Wolfe

The Good Jobs Strategy: How the Smartest Companies Invest in Employees to Lower Costs and Boost Profits by Zeynep Ton

Joy, Inc.: How We Built a Workplace People Love by Richard Sheridan

Joy at Work: A Revolutionary Approach to Fun on the Job by Dennis Bakke

Employees First, Customers Second: Turning Conventional Management Upside Down by Vineet Nayar

The Customer Comes Second: Put Your People First and Watch 'Em Kick Butt by Hal Rosenbluth

Patients Come Second: Leading Change by Changing the Way You Lead by Paul Spiegelman and Britt Berrett

It's Your Ship: Management Techniques from the Best Damn Ship in the Navy by D. Michael Abrashoff

Turn This Ship Around!: How to Create Leadership at Every Level by L. David Marquet

Small Giants: Companies That Choose to Be Great Instead of Big by Bo Burlingham

Hidden Champions of the 21st Century: The Success Strategies of Unknown World Market Leaders by Hermann Simon

Retail Superstars: Inside the 25 Best Independent Stores in America by George Whalin

The Soft Edge: Where Great Companies Find Lasting Success by Rich Karlgaard

Everybody Wins: The Story and Lessons Behind RE/MAX by Phil Harkins and Keith Hollihan

The Dream Manager by Matthew Kelly

Delivering Happiness: A Path to Profits by Tony Hsieh

Camellia: A Very Different Company (company publication)

Fans Not Customers: How to Create Growth Companies in a No Growth World by Vernon Hill

Like a Virgin: Secrets They Won't Teach You at Business School by Richard Branson

Good Business: Leadership, Flow, and the Making of Meaning by Mihaly Csikszentmihalyi

Enough: The Measures of Money, Business, and Life by John Bogle

An Everyone Culture: Becoming a Deliberately Developmental Organization by Robert Kegan and Lisa Laskow Lahey

6 A MANIA FOR TRAINING

MY STORY

MUCH AS I HATE TO ADMIT IT, I AM A SECOND-RATE ATHLETE.

All little boys are supposed to dream about making it to the major leagues. But me? I dreamed of making it from third-string guard to second-string guard on the junior varsity high school football team.

Well, I was never a star for sure, but the fact is that in 1962, I became the starting goalie on the Cornell varsity lacrosse team. And the reason in two words is: Ned Harkness.

I played lacrosse from about the age of eight or nine. That was requisite if you grew up in Maryland. I worked hard but didn't seem to get very far. (See my opening comment above.)

But I did keep at it, made it to my high school varsity team, made it to my Cornell freshman team. Hung in and hung on.

Then a magical thing happened. Ned Harkness became the coach of the Cornell varsity lacrosse team where I, in my sophomore year, was a second- or third-stringer. Ned had won national collegiate championships in both lacrosse and hockey. (He became, among other things, a successful National Hockey League coach.) At Cornell, he was the varsity hockey coach, but when the prior lacrosse coach left suddenly early in the 1962 season, Ned filled in for the rest of the year.

Here's the bottom line: Lousy jock that I was, I rose to the occasion under Coach Harkness. He was like no other I'd experienced. He got inside our heads, our horrible repetitive drills became fun, we learned new tricks of the trade by the bucketload, and we really got off on one another.

As for me, I was transformed in the space of two or three weeks. He believed I had two or three or ten times more potential than I'd ever exhibited, and he made *me* believe it. And, on the first game of the second half of the season, I became a varsity starter with, my God, the confidence necessary to do the job.

Thanks to Ned Harkness, I learned the meaning of great coaching, great practices, and performance that was orders of magnitude beyond what one could imagine one could do.

Lesson: *Great training is transformative: It can make you ten times the player (or whatever) you were a short time before, and it actually changes you dramatically as a person.*

The brief time with Coach Harkness made me a rabid believer in training. WRONG! The time with Coach Harkness made me a rabid believer in EXCELLENT training.

(I'd love to tell you there was some ending in which I became an All-American and helped Cornell to a championship. But the truth is, although I made huge strides thanks to Ned's tutelage, the next coach saw me for what I was—not much of an athlete. I lived down to his expectations, playing ceased to be fun, and I ended up exiting the team in order to put more time in on my absurdly challenging engineering courses. But, ah, those few months the prior year were joyous and a real eye-opener.)

(More generally and relative to The Excellence Dividend, I see training as anybody's or any organization's "Success Practice #1." And I am utterly dismayed, stunned, even enraged when others don't see it the way I do.

Moreover, I believe the "training/prep edge" is 10X or 100X more important in the midst of the age of disruption/tech tsunami in which we are embedded. With brand-new threats and opportunities, there may be challenging questions about the nature of the training, but there can be no question whatsoever about its importance.

This is the shortest chapter in the book. The training discussion was originally buried in chapter 5, but I decided it was too important—in 2018—to imbed in something else. It needed to stand out and stand alone. After all, I argue here with all the passion I can muster that training is any firm's single-most important capital investment.)

THE TRAINING NARRATIVE

6.1 TRAIN. TRAIN. TRAIN. TRAIN. TRAIN.

Training, TRAINING
and M-O-R-E
T-R-A-I-N-I-N-G.
> —Admiral Chester Nimitz, Commander in Chief,
> U.S. Pacific Fleet, communication to Chief of
> Naval Operations Ernest King in 1943.
> Fact: The U.S. Navy was woefully underprepared
> at the time of Pearl Harbor. The fix: TRAINING.
> (Note: The capitalization and punctuation and
> italics in the quote above are Nimitz's, not mine.)

I was never much of a game coach, but I was a pretty good practice coach.
> —Basketball coach John Wooden,
> perhaps the best coach of anything, ever

The will to succeed is important, but what's more important is the will to prepare.
> —Bobby Knight, basketball coaching legend

6.2 TRAINING = INVESTMENT #1!

In the army, three-star generals obsess about training. In most businesses, it's a ho-hum, midlevel staff function.

Intensive and extensive and expensive and constant training is obvious for:

- Army
- Navy
- Air Force
- Marines
- Coast Guard
- Football teams
- Baseball teams
- Archery teams
- Fire departments
- Police departments
- Theater companies
- Ballet companies
- University academic departments
- Etc.

In the military in particular, where the stakes are life and death:

Best training wins!
No issue.

So why the hell does "best training wins" not apply for the average business, and especially why not for the average small business?

It just seems so damned obvious to me.

Bottom line: **Training = Investment #1**

Damn it.

I have always thought training was important but would not have said "Investment #1." My altered tune stems from the animating idea of this book. To meet the tech tide from which the book title is derived, training, writ large, soars to the top of the list of organizational and individual opportunities.

6.3 TRAINING: FOREVER

Getting better and getting ready is an obsession of those moving to the top and particularly those attempting to stay there:

1. Winston Churchill's rule of thumb: ONE HOUR OF PREPARATION FOR ONE MINUTE OF A SPEECH
2. Tom Peters: TWO WEEKS' WORK TO GET READY FOR A FORTY-FIVE-MINUTE SPEECH
3. Jerry Seinfeld: SIX MONTHS (in small clubs) TO ADD THREE NEW MINUTES TO A STAND-UP ROUTINE
4. Abraham Lincoln: "GIVE ME SIX HOURS TO CHOP DOWN A TREE, AND I WILL SPEND THE FIRST FOUR SHARPENING THE AXE."

I acknowledge that I love the word *training*. Many prefer *development* or *preparation*. I get that. But when I think of my next speech, what I think about is, like football or theater, *training*. Then after weeks of getting ready (i.e., training!), I set the alarm for and wake up at 3:00 a.m. on the morning of the speech, and from 3:00 a.m. to 6:30 a.m. when I go downstairs from my hotel room, I will make probably two hundred or three hundred changes.

Development. Practice. Prep. Learning. Fine. But for me, perhaps idiosyncratically, those words are all part of *training*. Or, rather, and excuse the repetitiveness:

TRAINING.
TRAINING.
TRAINING.
DAMN IT.

6.4 THE TRAINING QUERIES: *IF NOT, WHY NOT?*

1. Is your chief training officer (CTO) your top-paid C-level job (other than CEO/COO)?
   If not, why not?
   (Of course I know you probably don't even *have* a CHIEF TRAINING OFFICER. For shame.)
2. Are your top trainers paid as much as and treated as well as your top marketers or engineers?
   If not, why not?
3. Are your training courses so good they make you tingle?
   If not, why not?

Someone at a seminar challenged me on this last question, saying it was unrealistic and, by the way, what the hell does "tingle" mean? I pointed to my sophomore year in college. For engineers, an introductory chemistry course was required. Most of us looked forward to it as the equivalent of a four-month-long root canal procedure. We had two well-known professors, Michell Sienko and Robert Plane. They were scholars of the first order and simultaneously entertainers of the first order.

Result: By the end of the course, probably half of us (among hundreds) wanted to be chemistry majors—that is, there are great teachers and great courses, and I do not understand why the corporate world can't develop or recruit the equivalents of the Sienkos and Planes. Billions upon billions of dollars (and survival) are at stake, and *great* on-payroll "profs" concocting *great* courses could do wonders for, say, recruitment, retention, quality, innovation, and productivity. (Companies spend megabucks recruiting computer science professors of great renown. Why not the same damn thing for top trainers?)

As to "tingle," I'm looking for something beyond *very good*; I'll accept *earthshaking* or *mind-blowing* or, for sure . . . **supercalifragilisticexpialidocious**.

4. If you randomly stop an employee in the hall, can she or he describe in detail her or his development plan for the next twelve months?
    If not, why not?

If the answer is "No," her or his boss should be sternly reprimanded ASAP. I would say *fired*, but you might accuse me of being over the top.

6.5 TRAINING: GAMBLIN' MAN

I'll bet (a pretty penny) . . .

Bet #1: Five of ten CEOs see training as an expense rather than an investment.

Bet #2: Five of ten CEOs see training as defense rather than offense.

Bet #3: Five of ten CEOs see training as a necessary evil rather than a strategic opportunity.

I'll bet (many, many a pretty penny) . . .

Bet #4: Eight of ten CEOs, in a forty-five-minute tour d'horizon of their business, would NOT mention training.

It's Bet #4 that drives me around the bend.

In that forty-five-minute conversation, the first fifteen minutes would most likely be devoted to "the changing environment" and business conditions in general. Then about fifteen minutes on strategy. And, say, ten minutes on "seriously cool software that cost us $87 million." And there you have it. Okay, maybe the last five minutes on people, but I bet with ever so much certainty based on a tractor-load of experience that during the five "people minutes" (which would focus on the quality of execs) there wouldn't be one bloody reference to training.

Damn it.
Damn it.
Damn it.

6.6 WHEN TIMES GET TOUGH, TRAIN! A POSITIVE EXCEPTION TO THE RULE

When a recession comes, most retailers cut back, probably way back, on training to save money.

Exception: In the last recession, Container Store DOUBLED training for in-store customer-contact employees.

Perfect time, they said, for best effort with any customers who still come our way during the economic turmoil. And the best plausible path is to double down on helping our closest-to-the-customer people grow.

FYI: A few years ago, Container Store was ranked as the number-one company to work for in the gigantic U.S. economy.

6.7 ONE MORE TIME: TRAINING = INVESTMENT #1

What is the very best reason to go bananas over training-training-training?

GREED.
(It pays off. BIG-TIME.)
(And, contrary to conventional "wisdom," damn near immediately.)

AXIOM I: Your (boss's) job is much safer if every one
of your team members is committed to training-led
radical personal development!

AXIOM II: The "training imperative" holds times **ten** or times **one hundred** for a small business; this is anything but a "Fortune 500 thing."

This last point should be unnecessary. If I have only nine employees on my payroll, then each one of them is of surpassing *strategic* importance. A no-holds-barred effort to train and develop each of these nine strategic pillars (people) should be as obvious as the end of one's nose.

Alas, it is not. Often one hears that damnable "Train 'em and they'll leave" or some other contemptible excuse.

Nine people on your payroll.
Nine peerless strategic opportunities.
TRAIN. TRAIN. TRAIN.

7 TECH TSUNAMI, WHITE-COLLAR APOCALYPSE, THE NEW MORAL IMPERATIVE

SECTION 1: TECH TSUNAMI, WHITE-COLLAR APOCALYPSE

MY STORY

I WAS SHOPPING ON A RAINY THURSDAY AFTERNOON IN MARCH 2017.

My wife called me while I was in the grocery store and said she had a problem (an "opportunity" for me). We had guests coming Saturday for lunch, and she'd just discovered that the vacuum bag was unusably full and that we were out of replacements. Did I have time to get some? I said, "Sure," finished the grocery run, went to the car, punched Home Depot in Dartmouth, Massachusetts, into my GPS.

A clerk pointed me in the right direction, but I soon discovered the bags I needed were not on the shelf. I caught the eye of another clerk, and he kindly agreed to take a look in the back and see if there might be some there. He was gone for three or four minutes, doubtless diligently searching. Though I appreciated his help and friendly attitude, this extra stop had me running late. Without thinking, really, I pulled my iPhone out of my pocket, went to my Amazon app, and punched in the vacuum bag specs. Needless to say, I found exactly what I wanted for less than the Home Depot price, and, thanks to Amazon Prime, it would arrive home tomorrow, Friday, leaving plenty of time for vacuuming. I felt badly that the clerk was trying to be helpful and I was effectively stiffing him and skipping out. Nonetheless, after about ten seconds of remorse, I pushed the One-Click order button. While the estimate is approximate, I am dead certain that the entire transaction from iPhone-out-of-my-pocket to iPhone-back-into-my-pocket took no more than ninety seconds, including "research."

And off home I went.

But, wait, "and off home I went" has a nontrivial backstory, too. I've probably been to Home Depot twenty times at least since my wife and I moved full-time from Tinmouth, Vermont, to Dartmouth, Massachusetts, about two years ago. Home Depot is only about three turns and seven miles from our house. Nonetheless, I am unsure of the way, including Step #1, coming out of the Home Depot parking lot, and went to my "favorites" on my Garmin GPS and punched in home.

So?

The "so" is this. When we moved, my wife, Susan, religiously eschewed her GPS. The simple fact is she can find her way from here to there without a hitch, including odd corners of New Bedford or Fall River or wherever. I pride myself on my sense of direction, but when we got to Dartmouth, I was lazy and did a "Full Garmin." It is not an exaggeration (I dearly wish it were!) to state that I can barely find my way out of *our* driveway. I am hardly alone; recent research indicates that we GPSDs (GPS Dependents) not only are perpetually lost but also measurably lose our innate sense of direction. The GPS rewires our brains, and not in a good way.

Technology is changing the world. The implications, especially for employment, are staggering. My little mini-sagas above pale by comparison.

Or do they?

The implications of the Home Depot story alone are affecting millions of retail jobs in the United States, from minimum-wage greeters to $100,000-a-year senior staff department folks; disruption is a frightfully overused word, but Amazon and an increasing number of like firms are indeed disrupting a big share of the economy, from corner mom-and-pop shops to multihundred store chains and, by the score, the shopping centers in which they are imbedded. As to the little GPS story, it foretells AI monkeying with our brains and changing the way we perceive the world. That's hardly a mini-saga.

THE TECH TSUNAMI NARRATIVE

7.1

7.1.1
MARC ANDREESSEN IS DEAD CERTAIN "SOFTWARE IS EATING THE WORLD"

What follows is a brief collection of quotes that capture a wee bit of the state of play—until tomorrow, when everything changes—in the topsy-turvy tech world. About three years ago, certain that I had fallen hopelessly behind, I started a crash reading program, now one hundred–plus books and no end in sight. In the end, I hardly felt expert; in fact, I was more confused than ever, but I had developed a relatively decent feel for the muddled state of play. Assuming you are not a major tech player, I urge you to consider launching a similar personal education program.

READ. READ. **READ**. **READ**. **READ**.

(Tom's Axiom 2018: **Outread the buggers!**)

The greatest shortcoming of the human race is our inability to understand the exponential function. —Albert A. Bartlett

VERY strong language: "greatest shortcoming." But I believe he has a critical point. The issue today is not "change," it is the *acceleration* of the rate of change—that damnable exponential function. Big phase shifts used to come along every, say, twenty-five years. Now the number, experts mostly agree, may be every five years. The business implications are huge, and the social implications boggle the mind.

Automation has become so sophisticated that on a typical passenger flight, a human pilot holds the controls for a grand total of just THREE MINUTES. [Pilots] have become, it's not much of an exaggeration to say, computer operators.
—Nicholas Carr, "The Great Forgetting," *The Atlantic*

Showstopper for me, among the most frequent of frequent flyers. There are many pluses and at least one big negative. The latter: Pilots are losing their ability to respond to ambiguous emergencies; that's been the conclusion after several major crashes.

The combination of new market rules and new technology was turning the stock market into, in effect, A WAR OF ROBOTS.　　　　　　　　　　　—Michael Lewis,
"Goldman's Geek Tragedy," *Vanity Fair*

Welcome to the era of insta-crashes, mega-crashes, maniacal trading to no fruitful end, and so on. Despite stacks of regulations, it's fair to say: NO ONE IS IN CHARGE.

Guaranteed: Michael Lewis is a superb guide.

Guaranteed: More—much more—unimaginable craziness and instability is on the way.

Almost all health care people get is going to be done— hopefully—by algorithms within a decade or two.
—Michael Vassar, MetaMed founder,
quoted in *New York* magazine

The process is well under way. For example, at one world-famous hospital in Greater Boston, M.D.s in some disciplines are not permitted to override the diagnostic conclusions spit out by the algorithms/Big Data.

Let's welcome our newest board member:

Just like other members of the board, the algorithm gets to vote on whether the firm makes an investment in a specific company or not. The program will be the sixth member of DKV's board.
—*Business Insider*: "A Venture Capital Firm Just Named an Algorithm to Its Board of Directors—Here's What It Actually Does"

No joke. A formal member of the board of directors. Apparently, the algorithm's track record surpasses that of its human counterparts.

Algorithms have already written symphonies as moving as those composed by Beethoven, picked through legalese with the deftness of a senior law partner, diagnosed patients with more accuracy than a doctor, written news articles with the smooth hand of a seasoned reporter, and driven vehicles on urban highways with far better control than a human.
—Christopher Steiner, *Automate This: How Algorithms Took Over Our Markets, Our Jobs, and the World*

DENIAL = PUNCH IN THE NOSE. Mr. Steiner tells a tale of a classical music–composing contest won by an algorithmically produced piece of music. At a subsequent high-level conference, the algorithm's creator was punched in the nose by a leading (human) composer.

7.1.2
JOBS APOCALYPSE

ALARMISM?
COLD TRUTH?

Up to 35 percent of Britain's jobs will be eliminated by new computing and robotics technology over the next 20 years, say experts [Deloitte/Oxford University].

> —*Telegraph*, "Ten Million Jobs at Risk from Advancing Technology," November 14, 2014

(A similar report featured on CNBC in March 2016 concluded that 50 percent of U.S. jobs were at "high risk" of being automated out of existence in the next two decades.)

Perhaps overstatement. Perhaps understatement. That there are such estimates being seriously discussed is in itself extraordinary. There are experts who fall into a category generally called "techno-optimists." They believe we will cope with the change—one talked of an "innovation tsunami"—and come out the other end whole. There are equally intelligent and seasoned "techno-pessimists" who have apocalyptic views. For what it's worth, and I in no way claim to be an expert, I view myself as leaning ever so slightly toward the techno-optimist end of the scale. In any case, the level of uncertainty is astronomical and the implications are astronomical.

7.1.3
YOU'RE A PROFESSIONAL. SO WHAT?

The intellectual talents of highly trained professionals are no more protected from automation than is the driver's left turn.
—Nicholas Carr,
The Glass Cage: Automation and Us

If you think being a "professional" makes your job safe, think again.
—Robert Reich

A bureaucrat is an expensive microchip.
—Dan Sullivan, consultant and executive coach

The last of the three quotes is a great laugh line—except it's not very funny for a staggering number of professional jobholders.

Message: **THE PROFESSIONS ARE NOT IN ANY WAY, SHAPE, OR FORM SAFE FROM ENCROACHING ARTIFICIAL INTELLIGENCE.**

No, all the lawyers and docs and engineers won't disappear. But there will be, in rather short order, virtually unimaginable dislocation.

Face it: "Professionals" in medicine or law are, in a fashion, no different from chefs or window cleaners. A few are excellent, many are okay, and some number are marginal. Following a botched root canal, a top-flight dentist cleaning up the mess said to me, and I remember ever so clearly, "Remember, Tom, half the dentists graduated in the bottom half of their class." I laughed through the pain, but the one-liner contains nontrivial employment, or rather unemployment, consequences.

7.1.4
THE GREAT RESTRUCTURING

The root of our problems is not that we're in a Great Recession or a Great Stagnation, but rather that we are in the early throes of a Great Restructuring. Our technologies are racing ahead but our skills and organizations are lagging behind.
—Erik Brynjolfsson and
Andrew McAfee, *Race Against the Machine*

This slim volume by two MIT professors played an oversized role in helping me develop a point of view. Their analyses are clear. Their conclusions are balanced. Their pedigree is unassailable.

Remember the term: **GREAT RESTRUCTURING.**

7.1.5
FYI: CHINA, TOO: MANUFACTURING EMPLOYMENT DOWN THIRTY MILLION

From Erik Brynjolfsson and Andrew McAfee, *The Second Machine Age: Work, Progress, and Prosperity in a Time of Brilliant Technologies*:

Since 1996, manufacturing employment in China itself has actually fallen . . . by an estimated 25 percent. That's over 30,000,000 fewer Chinese workers in that sector, even while output soared by 70 percent. It's not that American workers are being replaced by Chinese workers in that sector. It's that both American and Chinese workers are being made more efficient [replaced] by automation.

Just one Chinese company, Foxconn, is in the process of installing **ONE MILLION** new robots in the next two or three years; and one of its factories, in Kunshan, has already seen, courtesy of automation, employment plunge from 110,000 to 50,000.

The straightforward story: This phenomenon is universal. It is not limited to high-wage settings, though China's urban wages are soaring. In China's case, too, the social and political consequences of the worker dislocation caused by this trend, still picking up steam, boggles the mind.

I do not have an answer. I do not even have a strong point of view—that is, I'm all over the map. Sure of one thing one day, then something different the next. (I've got a lot of company, even in the expert class.) Something enormous *is* going down. You need not attempt to be an expert. You *do* need to try to be conversant in the great debate over the meaning of highly advanced AI.

One more time:

READ. READ. READ. READ.

READ! STUDY!

#1: *The Second Machine Age: Work, Progress, and Prosperity in a Time of Brilliant Technologies* by Erik Brynjolfsson and Andrew McAfee

And:

The Future of the Professions: How Technology Will Transform the World of Human Experts by Richard Susskind and Daniel Susskind

The Industries of the Future by Alec Ross

Superintelligence: Paths, Dangers, Strategies by Nick Bostrom

Rise of the Robots: Technology and the Threat of a Jobless Future by Martin Ford

Robot Futures by Illah Reza Nourbakhsh

The Glass Cage: Automation and Us by Nicholas Carr

Data-ism: The Revolution Transforming Decision Making, Consumer Behavior, and Almost Everything Else by Steve Lohr

Big Data: A Revolution That Will Transform How We Live, Work, and Think by Viktor Mayer-Schönberger and Kenneth Cukier

Glass Jaw: A Manifesto for Defending Fragile Reputations in an Age of Instant Scandal by Eric Dezenhall

Automate This: How Algorithms Came to Rule Our World by Christopher Steiner

Predictive Analytics: The Power to Predict Who Will Click, Buy, Lie, or Die by Eric Siegel

Addiction by Design: Machine Gambling in Las Vegas by Natasha Dow Schüll

Glass Houses: Privacy, Secrecy, and Cyber Insecurity in a Transparent World by Joel Brenner

Our Final Invention: Artificial Intelligence and the End of the Human Era by James Barrat

7.1.6
EXTREME PREDICTIONS COURTESY OF NON-EXTREME COMMENTATORS

The development of full artificial intelligence could spell the end of the human race.   —Stephen Hawking

AI is a fundamental existential risk for human civilization.
—Elon Musk

We think there could be a possibility where 95 percent of people . . . won't be able to contribute to the workforce.
—Sam Altman, Y Combinator

Correct or incorrect, such utterances by serious students are definitely in the air. The point of these three quotes is not alarmism. But they do underscore the extreme (unprecedented?) uncertainty that marks the times.

I also find it interesting that several of these most expert of the experts put science fiction at the top of their suggested reading lists—e.g., *Accelerando*, Charles Stross; *Robopocalypse* and *Amped*, Daniel Wilson; *Mother of Storms*, John Barnes; *Parasites Like Us*, Adam Johnson; *Snow Crash* and *Cryptonomicon* and others by Neal Stephenson; anything by William Gibson.

Hmmm . . .

7.1.7
CASE: ALPHAGO BEATS GO GRANDMASTER

This technology is going to cut through the global economy like a hot knife through butter. It learns fast and largely on its own. It's widely applicable. It doesn't only master what it has seen, it can innovate. For example: some of the unheard of moves made by AlphaGo were considered "beautiful" by the grandmaster it beat.

Limited AGI (Artificial General Intelligence, deep learning in particular) will have the ability to do nearly any job currently being done by human beings, from lawyers to judges, nurses to doctors, driving to construction—potentially at a grandmaster's level of capability. This makes it a buzzsaw.

Very few people (and I mean very few) will be able to stay ahead of the limited AGI buzzsaw. It learns so quickly, the fate of people stranded in former factory towns gutted by "free trade" is likely to be the fate of the highest paid technorati. They simply don't have the capacity to *learn fast enough* or be creative enough to stay ahead of it.

—John Robb, on his blog, *Global Guerrillas*, March 12, 2016

First it was chess, which in retrospect was straightforward—computation speed per se was the not-so-secret sauce. Then came *Jeopardy!*, far less rule driven. Now the ultimate expression of abstraction: Go.

The clause that most caught my eye was: "some of the unheard of moves made by AlphaGo were considered 'beautiful' by the grandmaster it beat."

BEAUTIFUL IS A VERY BIG WORD! IT GETS TO THE HEART OF WHAT IT MEANS TO BE HUMAN.

7.1.8
GRIN AND BEAR IT: MUCH, MUCH MORE TO COME

Genetics +

Robotics +

Informatics +

Nanotechnology =

????

7.1.9
ADDENDA FOR THE SHEER HECK OF IT: THE DULL OLD DAYS/LIFE BEFORE "DISRUPTION"

I like to laugh at myself as I huff and puff and proclaim these to be times of unprecedented exponential change. I love Henry Mintzberg's wonderful line, "It is the conceit of every age to say that we live in confusing times compared to the placid age the prior generation experienced."

Madness *is* the watchword of 2018, but my mom, Evelyn Peters, 1909–2005, lived through rather turbulent times as well:

The Model T, cell phones, satellites, TV, TV dinners, microwave ovens, jets, the Great Depression, Ty Cobb, Babe Ruth, Derek Jeter, the civil rights movement, gay pride, women's suffrage, Gandhi, Oklahoma and New Mexico and Arizona and Hawaii and Alaska become states, Churchill, World War I, World War II, the Holocaust, the A-bomb, the H-bomb, the Korean War, the Vietnam War, the

Iraq War, 9/11, the Cold War, the disintegration of the USSR, William Howard Taft (just missed Teddy Roosevelt!), FDR, Ronald Reagan, mainframe computers, PCs, the iPod, the Internet, air-conditioning, Weedwackers, Mickey Mouse, Frank Sinatra, Elvis, the Beatles, Madonna, Nancy Drew, the first five Harry Potter books, antibiotics, MRIs, polio vaccine, genetic mapping, man on the moon, more or less permanent space station. (But, alas, she didn't live long enough to see the Cubs win another World Series or to take a selfie.)

I will not retract a word in this chapter on madcap change, but I will acknowledge that we are not the first to experience a ceaseless string of immodest disruptions. Your call, but I'd stack the madness of my mom's ninety-five years with what's on the plate today.

SECTION 2: THE NEW MORAL IMPERATIVE

MY STORY

AFTER PETER DRUCKER'S DEATH, NUMEROUS ORGANIZATIONS COULD HAVE BEEN THE FIRST TO HOST A CONFERENCE TO CELEBRATE HIS LIFE'S WORK AS *THE* PIONEER OF MODERN MANAGEMENT THINKING.

The one that took the lead position was the Australian Institute of Management. Likewise, a lot of people could have been selected to give the keynote speech at that conference, but I was the one who got the nod. That was a bit odder than you might think; Mr. Drucker had never been much of a fan of my work, *In Search of Excellence* in particular. He thought Bob Waterman and I were playing to the masses and being mere popularizers of what he viewed as a very serious subject.

The fact is, *I* took and take Dr. Drucker *very* seriously, and AIM placed an enormous weight on my shoulders in handing me the opening talk at this landmark event. Can I put it in plain English? I was scared shitless and had no idea what to say that would live up to the event's gravitas and stellar attendee list that included Doris Drucker, Peter's wife and very active partner.

As usual, I went to the books—in this instance, Drucker's early work in particular.

I had been, perhaps, a typical Drucker reader. I'd glommed on to this message or that. For example, Drucker's riff on planning, in particular managers' need to take an hour out to think every day, had been my early career lodestone in my two years (1969, 1970) in the Pentagon as a junior U.S. Navy officer. I had cherry-picked and vastly oversimplified. I had woefully shortchanged the philosophical underpinnings of Drucker's corpus.

What I discovered in my deep Drucker immersion is what I call the "moral basis of management." Drucker was a refugee from Hitler, and he thought deeply about the human condition. My deep Drucker dive helped with preparing my speech and then seeped into everything I've subsequently done.

I don't believe in "magical writing." But as I pondered and pondered the AIM talk, at one point my computer keyboard more or less seemed to independently produce the following, in time transferred to PowerPoint presentation slides:

Organizations exist to serve.

Period.

Leaders live to serve.

Period.

Passionate servant leaders, determined to create a legacy of earth-shaking transformation in their domain (a 600-square foot retail space, a 4-person training department, an urban school, a rural school, whatever), must necessarily create organizations which are no less than cathedrals in which the full and awesome power of the Imagination and Spirit and native Entrepreneurial Flair of diverse individuals is unleashed in passionate pursuit of a jointly perceived soaring purpose (e.g., worthy of bragging about 25 years from now to your grandkids) and personal and community and client service Excellence.

Organizations as cathedrals for human development.

Phew.

Phew but true. Damn it.

I am pleased to report that the talk was well received, including by Mrs. Drucker. Perhaps in her nightly prayers she reported to her late husband that I wasn't quite the rube he had imagined me to be.

This Drucker-inspired paean to service and human development was written, as indicated above, in 2007. Reflect now on the first section of this chapter covering "The Tech Tsunami, White-Collar Apocalypse." With the wave of change bearing down on us, there is, as I see it, a new *moral* requirement of the utmost urgency to prepare all our team members for a madcap world in which only continuous "radical" growth increases the odds of professional survival.

Hence . . .

THE MORAL IMPERATIVE NARRATIVE

7.2

7.2.1
PEOPLE FIRST: A MORAL IMPERATIVE

Corporate Mandate/Your "Mandate 2018":

> **Your principal moral obligation as a leader is to develop the skill set of every one of the people in your charge—including semipermanent and temporary—to the maximum extent of your abilities and consistent with their "revolutionary" needs in the years ahead. (The bonus: This is also the premier profit maximization strategy!)**

The "employment contract," as we've known it for the last fifty years, is permanently severed. What will take its place? Certainly not job security in any form that resembles the past. Only sustained personal development will possibly stand up to the seismic forces at work. Thus developing one's associates is now indeed a *moral* imperative and the *first* imperative. As suggested, however, the good "business" news: It's also a precursor of enterprise durability and financial success.

7.2.2
SUPERIOR WORK ENVIRONMENTS ARE POSSIBLE— AND PROFITABLE—IN EVERY CORNER OF THE ECONOMY

1998–2014: *Fortune* reported that just twelve enterprises had been on its "100 best companies to work for in the United States" *every year*, for all sixteen years of the list's existence. Along the way, among other things, the Super Twelve created 341,567 new jobs; that amounts to job growth of 172 percent (shareholder returns, for the publicly traded companies, also dramatically outpaced the market as a whole).

The twelve:

> **Publix**
> **Whole Foods**
> **Wegmans**
> **Nordstrom**
> **Marriott**
> **REI**
> **Four Seasons**
> **Cisco Systems**
> **Goldman Sachs**
> **SAS Institute**
> **W. L. Gore**
> **TDIndustries**

BIG Note: Fully **7/12** (the first seven on the list) of the "best of the 100 best" are in so-called necessarily low-wage components of the service industry.

Performance example:

Retail turnover in general: 65 percent;
Publix (groceries, one of the 7/12) turnover: 5 percent.

7.2.2.1
THE "SUPER TWELVE'S" SUPER SECRET: PART-TIMERS ARE FULL-TIME MEMBERS OF THE FAMILY

Relative to the 2016 version of the best-to-work-for list, *Fortune* reported that the Super Twelve have "one thing in common:

They take generous care of their part-timers.

At some of the companies on the full list of top performers, the share of part-timers is low. But among the seven (of twelve) that are in industries such as hotels and retail, the numbers are sky high. Whole Foods, for example, has twenty-seven thousand part-timers, Nordstrom has thirty thousand—and Publix has a staggering one hundred thousand.

Perhaps the most important commonality (and indicator of corporate philosophy) among the twelve is that they all offer part-timers health care benefits. And most give part-timers paid time off for sick days, holidays, and so on. Nordstrom's part-timers, for example, have nineteen paid days off, Marriott's have eighteen paid days off, and REI's have twelve. Other examples of treating part-timers as full-time members of the family include Publix's (again) policy of making part-timers eligible for employee stock ownership plans that fund retirement savings.

Dare I ask: *Are your part-timers treated as full-time members of the family?*

7.2.3
ONE MORE: THE GOOD JOBS STRATEGY

In the book *The Good Jobs Strategy*, author and MIT professor Zeynep Ton reinforces the point made above about the seven employee-friendly superstars in theoretically low-wage, low-benefit industries:

> **Contrary to conventional corporate thinking, treating retail workers much better may make everyone (including their employers) much richer.**

One of Ton's primary exemplars, Costco, offers average hourly pay of $20.89, which is 40 percent greater than its number-one competitor, Sam's Club. Professor Ton persuasively argues that an obsession with developing people in retail is as important as it is at Google, and it pays, as firms such as Costco demonstrate.

7.2.4
LEAST LIKELY "BEST PLACES TO WORK" AWARD: TEA PLANTATIONS

The greatest satisfaction for management has come not from the financial growth of Camellia itself, but rather from having participated in the vast improvement in the living and working conditions of its employees resulting from the investment of many tens of millions of pounds into the tea gardens' infrastructure of roads, factories, hospitals, employees' housing and amenities. . . . Above all, there is a deep concern for the welfare of each employee. This arises not

only from a sense of humanity, but also from the conviction that the loyalty of a secure and enthusiastic employee will in the long-term prove to be an invaluable company asset.
                    —*Camellia: A Very Different Company*

Camellia—Latin for tea—is based in London. While the firm includes manufacturing, distribution, and a financial services arm among other assets, it sprung from the tea business and is today the world's second-largest private tea producer. A couple of years ago, Camellia had revenues of $600 million and after-tax earnings of approximately $100 million. The tea business can be an extraordinarily good commercial venture.

In the book extract above, Camellia's leadership attributes that effectiveness directly to employee and community development. Presumably, if you are like me, you do not think of *tea plantations* and *unwavering long-term commitment to employee development* in the same breath. Well, think again. I urge you to pass this quote out and perhaps reread it weekly. The significance borders on biblical.

Do the right thing for our people.
Startling results follow.
(Regardless of industry.)

7.2.5
OATH OF OFFICE: MANAGERS/SERVANT LEADERS

Our goal is to serve our customers brilliantly and profitably over the long haul.

Serving our customers brilliantly and profitably over the long haul is a product of brilliantly serving, over the long haul, the people who serve the customer.

Hence, our job as leaders—the alpha and the omega and everything in between—is abetting the sustained growth and success and engagement and enthusiasm and commitment to excellence of those, one at a time, who directly or indirectly serve the ultimate customer.

We—leaders of every stripe—are in the human growth and development and success and aspiration to excellence business. We leaders only grow when each and every one of our colleagues are growing.

We leaders only succeed when each and every one of our colleagues are succeeding.

We leaders only energetically march toward excellence when each and every one of our colleagues are energetically marching toward excellence.

Period.

This, too, was a by-product of my AIM speech. My "oath of office" was not an attempt to mimic Drucker's ideas, but it was offered in the spirit of his profoundly important work. And it *is* literally meant as a formal "oath of office," however grandiose that may seem at first blush.

7.2.6
SEVEN STEPS TO SUSTAINING SUCCESS

You take care of the people.

The people take care of the service.
The service takes care of the customer.
The customer takes care of the profit.
The profit takes care of the reinvestment.
The reinvestment takes care of the reinvention.
The reinvention takes care of the future.
(And at every step the only measure is EXCEL-
LENCE.)

And it all starts with **YOU** taking care of the people.

7.2.7
THE COMMITTED LEADER'S (GUARANTEED!)
MULTIPLIER; THE LAW OF LARGE NUMBERS

IF YOU (e.g., project manager, train-
ing department chief) WORK YOUR ONE
ASS OFF HELPING YOUR TEAM MEM-
BERS SUCCEED AND GROW, THEY WILL
WORK THEIR TEN ASSES OFF MAKING
YOU SUCCESSFUL.

7.2.8
THE TIM RUSSERT STORY (AND YOURS?)

In a way, the world is a great liar.

It shows you it worships and admires money, but at the end of the day it doesn't.

It says it adores fame and celebrity, but it doesn't, not really.

The world admires, and wants to hold on to, and not lose, goodness. It admires virtue. At the end it gives its greatest tributes to generosity, honesty, courage, mercy, talents well used, talents that, brought into the world, make it better. That's what it really admires. That's what we talk about in eulogies, because that's what's important. We don't say, "The thing about Joe was he was rich!"

We say, if we can, "The thing about Joe was he took care of people." —Peggy Noonan, "A Life's Lesson," on the life and legacy of journalist Tim Russert (*The Wall Street Journal,* June 20, 2008)

A wonderful story for the ages.
A requisite leadership excellence imperative for 2018.

8 JOB SECURITY IN AN INSECURE WORLD

MY STORY

THERE'S FRITZ ROETHLISBERGER AND THE HAWTHORNE EXPERIMENTS. AND ELTON MAYO . . .

Roethlisberger and Mayo were the godfathers of the employee involvement movement that actually dates back to the 1940s and their studies of ways to improve productivity at Western Electric's massive Hawthorne Works outside Chicago.

There were over the years many flavors:

Participative management.

Self-managed teams.

In modern times, a dozen varieties of "empowerment."

None of these really work for me. "Empowerment," for example, seems condescending in a way: "I've generously decided to let you occasionally think for yourself, dude."

Now segue to 1993 . . .

In 1993, in *The Tom Peters Seminar*, I went my own way, and it was meant to signal a leap in independent thinking (and acting) on the part of the average worker. The moniker was "every person a businessperson," or my ugly version, "businessing" every job.

The idea was this: Already in the early '90s competition was heating up, white-collar automation was digging in a little deeper, and outsourcing was gathering way. I viewed it as a big "lots-more-to-come-within-a-decade" threat and put it this way (apologies for quoting myself), "You [worker] will no longer survive as 'Hewlett-Packard Badge 2319 who shows up on time.' You will need to think more independently, think like a more or less independent 'holistic' [a cringe-worthy word, but it's appropriate here] 'businessperson,' rather than a mostly invisible 'employee,' even 'reliable employee.'" (I added that this indirectly [pretty damned directly, actually] amounts to a huge win for the employer—everyone thinking in wholes instead of parts, thinking about "the business," not just her or his hundred square feet of turf. That part of the story was a surprisingly hard sell; a bunch of folks with entrepreneurial bents running around was not exactly every boss's dream.)

In the *Seminar* book, I made this the topic of an entire chapter, titled "Beyond 'Empowerment,' Turning Every Job Into a 'Business.'" I spelled out what I thought 100 percent of us "thinking like a businessperson" meant. Then, somewhere along the way, the "businessing" idea morphed into Brand You. It took wings in the August–September 1997 issue of *Fast Company*, then a young magazine. Its cover story, with my byline, was titled "The Brand Called You." (The cover was a vividly colored rendering of a box of Tide detergent; the idea was that you and I and the brand-called-Tide were one and the same.) The response to the article was off the charts, and it still is twenty years later. When, for example, I look at my 2018 tweetstream, the reference to the 1997 article shows up regularly.

I still think, think more than ever, that twenty-five Brand Yous in a twenty-five-person company is the ultimate win for that company, or it can be—twenty-five folks hell-bent on growth, with the boss supporting them, can or will result, for instance, in a stunning commitment to the customer and continuous do-or-die innovation.

Brand You was born amid, and became associated with, the excesses of the "me decade" as the '90s were sometimes called. To be sure, Brand You does indeed call for significant distinction in your work and a commitment to radical personal growth; these are survival requisites for all of us, age twenty-two to eighty-two. But self-centeredness is precisely the wrong way to go—it is, in fact, the kiss of death.

The logic is simple. You are increasingly on your own; job security for that hardworking soul, Badge 2319, is DOA. Sucking up to the boss is a loser's strategy; the boss's job is likely to go before yours as companies flatten their hierarchies and dump middle managers by the busload. Hence, being an effective "Brand You 2018" means shifting your focus ninety degrees from vertical to horizontal. The emphasis shifts from "suck UP" to "suck SIDEWAYS," to becoming a highly valued—nay, irreplaceable—collaborator. Your future is a by-product of the word-of-mouth/ mouse reputation associated with your name; and make no mistake, a stellar word-of-mouth rep is primarily based on the "horizontal" supportiveness of your peers and your customers and other outsiders.

Today, every* person is a businessperson—or else.

Every person is distinctly good at something—or else.

Every person is a "professional development maniac"—or else.

Every person lives off her or his network of peers and customers—or else.

And "We ain't seen nothin' yet" is gross understatement!

THE JOB SECURITY 2018 NARRATIVE

8.1 DANCING IN THE RAIN

Life is not about waiting for the storm to pass; it's about learning to dance in the rain.
—Ted Rubin

Welcome, boys and girls, friends and foes, left-handers and right-handers, to 2018+.

* Every = Every. The "target audience" is not graduates of top universities. The best of the independent contractors who deal with plumbing, heating, et cetera, do so by becoming students—taking online courses and adapting to change with the same vigor as the Yale freshmen.

8.1.1
THE AGE OF UBIQUITOUS BRAND YOU AND THE UNASSAILABLE NECESSITY OF PERSONAL DIFFERENTIATION

> One of its defining characteristics [globalization and Web-driven innovation] is that it will be less driven by countries or corporations and more driven by real people. It will unleash unprecedented creativity, advancement of knowledge, and economic development. But at the same time, it will tend to undermine safety net systems and penalize the unskilled.
>
> —Clyde Prestowitz, *Three Billion New Capitalists*

> The new organization of society implied by the triumph of individual autonomy and the true equalization of opportunity based upon merit will lead to very great rewards for merit and great individual autonomy. This will leave individuals far more responsible for themselves than they have been accustomed to being during the industrial period. It will also precipitate transition crises, including a possible severe economic depression that will reduce the unearned advantage in living standards that has been enjoyed by residents of advanced industrial societies throughout the twentieth century.
>
> —James Davidson and William Rees-Mogg,
> *The Sovereign Individual*

The ecosystem used to funnel lots of talented people into a few clear winners. Now it's funneling lots of talented people into lots of experiments.
—Tyler Willis, business developer,
to Nathan Heller, "Bay Watched: How
San Francisco's New Entrepreneurial
Culture Is Changing the Country,"
The New Yorker, October 14, 2013

Career has a radically altered meaning; it does not play out within the bounds of a single, or even small number, of employers. Commitment to breakneck-speed perpetual learning and growth is a lifetime requirement for one an all. A supportive labor-market legal framework that deals with the likes of "gigs" and brief associations with companies is barely gathering way (e.g., Uber's high-frequency legal tussles over employee benefits). Education is woefully misguided.

Pretty much everything is up for grabs.

8.1.2
DISTINCT OR EXTINCT

We used this—**DISTINCT OR EXTINCT**—on T-shirts and posters in my Brand You seminars.

Are there exceptions to all this?

There are surely different paces in different places, but true exceptions?

Simply put, I don't think so.

If there is nothing very special about your work . . . no matter how hard you apply yourself you won't get noticed, and that increasingly means you won't get paid much either.

—Michael Goldhaber, *Wired*

More of the same.

THE RULE OF POSITIONING: If you can't describe your position in eight words or less, you don't have a position.

—Jay Levinson and Seth Godin, *Get What You Deserve!*

And more.
And on—and—on it could go.

8.2

8.2.1
SALLY HELGESEN'S DE FACTO BRAND YOU ROAD MAP

Sally Helgesen, author of the widely acclaimed book *The Female Advantage: Women's Ways of Leadership*, returned to the fray with *Thriving in 24/7*. In the crazy new security-is-dead world, she argues that professional survival will require a newly constructed package of skills.

The bedrock:

- **"START AT THE CORE."** Nimbleness is only possible if we "locate our inner voice," take regular inventory of where we are.

- **"LEARN TO ZIGZAG."** Think "gigs." Think lifelong learning. Forget "old loyalty." Work on optimism.
- **"CREATE OUR OWN WORK."** Articulate your value. Integrate your passions. ID your market. Run your own business.
- **"WEAVE A STRONG WEB OF INCLUSION."** Build your own support network and develop a reputation as a network builder.

I think that in a very few words Ms. Helgesen precisely captures the spirit of this chapter's argument.

8.3 NEW WORLD/NEW WORK SURVIVAL KIT 2018

Herewith, *my* version of Sally Helgesen's list above:

1. Mastery! (Absurdly good at *something*!)
2. Your Legacy (All work = Memorable/braggable WOW projects!)
3. "USP"/Unique Selling Proposition (That old favorite, USP, applies to each of us circa 2018)
4. Networking Obsession! (From vertical loyalty to horizontal loyalty)
5. Entrepreneurial Instinct (A sleepless eye for opportunity!) A "small" (actually, there is no such thing as small!) opportunity for independent action beats a faceless part of a monster project
6. CEO/Leader/Businessperson/Closer (CEO of Me Inc.)

7. Mistress of Improv (Play a dozen parts simultaneously, from chief strategist to chief toilet scrubber)

8. Intense Appetite for Technology (e.g., Are you a leading edge, fantastic user of social media?)

9. Embrace Marketing (You are your own CSO/Chief Story-telling Officer)

10. Obsessed with Renewal (Your own CLO/Chief Learning Officer)

11. Execution Fanaticism! (Show up early! Leave late! Sweat the details! Tuck the shower curtain in—recall chapter 1)

12. EXCELLENCE. PERIOD. (What else?)

If not this list, one like it. Brand You is an alpha-to-omega affair.

8.4 BRAND YOU = TEAM SPORT! FIRST ORDER OF BUSINESS: YOUR REPUTATION WITH YOUR PEERS

The Brand You idea, as noted in the chapter introduction, was seen by many as selfish (i.e., you or me attempting to trot out our wares, hog the spotlight, and elbow others out of the way).

Nothing could be further from the truth.

You must indeed be *very* good and noteworthy in terms of a useful skill. But—AT LEAST AS IMPORTANT—you must also be seen as a superb teammate.

Truth be known, when Jane Jones is assessing you as a help-mate for her next independent gig, your reputation as a supportive team player and the breadth and health of your external network may well outweigh your technical skills.

So:

First, you must BE a great teammate. (Give yourself a score on this every day. That's my suggestion. By which I mean, for example, did you go out of your way, and at some cost in time, to give someone a helping hand with something?)

Second, you must INVEST a substantial amount of time and emotional effort (lots and lots and lots) in networking. Remember Ms. Helgesen's commandment: "Weave a strong Web of Inclusion."

8.5 RE-RE-RE-RE-TOOL OR PERISH

The illiterate of the twenty-first century will not be those who cannot read or write, but those who cannot learn, unlearn and relearn. —Alvin Toffler

Knowledge . . . becomes obsolete incredibly fast. The continuing professional education of adults is the number-one growth industry in the next thirty years. —Peter Drucker

BRAND YOU "BRAND EQUITY"
Your specialness depreciation rate per annum:
15 percent?
25 percent?

Therefore, it is imperative that you develop a . . .
Formal **"Investment Strategy."**

> **PERSONAL DICTATE 2018**
> You **MUST** invest in skill development.
> You **MUST** have a Renewal Investment Plan.
> It **MUST** be formal.
> It **MUST** be bold.
> You **MUST** self-schedule a routine personal
> "Brand You Audit."

8.6 GETTING STARTED: TODAY

1. When you wake up, imagine that you are self-employed*:
   - Are you ready?
   - Are you organized?
   - Are your priorities clear?
   - Have you got an achievable to-do list?
     (Pare it down. Pare it down some more. And more.)
   - Are you clear about how to approach the first item on the list?
   - Most of all . . . IS YOUR ATTITUDE WHAT IT NEEDS TO BE?
     Success depends on your demeanor from the opening bell. Professional? Friendly? Cheerful? Organized?

---

* Many of you are, in which case this list may serve as a reminder.

2. Reconsider the project you are working on.
   - Does it have pizazz?
   - Can it have *more* pizazz?

     The job or task may be pretty damned mundane, and you may have been treating it accordingly. But my experience is that nine out of nine times you can add new twists here and there, get a couple of other people involved to widen the project's impact, and so on. I call this "Moving up the 'Wow Scale.' "
   - Are the immediate milestones clear and achievable?
   - If it is a team project, does everyone feel ownership?
   - Are you crystal clear as to who the "customers" are and what their expectations are? Think CUSTOMERS. *E-v-e-r-y* project, of one day or one year's duration, has customers!

3. Lunch
   - **LUNCH IS THE DAY'S OPPORTUNITY #1.**
   - Are you going to lunch with pals, or are you going with someone new whose brain you can pick about this, that, or the other? (And who you can add to your network.) Your pals are great and a blessing, but in this new world order, I suggest that 50–75 percent of your lunches should be calculated learning and network development and maintenance opportunities.

4. Homework
   - Do you have a weekly or monthly professional development plan—in less imposing terms, a list of "stuff" you want to learn and a to-do list for learning it?

5. Etc. This list is meant as a rough-thought starter and pot stirrer. It is not Holy Writ.

8.7 PARTING THOUGHTS ON "BRAND YOU"

All human beings are entrepreneurs. When we were in caves, we were all self-employed . . . finding our food . . . feeding ourselves. That's where human history began. As civilization came we suppressed it. We became "labor" because they stamped us, "You are labor." We forgot that we are entrepreneurs. —Muhammad Yunus, Nobel laureate and father of microlending

Entrepreneurial, Yunus asserts, is not a term reserved for the elite with 2018 technical degrees from Stanford or MIT. Look around you. Your neighbor, the freelance writer next door working from her spare bedroom, the electrician down the street, the interior decorator in the next block. Ordinary in the best sense of that word and full-fledged excellence-or-bust entrepreneurs in every sense of those words.

My personal breakthrough on this came in a so-called green room in New York in 1999. I was about to go on the CBS morning show to talk about Brand You soon after my book by that name had been published. In my mind, I pictured the viewer as a white-collar cubicle slave off to another dreary day at the office. It seemed rather ludicrous to imagine him or her as an entrepreneur. And thinking back to my days in Palo Alto, *entrepreneur* meant browser developer Marc Andreessen or Sun Microsystems' crazy founder Scott McNealy.

But then my mind shifted to my farm in Vermont and the week before my trip to New York. There had been an electrical problem, and our electrician and an assistant had driven out to fix it. There was also a stinky septic problem. And I, by the way, had been working with a solo Boston editor on a magazine article. All these people were genuine entrepreneurs/Brand Yous working on their own or with a very small team, probably supported by an hour-a-week bookkeeper who took care of business issues. These were normal folks, the de facto people next door. And they all wanted glowing word-of-mouth recommendations to keep on going. No, entrepreneur or Brand You was not just some wild-eyed Silicon Valley, Ph.D.-toting inventor—it was that metaphorical neighbor. And Brand You was indeed an achievable aim.

Last words:

You are the storyteller of your own life, and you can create your own legend, or not.   **—Isabel Allende**

Carpenters bend wood; fletchers bend arrows; wise men fashion themselves.   **—Buddha**

INNOVATION

9 WHOEVER TRIES THE MOST STUFF WINS, WHOEVER SCREWS THE MOST STUFF UP WINS

MY STORY

GRAB A PAIR OF GARDEN CLIPPERS, AND GO FORTH . . .

Call it . . . THE SUMMER OF BRUSH CUTTING.

But it turned out to be so much more.

Much, much more.

It started as a simple task: cleaning out some annoying brambles on a walking path—an irritating item to be checked off the spring to-do list. So off I went with minimal enthusiasm. A day or two later, scratches from head to toe, I had an intriguing sense of accomplishment; rooting around for hours on end in the bramble patch, I saw things I'd never seen before. So I tentatively expanded my effort to clearing a little addition to the main path, aiming to get a better view of one of our Vermont farm ponds.

That next bit somehow revealed something else, to my (continuing) surprise.

Then, at a casual dinner, I sat next to a landscaper, and we got to talking about our farm and my nascent skills with hand clippers, handsaw, and so on. In particular, she suggested that I do some clearing around a few of our big boulders. "Start a second career as a rock sculptor," she said with a laugh.

Amused by her comment, I set about that boulder clearing on our main trail, and I was again surprised—rather taken aback, actually—by the striking result. (Maybe there *was* a sort of second career here?)

My growing artistry led to attacking some dense brush and brambles around some barely visible rocks that had often caught my attention, which, then, as the iterations accelerated, led to finding, in effect, a great place for a more or less Zen garden, as we subsequently came to call it.

Which led to more and more.

And more.

Surprise after surprise after surprise.

Especially a massive rock outcropping I unveiled on a steep hillside featuring three towering somber granite faces I call the Cardinal, the Pope, and the Monsignor. A good friend, a Catholic priest from Chicago, informally blessed the trio.

To make a long story short:

I proceeded by trial and error and instinct, and each experiment signaled possibilities for another experiment (or two or ten) and to a greater understanding and appreciation of overall potential—the kindasortaplan, though there was none, in fact, made itself. And it was far, far better (more ambitious, more interesting, more satisfying) than I could have imagined. In fact, the result bore ZERO resemblance to what I was thinking about at the start—a trivial self-designed chore that became the engine of a decade's at-home activities.

With a nod to my landscaper friend, I called my imaginary one-person "outfit" the Rock Revelations Corporation.

(Note: We recently moved from Vermont to Massachusetts, and the process began to repeat itself—this time in a sizable patch of wetlands. I guess I need to rename my venture?)

I suspect that your interest in "Tom's Vermont brush-cutting thing" may be modest at best. The point here, obviously, is much more general:

JJI/Just Jump In

There was no grand plan.

There was no plan at all.

The starting point was STARTING, a boring task with about a week's expected duration.

The doing grew into something totally different from anything I could have imagined at the start.

As I see it, the minisaga of "Tom's Brush-Cutting Transformation" (I ordinarily dislike that grandiose T-word—*transformation*—but it's merited here) is in fact the basic story of innovation in general.

(The Nobel-winning economist F. A. Hayek said the secret of market-driven capitalistic economic growth is what he labeled a "spontaneous discovery process." I expect no Nobel, but what I just described was indeed a textbook spontaneous discovery process. And it surely, from its insignificant beginnings, upended my life; now I hope to upend yours.)

Off we go to the land of WTTMSW/Whoever Tries the Most Stuff Wins!

Huh?

Read on . . .

THE WTTMSW NARRATIVE

9.1 INNOVATION I: WTTMSW/WHOEVER TRIES THE MOST STUFF WINS

I'm in the habit of saying that this—WTTMSW, the lead item in the chapter—is the only thing I've learned *for sure* in the last fifty years. Here's what I mean. My training is scientific, and science's Axiom #1 is that nothing is for certain or settled and that for every hypothesis there is a competing hypothesis—or ten or twenty—waiting in the wings. That makes sense . . .

Except in this instance.

I can find no counterhypothesis to the notion of . . .

WTTMSW/Whoever Tries the Most Stuff Wins.

Consider several manifestations of my WTTMSW story:

9.1.1
WTTMSW/ROSS PEROT VERSUS GM

Ross Perot founded Electronic Data Systems, which was the first of the big systems software houses. He eventually sold the giant firm to General Motors. Describing the differences between the two enterprises, Perot said that the EDS strategy was . . .

READY. FIRE. AIM.

GM's, by contrast, he claimed, was "Ready. Aim. Aim. Aim. Aim . . ."

The "try it fast" mantra has in recent times become the mainstay in Silicon Valley software firms. The Valley manifestation of the WTTMSW doctrine actually started up north, in Seattle, where Microsoft's alternative to Apple's perfectionism was to launch, with blazing speed, big systems updates, often significantly flawed; and then they'd correct the at-launch problems with an endless stream of rapid upgrades. That strategy, among other things, brought and sustained for decades an operating system market share of above 80 percent. (Microsoft once bailed Apple out with a large loan aimed at keeping Steve Jobs's firm alive to avoid Microsoft's becoming a real rather than de facto monopoly and even more in the sights of the federal trustbusters than was normally the case.)

Here's my historical take on WTTMSW/RFA:

1950–1980/Age of GM:
RAF/Ready. Aim. Fire.

1981–2000/Age of Microsoft:
RFA/Ready. Fire. Aim.

2000–20??/Age of Google/Facebook/You/Me:
FFF/Fire. Fire. Fire.

MORE FLAVORS OF WTTMSW

9.1.2
WTTMSW/NAPOLÉON

On s'engage et puis on voit! **(One jumps into the fray, then figures out what to do next!)**   —Napoléon

9.1.3
WTTMSW/RICHARD BRANSON

Screw It, Let's Do It: Lessons in Life
                                        —Richard Branson (book title)

9.1.4
WTTMSW/JOHANN SEBASTIAN BACH

Malcolm Gladwell authored a *New Yorker* article titled "Creation Myth." In the myth-busting part of the piece, he ups the de facto WTTMSW ante by suggesting it even holds in the heavens—that is, in the stratospheric world of J. S. Bach:

> The difference between Bach and his forgotten peers isn't necessarily that he had a better ratio of hits to misses. The difference is that the mediocre might have a dozen ideas, while Bach, in his lifetime, created more than a thousand full-fledged musical compositions. A genius is a genius, [psychologist Paul] Simonton maintains, because he can put together such a stagger-

ing number of insights, ideas, theories, random observations, and unexpected connections that he almost inevitably ends up with something great. "QUALITY," Simonton writes, "IS A PROBABILISTIC FUNCTION OF QUANTITY."

(At the time of Steve Jobs's death, several tributes referred to Jobs as a great tinkerer, akin to Thomas Edison. He did not pull a great invention out of thin air. Instead, he took some eighth-baked idea and tinkered and tinkered and tinkered his way to near perfection. More or less WTTMSW or Bachian "quality is a probabilistic function of quantity.")

9.1.5
WTTMSW/JOE MURRAY'S NOBEL

My summer neighbor, several years back, was Joe Murray, recipient of a Nobel Prize in medicine for performing the first successful organ transplant. I once, half joking, asked him, "So what's your secret?"

He replied with a smile, "*We did more procedures.*"

That is, while his peers theorized, Dr. Joe headed for the OR, put on his surgeon's gown and gloves, asked the head nurse for his scalpel, and went to work.

More time in the operating room.

More tries.

WTTMSW.

Mantelpiece ornament: **Nobel Prize**.

9.1.6
WTTMSW/HERB KELLEHER ON STRATEGY

Southwest Airlines founder Herb Kelleher offers his version of WTTMSW:

We have a "strategy" at Southwest. It's called "doing things."

9.1.7
WTTMSW/I WANNABE . . .

I want to be a Photographer.
 Take a ton of photos. Start a photo blog.
 Organize an art show for your best work.
 MAKE STUFF.

I want to be a Writer.
 Write a ton of pieces. Establish a voice on social media.
Start a blog. Write guest posts for friends.
 MAKE STUFF.
 Talk is cheap.
 JUST MAKE STUFF.
> —Reid Schilperoort, brand strategist, on the
> "one piece of advice" that has helped
> him overcome creative blocks

(Variation on a theme: **"Butt in chair."**

Anne Lamott: "How to write. Butt in chair. Start each day anywhere. Let yourself do it badly. Just take one passage at a time. Get butt back in chair.")

9.2 WTTMSW/ACTION AND EXCELLENCE

In Search of Excellence/1982/The Bedrock "Eight Basics"

1. **A Bias for Action**
2. Close to the Customer
3. Autonomy and Entrepreneurship
4. Productivity Through People
5. Hands-On, Value-Driven
6. Stick to the Knitting
7. Simple Form, Lean Staff
8. Simultaneous Loose-Tight Properties

In Search of Excellence was organized around "Eight Basics" of success and excellence. Pride of place went to "A Bias for Action"—and so it would be, times ten or times one hundred, in a rewrite in 2018. To repeat:

WTTMSW.
QED.
(I am quite serious when I claim WTTMSW is the only thing I know "for sure.")

9.3 WTTMSW/SERIOUS PLAY

MIT Media Lab stalwart Michael Schrage wrote an important book titled *Serious Play*. The basic thesis:

You can't be a serious innovator unless and until you are ready, willing, and able to seriously play. "Serious play" is not an oxymoron; it is the essence of innovation.

This idea—serious play—is indeed worthy of an entire book. WTTMSW is relatively easy to describe, and it's also relatively easy to make a strong case for it. But there is a big catch:

WTTMSW requires a WTTMSW culture.

And at the heart of that culture, I believe, is a pervasive spirit of **"playfulness."**

To perhaps state the obvious, *play* in no way suggests a lack of seriousness of purpose. It speaks instead to teammates taking immense pleasure in the messy process of many approximations and wrong turns and dead ends on the way to market.

(Note: problem/opportunity: *Alas, more to come,* playful *is hardly the word that comes to mind when one conjures up the purchasing or HR department, particularly in a giant firm. Yet, circa 2018, enterprise survival demands constant innovation—hence playfulness—from those units as much as from the marketing and new product gangs.*)

SERIOUS PLAY: WOBBLING TOWARD SERENDIPITY

The late Robert Altman was once asked how, when filming, he knew when enough was enough. He replied:

> **We normally shoot a few takes, even if the first one is terrific . . . because what I'm really hoping**

for is a "mistake." I think that most of the really great moments in my films were not planned. They were things that naturally occurred and we said, "Wow, look at that—that's something we want to keep." That's when you hit the truth button with the audience.

THE 3PS OF SERIOUS PLAY

Elliott Masie is the pioneer's pioneer of e-learning. He was once asked how he moved forward in his work; he replied, "I want a 'sandbox partner.'"

My translation:

- Playmate!
- Playpen!
- Prototype!

The "playmate" can be an interesting client, an innovative, small supplier; in a large enterprise, a like-minded insider. As to the playpen, if, again, you are in a sizable enterprise, the Golden Rule is the further from headquarters and the beady-eyed bureaucrats typically therein, the better. As to prototyping, see the next section.

SERIOUS PLAY: MEASURE IT!

SCALE OF 1–10: How would you rate your organization on "devotion to serious play"? This is a query of the utmost strategic importance!

(*Organization* here may mean a giant firm. And it also might mean a ten-person training department or a fifty-person logistics department. The idea—a recurring theme in this book—knows no bounds.)

9.4 WTTMSW/A CULTURE OF PROTOTYPING

More wisdom from Michael Schrage:

Effective prototyping may be the most valuable core competence an innovative organization can hope to have.

Gospel as far as I'm concerned. But the critical notion is accompanied by the usual problem surfaced above: The implementation issue is "cultural."

I've not found a more lucid translation of the prototyping idea than is provided here by Michael Bloomberg, in his book *Bloomberg by Bloomberg*:

> **We made mistakes, of course. Most of them were omissions we didn't think of when we initially wrote the software. We fixed them by doing it over and over, again and again. We do the same today. While our competitors are still sucking their thumbs trying to make the design perfect, we're already on prototype version #5. By the time our rivals are ready with wires and screws,**

we are on version #10. It gets back to planning versus acting: We act from day one; others plan how to plan for months.

One more take, courtesy of Nicholas Negroponte:

DEMO OR DIE!

This was the approach championed by Negroponte that vaulted his MIT Media Lab to the forefront of IT-multimedia innovation. It was his successful alternative to the traditional academic "*publish or perish.*" Negroponte's rapid-prototyping version was emblematic of the times and the pace and the enormity of the opportunity.

9.5 WTTMSW/WORLDWIDE WINNING HAND

Success Tactic #1: EXPERIMENT FEARLESSLY.
—Bloomberg Businessweek,
"Type A Organization Strategies:
How to Hit a Moving Target"

(Yes, *Bloomberg Businessweek* gave it the **#1** ranking on the success tactics list.)

RELENTLESS TRIAL AND ERROR.
—The Wall Street Journal, on the most
effective approach to adjusting company
portfolios in the face of changing and
uncertain global economic conditions

These two assessments describe WTTMSW at the highest level—the engine of overall economic success.

Fact: **Capitalism = WTTMSW.**

Recall my reference to F. A. Hayek's "spontaneous discovery process" in the chapter-opening vignette.

9.6

9.6.1

WTTMSW/COROLLARY #1: FAIL FASTER. SUCCEED SOONER. (WSTMSUW/WHOEVER SCREWS THE MOST STUFF UP WINS.)

The idea is straightforward: If trying a lot of things at a breakneck pace is Innovation Success Key #1, then screwing things up at a breakneck pace is part and parcel of the story.

(The issue raised by this assertion is straightforward, too. Starting at home and in kindergarten, research shows that the use of the word *no* exceeds the use of the word *yes* by as much as an order of magnitude. Coming out of the starting gate, "Don't screw it up," alas, wins out over "Screwups are normal and invaluable" by twenty furlongs.)

The winners:

FAIL FASTER. SUCCEED SOONER.

—David Kelley, founder, IDEO

FAIL. FORWARD. FAST.   —High Tech CEO, Philadelphia, seminar participant

NO MATTER. TRY AGAIN. FAIL AGAIN. FAIL BETTER.
—Samuel Beckett

IDEAS ECONOMY: CAN YOUR BUSINESS FAIL FAST ENOUGH TO SUCCEED?
—Advertisement, *Economist* conference

SUCCESS REPRESENTS ONE PERCENT OF YOUR WORK, WHICH RESULTS ONLY FROM THE NINETY-NINE PERCENT THAT IS CALLED FAILURE.
—Soichiro Honda

Now add a powerful twist:

REWARD excellent failures.
PUNISH mediocre successes.
—Phil Daniels, successful businessman, Sydney

Actually, Daniels said in full, *"I owe my success to six words . . ."*

I used this quote at a seminar for senior staff of a giant financial services company. The CEO came up to me afterward and said, with an almost violent head shake, "Tom, more than any other one thing you mentioned, I am bedeviled by the 'mediocre success' phenomenon. We launch a project with fanfare and high hopes and liberal funding. Over time, it's dumbed down and down and down. We end up with a technical 'success,' but it's so diluted from the original that we might well not have bothered and saved ourselves a lot of money and effort."

Call his (all too common) rendition: "stagnation by mediocre success."

9.6.2
GOING ALL THE WAY: PUTTING A POSITIVE SPIN ON SCREWING UP

What really matters is, companies that don't continue to experiment, COMPANIES THAT DON'T EMBRACE FAILURE, they eventually get in a desperate position where the only thing they can do is a Hail Mary bet at the very end.

—Jeff Bezos

EMBRACE. NOT TOLERATE.

It is not enough to "tolerate" failure—you must "CELEBRATE" failure. —Richard Farson, with Ralph Keyes,
Whoever Makes the Most Mistakes Wins

CELEBRATE. NOT TOLERATE.

In business, you reward people for taking risks. When it doesn't work out you PROMOTE THEM—because they were willing to try new things. If people tell me they skied all day and never fell down, I tell them to try a different mountain.
—Michael Bloomberg, *Bloomberg Businessweek*, June 25, 2007

PROMOTE BECAUSE OF FAILURE. NOT MERELY TOLERATE.

Key Words:

- REWARD!
- EMBRACE!

- CELEBRATE!
- PROMOTE!

The point: TAKE THIS PRECISE LANGUAGE—REWARD/
EMBRACE/CELEBRATE/PROMOTE—SERIOUSLY. OPER-
ATIONALIZE IT.

9.7 BOTTOM LINE/WTTMSASTMSUTFW:

WHOEVER TRIES THE MOST STUFF AND SCREWS THE MOST STUFF UP THE FASTEST WINS

9.8

9.8.1
WTTMSW/ENTERPRISE AS LEARNING LAB

- Our mantra: WTTMSASTMSUTFW/Whoever Tries The Most Stuff And Screws The Most Stuff Up The Fastest Wins.
- Celebrate small wins (and interesting screwups). The idea is to build a rockin'-and-rollin' ethos—all hands trying stuff all the time.
- Celebrate small wins (and small screwups) on a *daily* basis! Momentum! Momentum! Momentum!
- Rapid prototyping. "Demo or die."
- Readily available prototyping budget. Make it easy for

virtually anyone to obtain small sums for quick tests of pretty much anything.

- One percent of the operating budget as "play money"/"seed money." And it must be spent.
- Transparency (all info available and visible to all).
- The bosses **ALWAYS** ask anyone and everyone as a matter of routine: **"WHAT ARE YOU PLAYIN' WITH TODAY?"**
- Who are our innovators: **100 PERCENT OF US.** Make that clear!

This is a straightforward list. But the underlying idea is not simple to implement; it's about creating and constantly nourishing a full-bore "try it" culture. Needless to say, recalling chapter 5, this rockin'-and-rollin' cultural aspiration must be directly reflected in hiring, evaluating, and promoting processes and decisions.

(Please take the word *lab* in the title seriously. A laboratory is dedicated to and exists for experimentation. So, too, our organizational units—each and every one of them, from R&D to Purchasing and HR.)

9.8.2
"TRY IT" CULTURE CASE: MICKEY DREXLER/THE GAP/J. CREW

For more than three decades, Mickey Drexler was one of America's most preeminent fashion retailers. The list below is primarily sourced from an article in *The New Yorker* on his approach to success in an insanely competitive, mercurial, fast-moving industry:

- Bias for instant action/towering impatience with inaction
- Impatient but not brutal
- Relentless speed-of-light experimentation; more tests ASAP if something is working well, drop ASAP if not
- Vibrates with energy
- Always on the prowl—anywhere, everywhere—for ideas
- Lots of instances of the team standing around making quick assessment decisions with all contributing
- Likes working with women more than men because, he observes, females are more intuitive than males
- Dresses like the brand
- Offense, not defense
- Communicates all the time; everyone, including the most junior members, purposefully drawn in to be and to feel like part of the decision-making team
- Listens attentively regardless of age or seniority
- Obvious in his transparent respect for young employees
- Trusts intuition plus fanatic about the numbers
- Expects everyone to know their numbers cold with no assistance from an electronic device
- An obsession with MBWA/Managing by Wandering Around
- Constant customer contact-dialogue and reacts instantly to customer feedback

I have had the opportunity to spend time with Mr. Drexler. The material above squares with my observations.

9.8.3
NOT SO FAST!

I want to make this AS DIFFICULT AS POSSIBLE. It's reasonably easy to concoct lists like the two immediately above. But, if it ain't there already, it is gut-wrenchingly difficult to instill that requisite try-it culture, even in small organizations. "Playing with stuff" comes naturally at age four, but it's virtually all downhill from there. We are taught in most schools that errors are bad and to be avoided. Most jobs reinforce this bias. Again, *serious play* doesn't mean sloppiness or less than an all-out effort. But it does mean that we cherish the damn good try that goes awry and from which we learn something of value. I emphasized above the idea of the boss who routinely asks, "Whatcha playin' with right now?" And she takes as much or more pleasure from those interesting screwups as from the steps forward.

WORK ON IT. A DAY AT A TIME. AN HOUR AT A TIME. STARTING TOMORROW. OR THIS AFTERNOON.

9.9

9.9.1
CONCLUDING NOTE I: WTTMSW/WTTMSASTMSUTFW

"What makes God laugh?"
"People making plans."

**Innovation is messy.
Innovation is nonlinear.
Innovation is a circus.
Innovation depends in full on a robust culture of "try it now."**

**Innovation is fun.
Innovation is heartbreaking.
Innovation is not for sissies.**

**If you know where you're heading, you're not innovating.
If things work out as planned, you weren't chasing anything interesting.**

9.9.2
CONCLUDING NOTE II

YOU MISS 100 PERCENT OF THE SHOTS YOU DON'T TAKE.
—Wayne Gretzky

This quote is my favorite—**number one**—in my five thousand–slide library!

10 WE ARE WHO WE HANG OUT WITH

MY STORY

ON THE WAY HOME TO MASSACHUSETTS FROM MY NORTH AMERICAN WINTER SOJOURN IN NEW ZEALAND, I MADE A STOP IN SAN FRANCISCO.

I lived in San Francisco from 1974 to 1981, and in the Bay Area from 1970 to 2000. I have a special fondness for the city. I had lunch with an old friend on Hayes Street, about thirty blocks from my hotel, then walked back.

I was staggered. I'd read and heard about San Francisco's severe homeless situation, but now I was in the midst of it. It was sad, unnerving, a little scary, and a true shock to the system. (San Francisco has the second-worst homeless stats, a bit behind New York.)

In addition to the extremely troublesome situation, I realized something else—something obvious. I realized anew that having all one's senses totally immersed in a situation causes an awareness that sticks, sticks big-time, and that is ten times or one hundred times more profound than reading, watching video clips, or even having serious conversations with people in the know.

And that is, in effect, the topic of this chapter. Innovation is about new ways of looking, new ways of sensing, seeing something at the end of your nose for the first time or in a remarkably new way.

The topic here, in short: We are what we eat. We are who (or what) we hang out with.

Hardly a profound statement—or is it indeed profound?

We talk constantly about new things—how could we not amid today's madness? But do we with great regularity and systematically immerse ourselves in new situations: new contexts, new physical locations, and make contact with new people? Do we have lively and indeed deep discussions about homelessness but fail to wander the streets for hours upon hours and engage all of our being with the actual situation?

I was superbly trained prior to my arrival in Vietnam in August 1966. But in a hundred ways, I learned more in my first hour on the ground than I had in six months of preparation. There was no combat—just an unremarkable one-hour jeep ride from the Danang airfield to the camp where I would be headquartered for the next ten months. But that hour, all the sensations of that night, the smells and sounds and scenes, turned my world truly upside down in sixty officially uneventful minutes.

The same thing happened when I made my first presentation, as a youngish McKinsey consultant, to a big company's exec team in a big company boardroom. I was technically overprepared, waaaay overprepared, but the actual full set of sensations associated with that twenty-five-minute submersion, yes, turned my professional life upside down. I don't mean to lump McKinsey presentations with homelessness in San Francisco and war in Vietnam, but all three events, true full-body immersion in the new, are illustrative of the key idea in this chapter.

To deal effectively and creatively with a given context, we must push ourselves hard, very hard, systematically, one day at a time, one hour at a time, to become fully engaged with novelty.

Novel settings.

Novel people.

Novel everything.

While, as I said in the introduction, there is much, much more I could offer on the topic of innovation, I have chosen to make two points. WTTMSW/Whoever Tries The Most Stuff Wins/ Whoever Screws The Most Stuff Up Wins in the last chapter. And in this chapter, realization (and action associated therewith) that we are shaped by the people we cavort with and the situations we are immersed in—and if those situations do not constantly challenge what we think we know, we haven't a snowball's chance in hell of regularly innovating.

One feature of this discussion will be to question whether our extraordinary new level of connectedness, courtesy of new technologies, is a true connectedness that leads to breakthroughs in our thoughts and actions.

It is so, so, so easy—even in 2018, or perhaps especially in 2018 (think working from home)—to fall into the Great Same-Same Trap. And make no mistake, that same-same trap is the death knell of creativity.

Hence . . .

THE HANG-OUT NARRATIVE

10.1 ALL YOU NEED TO KNOW

You will become like the five people you associate with the most. This can be either a blessing or a curse.

—Billy Cox, sales training guru

10.2

10.2.1
INNOVATION/DIVERSITY ON STEROIDS: WE ARE WHO WE HANG OUT WITH. WEIRD TIMES CALL FOR WEIRD MATES.

Opener/Take #1/Fact:

**We Are What We Eat.
We Are Who We Hang Out With.**

Opener/Take #2/Vernacular:

Hang out with "cool" and thou shalt become more cool. Hang out with "dull" and thou shalt become more dull.

On my scorecard, the "hang-out factor" gets equal billing with WTTMSW/WSTMSUW:

1. WTTMSW/WSTMSUW: Insist that everybody be trying anything and everything all the time and as quickly as

possible, with hoopla and incentives offered for cool screwups.

2. DIVERSITY: In upside-down times, demand/ensure constant, deep contact with those who are way ahead of the game and those who get under our skin—and thereby potentially save our professional lives.

10.2.2
INNOVATION/DIVERSITY ON STEROIDS: MESSAGE NINETEENTH CENTURY = MESSAGE 2018

It is hardly possible to overrate the value of placing human beings in contact with persons dissimilar to themselves, and with modes of thought and action unlike those with which they are familiar. Such communication has always been, and is peculiarly in the present age [19th century], one of the primary sources of progress.

—John Stuart Mill (1806–1873)

No less than a "primary source of progress"—makes perfect sense to me. On the one hand, such a straightforward assertion. On the other hand, it's hard (mind-boggling?) to believe how often this axiom is still violated in, God help us, 2018.

Regarding "diversity qua diversity," the central idea here is diversity on any dimension you can name:

Short, tall, fat, thin,
Stanford degree, no degree,
techie, artist, philosopher,

gardener, collector of vintage model aircraft,
small-town roots, urban roots,
black, white, male, female . . .

10.2.3
INNOVATION/DIVERSITY ON STEROIDS: DIVERSITY TOPS EXPERTISE

Another—modern times, in this instance—endorsement of diverse groups, from Scott Page's superb book, *The Difference: How the Power of Diversity Creates Better Groups, Firms, Schools, and Societies*:

Diverse groups of problem solvers—groups of people with diverse backgrounds—consistently outperformed groups of the best and the brightest. If I formed two groups, one random (and therefore diverse) and one consisting of the best individual performers, the first group almost always did better. . . . DIVERSITY TRUMPED ABILITY.

This is an exceptionally powerful and counterintuitive conclusion. And the practical implications are clear: diversity—once again, on any and all dimensions—leads to better thinking, better problem solving, and greater creativity. Diversity qua diversity beats the "experts."

Note that Scott Page, a University of Michigan professor of complex systems, political science, and economics, devotes an entire book to this topic and presents a truckload of sound research to bolster his argument. While I have long and unequivocally bought into the diversity idea, I was startled by the ability to propose and support such an encompassing and strong argument for diversity.

(*Please. Stop, reread the Scott Page quote above and perhaps his entire book. Consider the practical implications, in particular the tendency to over-rely on experts [e.g., you and your leadership team].*

Should, for example, every major decision, from strategy to a critical promotion, involve or be reviewed by a panel of nonexperts?)

10.3 INNOVATION/DIVERSITY ON STEROIDS: EVERY DECISION!

At its core, every relationship, partnership, location, time allocation decision, and so on is a strategic diversity (of perspective] decision. INNOVATE, YES OR NO?

Diversity (INNOVATION!) decisions:

- Staff selection and promotion
- Choice of external consultants
- Customers (Adrian Slywotzky, Mercer Consultants: "Future-defining customers may account for only 2 percent or 3 percent of your total, but they represent a crucial window on the future.")
- Outsourcing partners (exceedingly important!)
- Vendors (Wayne Burkan, *Wide Angle Vision: Beat the Competition by Focusing on Fringe Competitors, Lost Customers, and Rogue Employees*: "There is an ominous

downside to strategic supplier relationships. A strategic supplier is not likely to function as any more than a mirror to your organization." Suggestion: Read Burkan's book—another full volume on diversity qua diversity.)

- The whole wide world/crowdsourcing (*every damn thing!*)
- Calendar/time allocation (This is critical. Assess your calendar, and odds are one month looks pretty much like the rest—only a day-at-a-time evaluation will lead you in the direction of planned variety of time allocation.)
- Product portfolio (Too many line extensions, not enough pioneering efforts? A former Ford chairman: "If I make a new product decision and am not anxious, I am fearful I've approved no more than a look-alike.")
- HQ location (GE moves from Fairfield, Connecticut, to Boston to expose itself to a more broadly innovative community as it follows its bet-the-company strategic thrust into the IoT/Internet of Things.)
- Lunch (220 WORKING DAYS PER YEAR = 220 DIVERSITY OPPORTUNITIES. THIS IS A VERY BIG DEAL; A MATCHLESS GOLDEN OPPORTUNITY AVAILABLE TO ONE AND ALL STARTING TODAY. TODAY = TODAY. AND YES I AM RE-REPEATING MYSELF.)
- Board of directors composition (NO "SAME-SAME." See below.)

On each dimension above: Do we go with the safe bets, or do we DARE embrace a rich portfolio of edgy partners (employees, customers, etc.) who will drag us, kicking and screaming if necessary, into the eye of 2018's perfect storm? Recall in the section on hiring (5.4.1) that Soichiro Honda preferred "people who had been in trouble"—now that's anticipating the spirit of 2018!

10.4 INNOVATION/DIVERSITY ON STEROIDS: A BOARD FIT FOR 2018

Strategy guru Gary Hamel speaks in plain and profound terms to the worst of all manifestations of myopia:

The bottleneck is at the . . . top of the bottle. Where are you likely to find people with the least diversity of experience, the largest investment in the past, and the greatest reverence for industry dogma . . . at the top.

In fact, the most poisonous example of same-same is frequently the board of directors.

Here is my (tongue nowhere near cheek) response, inspired by Mr. Hamel:

TEN-MEMBER BOARD OF DIRECTORS FIT FOR 2018

- At least two members under age twenty-five. ("New youth" with new tech have had a different developmental experience than their elderly—say thirty-five-year-old—peers.)
- At least three or four women. (Boards with a balance of females and males produce very high relative performance—see chapter 15.)

- One IT/data analytics *superstar.* (Not an "IT representative" but a certified goddess or god from the likes of Google.)
- One or two entrepreneurs and perhaps a VC. (The entrepreneurial bent must directly infiltrate the board.)
- One or two people of stature with "weird" backgrounds—artist, musician, shaman, etc. (We need regular, uncomfortable oddball challenges.)
- A certified design guru. (Design presence at board level is simply a must in my scheme of things. See chapter 11.)
- No more than three with MBAs. (Why? The necessity of moving beyond the typical MBA, linear, analytic, over-quantified mind-set.)

Partial inspiration for this: Cybernetics pioneer W. Ross Ashby's Law of Requisite Variety. The diversity of the board should more or less match the diversity of the overall business environment.

10.5 INNOVATION/DIVERSITY ON STEROIDS: THE POWER AND NECESSITY OF DISCOMFORT

Legendary ad man Jay Chiat tells us:

I'm not comfortable unless I'm uncomfortable.

I treat Chiat's remark as a logical and literal command.

Or consider this version of Chiat's formulation from Eleanor Roosevelt:

Do one thing every day that scares you.

Mrs. Roosevelt's edict is so much easier said than done. In general, "same-same" is invariably our default position. So, how do you or I channel Eleanor Roosevelt, a woman who thrived on what others called the impossible? The obvious answer is the only answer: conscious, continuous, self-monitored effort one day at a time.

Federal Express founder and CEO Fred Smith casually asked me, "Tom, who's the most interesting person you've met in the last ninety days? And how do I get in touch with them?"

Several years ago, Smith and I sat together on a CNN economics panel. In the green room before our appearance, he popped the "most-interesting-person" question above. Frankly, I didn't have a good answer, and I am still mortified by that experience. For heaven's sake, exposure to interesting people is what I supposedly do for a living—how else keep up or stay ahead of the herd?

SO HAVE YOU GOT A GOOD ANSWER TO MR. SMITH'S QUESTION? AND IF NOT, WHAT DO YOU PLAN TO DO ABOUT IT ASAP?

10.6 INNOVATION/DIVERSITY ON STEROIDS: ALL CONNECTED TO ALL

The Billion-man Research Team: Companies offering work to online communities are reaping the benefits of crowdsourcing.
—Headline, *Financial Times*

Connectional Intelligence [labeled CxQ by the authors] is the ability to combine the world's diversity of people, networks, disciplines, and resources, forging connections that create value, meaning, and breakthrough results.
—Erica Dhawan and Saj-nicole Joni,
Get BIG Things Done: The Power of Connectional Intelligence

Simply put, the ability to tap in to global diversity has expanded exponentially. The implications range from the work of giant companies and laboratories to the smallest of local projects.

Consider two extremes . . .

10.6.1
CONNECT. CONNECT. CONNECT: RESEARCHGATE/ CONVERSATIONS AMONG ELEVEN MILLION SCIENTISTS

ResearchGate was founded in Boston in 2008 by virologist and computer scientist Dr. Ijad Madisch. It now has over eleven million vetted members from throughout the science and research community. Here is a partial description taken from Wikipedia:

ResearchGate is the largest social networking site for scientists and researchers to share papers, ask and answer questions, and find collaborators. . . . [Those who] wish to use the site need to have an e-mail address at a recognized institution or to be manually confirmed as a published researcher in order to sign up for an account. Members . . . can upload research output, including papers, data, chapters, negative results, patents, research proposals, methods, presentations, and software source code. Users may also follow the activities of other users and engage in discussions with them.

The possibilities are infinite.

The results have surpassed expectations by many a mile.

10.6.2
CONNECT. CONNECT. CONNECT: MS. MARX HOSTS HER BOOK GROUP

The prospect of contracting a gofer on an à la carte basis is enticing. For instance, wouldn't it be convenient if I could outsource someone to write a paragraph here [at this point in the *New Yorker* article], explaining the history of outsourcing in America? Good idea! I went ahead and commissioned just such a paragraph from Get Friday, a "virtual personal assistant" firm based in Bangalore. . . . The paragraph arrived in my in-box ten days after I ordered it . . . it was 1,356 words. . . . There was a bibliography with eleven sources. . . . At $14 an hour for seven hours of work, the cost came to $98.
—Patricia Marx, "Outsource Yourself," *The New Yorker*

In this wonderful article, Marx describes in detail crowdsourcing everything associated with hosting her book club. That included seeking out witty comments on Proust for her to make, since she hadn't had time to read the book. In fact, a set of excellent comments only set her back five dollars. ***The writer/contractor/ Proustian expert was a fourteen-year-old girl from New Jersey.***

All connected to all: from eleven million scientists to a local book group.

Message 2018: Stoke the Fires of Innovation . . .

Connect.
Connect.
Connect.
With anyone.
And everyone.
From anywhere.
And everywhere.
All the time.

The usual and all-important! caveat and reminder is in order: Technology is the enabler, but ATTITUDE and CULTURE are the "last 90 percent."

Connecting in the end is a disposition, not a tech trait.

10.6.3

ALL CONNECTED TO ALL, VERSION 2018: MORE—OR LESS!—THAN MEETS THE EYE

"Connected" ain't what it used to be. Connected was "songlines" in the Australian bush (see Bruce Chatwin's marvelous book *The Songlines*). Connection was the Pony Express in the American West. And then the trains. The real breakthrough and accelerator was the telegraph, called by some the "Victorian Internet." Then phones, and most recently, of course, the Internet itself and its derivatives such as smartphones.

All these landmarks were forms of "CONNECT. CONNECT. CONNECT." Today, we live in the age of Facebook. And, age six or sixty, *connection* means thousands upon thousands of "friends." It *is* connection. And it *is* nontrivial. On a deeply serious note, new connection tools enable the "billion-man research team" that kicked off this section.

But I do mean to remind you/me/us that there are connections, and then there are connections.

As I've said and will keep saying, **RELATIONSHIPS** are the heart and soul of excellence.

But the relationships I mostly point to—with employees, customers, our community—are relationships that take time. **LOTS AND LOTS AND LOTS OF TIME TO DEVELOP AND THEN LOTS AND LOTS OF TIME TO NURTURE.**

By hook or by crook, we must invest dearly in deep connections. Please do not forget that for a single moment.

10.7 INNOVATION/DIVERSITY ON STEROIDS: HANG-OUT FINAL WORDS

Your "hang out with" portfolio can be and should be as carefully concocted—and managed and evaluated—as your budget or strategic plan. It IS your de facto strategic plan!

Who you spend your time with may well be the single-most important variable associated with your personal and enterprise success.

10.8 WTTMSW/WSTMSUW/DIVERSITY/ SUMMARY: UBIQUITY AND SCORING BIG ON THE "HOLY SHIT" SCALE

IRON INNOVATION EQUALITY LAW: The quality and quantity and imaginativeness of innovation and formal R&D shall be the same in all functions (e.g., in HR and purchasing and logistics as much as in marketing or product development).

Wild and Woolly HR Department. YES!
Wild and Woolly Purchasing Department. YES!
Wild and Woolly Logistics Department. YES!

PROJECT INNOVATION EVALUATION INDEX: List your top-five active projects: How many score eight or higher

on a ten-point "Knock Your Socks Off"/"Wow!"/"Holy shit!" Scale?

If less than three, WORRY.

Worry A LOT.

Get on it.

NOW.

NOW = NOW.

ADDING VALUE, A "TOP LINE" OBSESSION

11 A PASSION FOR DESIGN, DIFFERENTIATOR #1

MY STORY

ON A LATE FEBRUARY DAY IN 2016, IT RAINED CATS AND DOGS IN TAKAKA, NEW ZEALAND . . .

I was coming out of the hardware store and had my iPhone, as usual, deep in my pocket when the surprise storm hit. But pocket protection was not enough. The water snuck in somehow. The phone was inoperable, kaput—though I tried every trick to revive it known to man and the Internet.

Gorgeous.

Functional.

And done in by a bit of rain.

Bottom line: bad design.

(Sorry, ghost of Steve.)

Well, it ain't gonna happen twice. Now, if there's even a single cloud in the sky, I carry my phone safe in a Ziploc bag.

Ziplocs!

How do I love thee?

Let me count the ways.

I do love my any-and-all-purpose Ziplocs so much so that I've got a reputation for Wretched Ziploc Excess. For my sixtieth birthday, one of my business partners put together a book of letters he'd collected from my various friends and colleagues wishing me well. The book was touching. Touching and at times hilarious. Those present at the subsequent birthday bash read their contributions.

The partner and pal who pulled all this together had contributed a piece of his own, which he read with gusto to the gathered guests. The entire piece—about six hundred words—was about me and my Ziplocs.

There's a whole drawer in my office filled with Ziplocs of every size, from the sandwich size (useful in a thousand ways!) to the two-gallon giants, sometimes hard to find, and without which I simply could not exist.

I think my Ziplocs have as much beauty as they do utility. One of my favorite aspects of the bags is that when you seal them up, there is a memorable clicking sound that tells you that you've done it right. No rain will intrude to ruin a several-hundred-dollar iPhone, that's for damn sure.

Why in the world am I relating this story?

Simple!

I LOVE, LOVE, LOVE THINGS THAT ARE BRILLIANTLY DESIGNED.
PEERLESS FUNCTIONALITY.
AESTHETICALLY PLEASING.
EMOTIONALLY IRREPLACEABLE.
(AND I HATE, HATE, HATE THINGS THAT ARE DESIGNED IN A SLOVENLY OR CARELESS FASHION. THEY ARE NOT "PROBLEMATIC." THEY ARE INSULTING.)

I fear I have nary an artistic bone in my body. I dropped out of architecture school after one semester; it was clear to me that the artistic bit and I would never co-reside. (I shifted to civil engineering, from which perch my colleagues and I could criticize the architects for the un-buildability of so many of their gorgeous-on-paper concoctions.)

No, I'm not an artist, but I have an appreciation and an abiding affection for things whose design does no less than blow me away—from those Ziplocs to my Tuf-E-Nuf Mini Striker Stubby Claw Hammer and, as Steve Jobs intended and obsessed on, the attractive, smoothly functioning *boxes* in which Apple products arrive at your door.

Let's pause and turn to the bigger picture of me and design: I had just had a GZE/Great Ziploc Experience, about twenty-five years ago when I was on the verge of giving a speech to packaging equipment dealers. In that speech, I sang a Ziploc love song and, unschooled though I was, turned that riff into a paean on the love or hate (not "like" or "dislike") engendered by design in general. From there, it was off to the races.

I rarely do things halfway. (My given name is Thomas J. Peters. My wife insists it's Thomas E. Peters, where the *E* stands for *excess*.)

So after that first talk, I kept turning up the volume—and started doing my homework. Design, I concluded way back when, was arguably "Differentiator #1" of any damn thing—for good or for ill. I ranted and raved and deepened my design appreciation, positive and negative, to the point that, for example, I ended up key-noting (ranting and raving) at top-drawer design conferences in New Zealand and in the United Kingdom. And one of America's most prominent designers, IDEO founder David Kelley, labeled me "the business world's leading ambassador of design."

Well, damn it, there are still far too many who don't get it, who remain oblivious to the allure of great design and are unaware of how the tiniest design boo-boo can enrage a customer. Great design moves mountains and vaults market share to the heavens. I think that's pretty much always been the case, but a design emphasis today is many many times more important than in the past. In the age of ubiquitous robotics and algorithmic this and algorithmic that, standing out from the crowd is getting tougher and tougher.

Well, I think standing up and standing out can be done. I will in fact present design and eight other differentiation strategies in this section. But not one of them is more important than the first-by-acclamation on the list: design that engenders no less than love.

Zippety doo dah Ziplocs (and much, much more) . . .

THE DESIGN NARRATIVE

11.1 DESIGN/D[ESIGN]-DAY: AUGUST 10, 2011

DESIGN rules!

APPLE market capitalization is number one, surging past ExxonMobil.

When Apple's market cap exceeded ExxonMobil's on August 10, 2011, there should no longer have been any issue about "DESIGN POWER." Now only idiots will ignore it in enterprises of any and every size and flavor.

For two decades, I'd been ranting and raving on the topic of design. The struggle was uphill and mostly futile. You could almost say that everything changed that day when Apple shot past Exxon. That, of course, overstates; but the D-day 2011 event surely did make the design message hard to dismiss, even, or perhaps especially, among the number munchers in the finance department.

11.2

11.2.1
DESIGN = CARE

Design = Care
Design = Elegance
Design = The Best of Human Achievement

Design = Contribution to Human Culture
Design = Respect
Design = Thoughtfulness
Design = Avoiding Insult

Huge degree of *care.*   —Ian Parker, *The New Yorker*,
on Apple design chief Jony Ive's
approach to creating products

Steve and Jony would discuss corners for hours and hours.
—Laurene Powell Jobs

**Expose yourself to the best things that humans have done
and then try to bring those things into what you're doing.**
—Steve Jobs

**In some way, by caring, we're actually serving humanity.
People might think it's a stupid belief, but it's a goal—it's
a contribution that we hope we can make, in some small
way, to culture.**   —Jony Ive

**[Apple's] great design secret may be avoiding insult. [Their
thoughtfulness is] a sign of respect. Elegance in objects
is everybody's right, and it shouldn't cost more than ugli-
ness. So much of our manufacturing environment testifies
to carelessness.**   —Paola Antonelli, MOMA

Great design is "Wow."
Great design is utility.

Great design is ease of use.

I believe those three statements.

Passionately.

But let's go further. Consider the words in the title of this section and in the quotes from which they were drawn: *Care. Elegance. The best of human achievement. Contribution to human culture. Respect. Thoughtfulness. Avoiding insult.*

I would like to raise the stakes and the bar as high as possible in this section. I hardly suggest that you or I are Steve Jobs clones. And our playground decidedly is not Apple.

But that's no excuse for not raising that bar to the sky in everything we do for our customers—and, for that matter, for our colleagues and our communities.

Consider care and corners. In your organization (of 1 or 101 people), does care enter into every discussion of customer connections, from the sales pitch to Web presentation to next client e-mail to supporting logistics systems to the delivered product or service itself? Are our corners—the tiniest bits of those products and services—given something like the attention that Jony and Steve gave to Apple product corners?

"Contribution to human culture" is a lot to ask of the blog I am about to post. Or is it? I have neither the time nor resources—nor skill—to match Jony and Steve in my blog post. But I *can* think about it. I *can* slow down and reread two—or three or four or five—times. I *can* wonder if a few word changes might make the blog post sing and have emotional impact on those who choose to read it.

I sure as hell can work on "avoiding insult." No lousy grammar. No carelessness of any sort. A little more time on word choice, a little more original and a little less management babble-ish. And so on.

I think these words and terms—*care, elegance, best of human achievement, contribution to human culture, respect, thoughtfulness, avoiding insult*—can be etched in the back of my mind, challenges that I can try to grab hold of in some way or other. Day in and day out. Hour in and hour out.

There is no damned excuse for being careLESS or thought-LESS in any interaction. In my case, no damned excuse for not attempting to get into the heads and hearts of every single one of the seven hundred–plus people who will be in my audience this morning in Edmonton, Canada, people who have generously given me an hour of their precious time as they listen to my talk. (If I don't give my all and then some, I'll have the ghost of John F. Kennedy on my case for sure; JFK told us never to open our mouths in public if our goal was not to change the world. Too grand for you or me? Perhaps. But then again, maybe not.)

Yes, my design-is-all riff is an unabashed, unadulterated sermon.

And I pray it just might make the tiniest bit of difference.

Try this out:

Design is everything.
Everything is design.
We are all designers.

—Richard Farson, *The Power of Design:*
A Force for Transforming Everything

It took me and my colleagues and our designer, Ken Silvia, two years of on-and-off dialogue and presentations to create the logo for the Tom Peters Company. And what did that painstaking two-year effort result in? Our logo is a standalone red exclamation mark. That's it, the whole deal, the whole kit and caboodle.

And I could not—twenty-five years later—be happier.

What I try to do every day in every interaction—including every tweet, and I've produced well over fifty thousand—is to be a . . .

Red.

Exclamation.

Mark.

To challenge.

To provoke.

To make a smidgeon of impact.

As I see it, there is no reason that you and I can't make big waves in our local market by grabbing hold of and living a design excellence obsession.

That is the message of this section. And it is the message of this book. The "excellence dividend" is about going on offense, about creating products and services and organizational climates and customer and community attachments that will more than survive any technology onslaught.

11.2.2
DESIGN/WHAT MATTERS: LEAVING "A BIT OF YOUR HEART" BEHIND

He said for him the craft of building a boat was like a religion. It wasn't enough to master the technical details of it. You had to give yourself up to it spiritually; you had to surrender yourself absolutely to it. When you were done and

walked away from the boat, you had to feel that you had left a piece of yourself behind in it forever, a bit of your heart.
—Daniel James Brown, *The Boys in the Boat: Nine Americans and Their Epic Quest for Gold at the 1936 Berlin Olympics*, on the world's premier racing shell designer and builder, George Yeoman Pocock

The bestselling *Boys in the Boat* is the heartwarming saga of the American eight-man crew from the University of Washington that won at the 1936 Olympics. In addition to the oarsmen, one of the heroes is Pocock. The technical bits of rowing shell design are intimidatingly complex. But, in Pocock's view, that's just the start of the story. The heart of the matter is: "*You had to give yourself up to it spiritually; you had to surrender yourself absolutely to it.*"

That makes sense to me. And as I compose this sentence, I'd say precisely the same thing is true about writing a book. You need good material. You need to be a halfway decent craftsman in putting prose together. But, like Pocock, I believe that's just the start. There must be some spiritual attachment to the material, which has, I hope, from time to time been transmitted through the pages you are reading.

My point is neither racing shells nor this book.

It is you.

Consider the layout of the restaurant you are planning to open and for which you have shelled out every penny of your net worth and then some. The layout must work and be within budget. But for your dream to come true, even if you have a superb chef, there must be, from day one, something spiritual about the restaurant. Or, I'd almost guarantee, it'll be either ho-hum or an outright flop.

And I would use exactly the same words to describe your efforts to design a new training course or marketing campaign, if that's the focus of your professional life.

11.2.3
DESIGN THAT IS TRANSFORMATIVE: "EPIC SCREWS WITH DEEPER MEANING"

[Nest founder Tony Fadell] admitted, "Every business school in the world would flunk you if you came out with a business plan that said, 'Oh, by the way, we're going to design and fabricate our own screws at an exponentially higher cost than it would cost to buy them.' But these aren't just screws. Like the thermometer itself, they're better screws, epic screws, screws with, dare I say it, deeper meaning. Functionally, they utilize a specific thread pattern that allows them to go into any surface, from wood to plaster to thin sheet metal. And the [custom] screwdriver feels balanced to the hand; it has the Nest logo on it and looks 'Nest-y,' just like everything from Apple looks 'Apple-y.'"
—Rich Karlgaard, *The Soft Edge*

Pause.

Please.

Epic screws with deeper meaning.

Please try to translate Fadell's sentiment into the at-first-glance mundane project you are working on right now. I know not what the substance of that project is, but I am dead certain that Mr. Fadell's words apply to that project and to you!

11.2.4
DESIGN: "OSCAR" FOR MOST SMILES

It is fair to say that almost no new vehicle in recent memory has provoked more smiles.

—*The New York Times* review of the
MINI Cooper S, reported in Donald Norman's
Emotional Design: Why We Love (or Hate) Everyday Things

Donald Norman is a highly influential and longtime champion-in-chief of design functionality, as opposed to the traditional "aesthetics first" definition of design.

Yet, in a more or less epiphany, he came over a period of decades to appreciate the limits to both aesthetics and functionality; hence his superb book that is one long paean to "emotional design."

Emotional design = "More smiles."

(FYI: As a companion to Norman's book, peruse Guy Kawasaki's *Enchantment: The Art of Changing Heart, Minds, and Actions*. Among many other things, Kawasaki was a principal player in the design and marketing of the first Apple Macintosh.)

11.2.5
DESIGN AS "RELIGION"/BMW

Design is treated like a religion at BMW.

—Fortune

I am not a Beemer owner. But I did rent a floor of my office building in Palo Alto to BMW. They treated the styling of their tiny "Silicon Valley outpost," as they called it, with the same degree of reverence they shower on the creation of their cars—it's all of a piece, and an integral part of the BMW way of being, as far as they're concerned.

BMW: **Office space = Auto = Religion.**

11.2.6
DESIGN AS "SEE, TOUCH, HEAR, SMELL OR TASTE"/ STARBUCKS

With its carefully conceived mix of colors and textures, aromas and music, STARBUCKS is more indicative of our era than the iMac. Starbucks is to the Age of Aesthetics what McDonald's was to the Age of Convenience or Ford was to the Age of Mass Production—the touchstone success story, the exemplar of . . . the aesthetic imperative.

"Every Starbucks store is carefully designed to enhance the quality of everything the customers see, touch, hear, smell or taste. All the sensory signals have to appeal to the same high standards. The artwork, the music, the aromas,

the surfaces all have to send the same subliminal message as the flavor of the coffee," writes CEO Howard Schultz.
—Virginia Postrel, *The Substance of Style: How the Rise of Aesthetic Value Is Remaking Commerce, Culture, and Consciousness*

STARBUCKS AND DESIGN AND ROMANCE AND SOUL LOST AND (RE)FOUND

Starbucks had become operationally driven, about efficiency as opposed to the romance. We'd lost the soul of the company.
—Howard Schultz on Starbucks' problems that caused him to reclaim the CEO job (Schultz, by the way, calls his association with Starbucks "a love story." FYI: Since Schultz returned, Starbucks has indeed gotten its mojo back!)

ROMANCE: Add *romance* and/or *love story* to your thoughts-on-design notebook. (CAUTION FLAG: The Schultz vignette also demonstrates how almost inevitable it is that "romance" fades with rapid growth; keeping a culture fresh and a romance alive is a monumental task—see chapter 3.)

11.2.7
DESIGN: LOVEMARKS

Shareholders very seldom love the brands they have invested in. And the last thing they want is an intimate relationship. They figure this could warp their judgment. They want measurability, increasing returns (always) and

no surprises (ever). Imagine a relationship with someone like that!

No wonder so many brands lost the emotional thread that had led them to their extraordinary success and turned them instead into metric-munchers of the lowest kind. Watch for the sign: Heads, not hearts, at work here. . . .

When I first suggested that Love was the way to transform business, grown CEOs blushed and slid down behind their annual accounts. But I kept at them.

I knew it was Love that was missing. I knew that Love was the only way to ante up the emotional temperature and create the new kinds of relationships brands needed. I knew that Love was the only way business could respond to the rapid shift in control to consumers.

—Kevin Roberts, former CEO, Saatchi & Saatchi,
Lovemarks: The Future Beyond Brands

Kevin has been a mentor of mine for years. I've given away dozens of copies of his book *Lovemarks*. It is original and challenging, and as the message of this chapter, it applies to all of us and to our every project.

11.3

11.3.1
DESIGN: THE THIRD DIMENSION (AND WHY IT MATTERS NOW FAR MORE THAN EVER BEFORE)

Design means buying the act (remember, Apple >> Exxon), then "taking the plunge" and hiring a first-rate designer or two. Then let 'em have at it. But as I've tried to illustrate in the quotes above, design with impact, design that changes everything is much, much more.

Effective design *is* about superior usability. (Check.)

It's also about aesthetic excellence. (Check.)

And then there is that "third dimension" called *heart* or *care* or *romance* or *surrender*—or, why not, *Lovemark*. Design that turns perceptions upside down—in the corner store as well as at Apple or BMW—involves achieving some form of spiritual connection with the customer and, thence and first, among ourselves.

I normally run like the dickens from terms like *spiritual*, but not in this instance. It is simply misleading to talk about compelling, lasting, shape-shifting, love-affair-inducing differentiation by design without using such words. And somehow or other bringing them to life in every corner of the large, small, or tiny enterprise.

Axiom: This *care* or *heart* holds equally for *internal products* such as training courses and business processes. BELIEVE IT.

Hypothesis: This "third dimension" will have great pragmatic importance beyond traditional product/service differentiation. As technology (AI, etc.) vacuums up more and more of

the standardized work of the organization, activities associated with this so-called third dimension will be the centerpiece of the role that humans continue to play.

11.3.2
DESIGN: THE LIST

Care

Respect

Thoughtfulness

Corners

More smiles

A bit of your heart

Epic screws with deeper meaning

Religion

Romance

Soul

Lovemark

Spirituality

(Apple >> Exxon)

11.3.3
DESIGN IS . . .

- The reception area
- The restrooms!
- Dialogues at the call center
- *Every* electronic or paper form
- *Every* business process "map"

- *Every* e-mail
- *Every* meeting agenda, setting, and so on
- *Every* square meter of every facility
- *Every* new product proposal
- *Every* manual
- *Every* customer contact
- A consideration in *every* promotion decision
- The presence and ubiquity of an "aesthetic sensibility"/ "design mindfulness"
- An encompassing "design review" process for more or less everything (every project, every system, etc.)
- Etc.

Typically, design is a vertical stripe in the chain of events in a product's delivery. [At Apple, it's] a long, horizontal stripe, where design is part of every conversation.

—Robert Brunner, former Apple design chief

Every conversation!

(There is no reason—none, **ZERO**—that this formulation should not apply to a one-person accountancy or four-person lawn maintenance service.)

Read! Study!

Emotional Design: Why We Love (or Hate) Everyday Things by Donald Norman

Enchantment: The Art of Changing Heart, Minds, and Actions by Guy Kawasaki

Lovemarks: The Future Beyond Brands by Kevin Roberts

The Business Romantic: Give Everything, Quantify Nothing, and Create Something Greater Than Yourself by Tim Leberecht

11.4

11.4.1
DESIGN: THE LAST WORD(S) I

Rikyu was watching his son Sho-an as he swept and watered the garden path. "Not clean enough," said Rikyu, when Sho-an had finished his task, and bade him try again. After a weary hour the son turned to Rikyu: "Father, there is nothing more to be done. The steps have been washed for the third time, the stone planters and the trees are well sprinkled with water, moss and lichens are shining with a fresh verdure; not a twig, not a leaf have I left on the ground." "Young fool," chided the tea-master, "that is not the way a garden path should be swept." Saying this, Rikyu stepped into the garden, shook a tree and scattered over the garden gold and crimson leaves, scraps of the brocade of autumn! What Rikyu demanded was not cleanliness alone, but the beautiful and natural also.

—Kakuzo Okakura, *The Book of Tea*

In her inspiring book *The Art of Imperfection*, Veronique Vienne adds her own version of the scattered leaves: "In the Zen tradition, 'wabi-sabi' objects, carefully crafted to be intentionally imperfect, impermanent, or incomplete, are considered most beautiful—their humble elegance transcending fads and fashions." Likewise, Kevin Roberts, in *Lovemarks*, adds, "When we were working through the essentials of a Lovemark, Mystery was always at the top of the list."

BREAKAWAY DESIGN = FUNCTIONALITY + AESTHETICS + SPIRIT/HEART/THE BROCADE OF AUTUMN/IMPERFECTION/MYSTERY

Sign in a recording studio in Vermont: **YOUR MOST "PERFECT" TAKE IS NOT THE TAKE YOU SHOULD KEEP. THE ONE YOU SHOULD KEEP WILL HAVE IMPERFECTIONS, BUT THE IMPERFECTIONS WILL IN FACT BEST CONVEY YOUR PASSION, YOUR LOVE, YOUR COMPELLING NEED TO TELL THE SONG'S STORY.**

11.4.2
DESIGN: THE LAST WORD(S) II

Only one company can be the cheapest. All others must use design. —Rodney Fitch, Fitch & Co. (from *Insights*, the Design Council UK)

12 THE RELENTLESS PURSUIT OF TGRS/ THINGS GONE RIGHT (AND EIGHT OTHER VALUE-ADDED STRATEGIES)

EIGHT VALUE-ADDED STRATEGIES

1. Maximize TGRs/Things Gone Right/Explicitly Manage the TGR Process/Little>>>Big
2. It Helps to Be as Helpful as You Can Be: Services (of Every Conceivable Flavor) Added
3. Social Business: Who? EVERYONE!/No Halfway!
4. Big Data/Mammoth Opportunities, Underexamined Downsides
5. IoT/Internet of Things, IoE/Internet of Everything: A First-Order Game Changer
6. Underserved Markets I: Women As Overwhelmingly Predominant Customer for EVERYTHING
7. Underserved Markets II: The ENORMOUS Aging Market/ Oldies Are Beautiful with a Lotta Years to Go and Have ALL the Money

8. The "Big Duh": Our People/Fully Engaged/Innovators All/#1 Value-Added Driver!

I make no suggestion that this list is complete. But I am dead certain that each of these well-tested ideas is important—in fact *very* important—and each encompasses a humongous opportunity in terms of customer fulfillment and delight, enterprise growth, and profitability. (*Excellence Dividend* raison d'être: a great way to keep and add jobs.)

Moreover, working at some combination of these strategies in the age of same-same-looks-like-every-other-app-car is ten times more important than ever before.

Products and services: Differentiate or Die.

Workers: Distinct or Extinct.

All yours.

A long list.

12.1 THE TGR NARRATIVE

CHERRY-PICK TO YOUR HEART'S CONTENT, MAXIMIZE TGRS/THINGS GONE RIGHT, EXPLICITLY MANAGE THE TGR PROCESS

12.1.1
TGRS/THINGS GONE RIGHT: ADDRESSING THE GREAT 8/80 CHASM

Customers describing their service experience as "superior": 8 percent

Companies describing the service experience they provide as "superior": 80 percent

— Bain & Company survey of 362 companies

Yikes.

40–60, sure.

But **8–80?**

ONE RESPONSE TO "THE GREAT 8/80 CHASM": MAXIMIZE TGRs/THINGS GONE RIGHT

Consider TGWs/Things Gone Wrong. In days past, TGWs were the automotive industry's measure of quality or lack thereof. Car types were formally graded for quality via their TGW score. TGWs were damned important when I cowrote *In Search of Excellence* in 1982. In short, the American auto industry was getting hammered in large measure because Japanese auto producers offered up vehicles with noticeably fewer TGWs (i.e., better quality) than ours.

Segue to 2018. Most things at every price point work pretty well. I got in trouble, more or less intentionally, a couple of years ago by saying in public—in Frankfurt, Germany!—that the quality (in terms of TGWs) of a Subaru is about as high as the quality of a Mercedes (e.g., my 2007 Subaru Outback has logged 156,000 miles as I write and shows ZERO signs of being on its last, or even next-to-last, legs). Yes, minimizing TGWs *is* essential, but top quality is not the differentiator it once was.

Consider the flip side of the coin, what I call TGRs, or Things Gone Right—that is, the differentiation battlefield has effectively switched to maximizing the good stuff rather than minimizing the bad stuff. You might even go so far as to call it the Age of TGRs. I'd go that far.

12.1.2
TGRS/FOCUS ON THE "EXPERIENCE": (WAAAY) BEYOND "SATISFACTION"/ "SATISFACTORY"

EXPERIENCES are as distinct from services as services are from goods. —Joe Pine and Jim Gilmore, *The Experience Economy: Work Is Theatre & Every Business a Stage*

I freely admit that when I was first introduced to the "experience" notion, some two decades ago, I snickered, "Sounds like a good way for consultants to earn a few extra bucks." But now I've come full circle: Focusing on the functional and emotional way in which we experience—connect with—a service or product is of surpassing importance, and is indeed on an entirely different planet from "satisfaction," which, after all, is derived from "satisfactory" (i.e., "not bad").

At our core, we're a coffee company, but the opportunity we have to extend the brand is beyond coffee; IT'S ENTERTAINMENT. —Howard Schultz, Starbucks

When Pete Rozelle ran the NFL, it was a football business and a good one. NOW IT'S TRULY AN ENTERTAINMENT BUSINESS. —Paul Much, investment adviser

Jungle Jim's International Market, Fairfield, OH: "AN ADVENTURE IN SHOPPERTAINMENT." —George Whalin, *Retail Superstars*

Boston Globe: **"Why did you [Berkshire Hathaway] buy Jordan's Furniture?"**
Warren Buffett: **"Jordan's is spectacular. IT'S ALL SHOWMANSHIP."**

12.1.3
TGRS/ FOCUS ON THE "EXPERIENCE": WHERE THE HELL ARE THE CARS? (I.E., WHY AREN'T THERE CARS IN THE SHOWROOM?)

"SHOWROOM" = BEST EVER FLORAL DISPLAY!

I learned a lot from Carl Sewell. He has a string of successful car dealerships, among them his keystone store, Sewell Village Cadillac, in Dallas. Go into the dealership as I did and you'd not find any cars in the showroom. Huh?

The signature instead was glorious displays of flowers. The showroom design came courtesy Carl's pal, the late Stanley Marcus. (Yes, the *Marcus* in Neiman Marcus.) You'd also find a wonderfully appointed sitting room, with a video always running. The video was not peddling cars; it was introducing you to the dealership itself. The undisguised message was:

Welcome to the Sewell Village Family. We will take care of your transportation and logistics needs.

Carl and his colleagues wanted you and your family to "join up."

When you were finished with the showroom that had no cars, it was off to the service bay, where, for starters and to repeat the old saw, one could eat off the floor. Touring that service bay was a big part of the intro to "the family"—among other things, you'd be introduced to several of the personable (remember hiring at Southwest: "caring, being warm . . .") and well-uniformed mechanics.

Carl overlooked nothing. Stepping backward in the process, he even bought a street sweeper—hey, the first thing the prospect would see is the road in front of the dealership, right? It's not that the city of Dallas did a lousy job on the streets; it's that Carl wanted to orchestrate the entry as well as, say, Disney does in its theme parks. (Disney lavishes special attention on the parking process; among other things, employment selection for parking lot attendants is rigorous to a fault. Why all this bother? Duh: First and last impressions overwhelm all the other variables, including the theme-park rides themselves, in assessing an experience.)

I've overlooked a zillion things—for more, see Carl's book *Customers for Life*. The bottom line: Carl Sewell has been a longtime master of . . . **THINGS GONE RIGHT**.

12.1.4
EMPHASIZING TGRS: DESIGNATE A <u>C</u>X<u>O</u>

Even in a small enterprise, Designate a (full-time/part-time) C<u>X</u>O/Chief e<u>X</u>perience Officer

A key word here is *small*. The "experience thing" applies as much—or more!—to a sole proprietor as it does to Starbucks or Jungle Jim's.

EMPHASIZING EXPERIENCE/Suggestion:
For every engineer and marketer on the experience design and development team, you need an artist, psychologist, musician, theater director, and perhaps a shaman.

Well, maybe I'm only half serious about the shaman. But I'm sure you get the idea. Creating a fabulous experience is not likely to come all that naturally to an engineer or MBA. Fact, not hypothesis. Sorry. At least the snarky comment comes from an engineer/MBA—me.

12.1.5

BEYOND "ENGINEERING": SUSTAINABLE EMOTIONAL ENGAGEMENT (OR THE LACK THEREOF)

I've been having some trouble with the "experience marketing" idea. The possible implication, as I see it, is that you can "engineer" an excellent experience. Certainly an excellent experience has superb systems lying beneath the surface. But when, say, the systems rule the roost, the trouble starts.

Experiences that stick are about emotional engagement. And emotional engagement is about intangibles, about artistry, about surprise, about the smiles that the MINI Cooper S engendered.

The experience fetish has, alas and all too often, "gone metric." Metrics for this, metrics for that. Metrics, metrics, metrics. I recently went to my car dealership for a regular checkup. They did a fine and timely job. But no fewer than three times the service boss reminded me to fill out my online assessment of the visit and asked me if he could do anything more that would improve my assessment.

Guess what: **KISS THE EMOTIONAL ENGAGEMENT GOOD-BYE.**

While I want the guy to get his bonus (even employment hinges on those scores upon occasion), my *feeling* about the service went down rather than up.

12.1.6
MORE TGRS: LITTLE >>> BIG

Courtesies of a small and trivial character are the ones which strike deepest in the grateful and appreciating heart.
—Henry Clay

Let's not forget that small emotions are the great captains of our lives.
—Vincent van Gogh

In the world of real human beings with real human emotions, *small* is often bigger than *big*—that is, it's the little "human stuff" that sticks in our minds longest (e.g., I don't remember much about the Cadillac at Carl Sewell's dealership—but I have an indelible memory, twenty years later, of the showroom floral display that Mr. Marcus designed).

LITTLE >>> BIG: SIX CASES

1. CLEAN GLASSES = LIFELONG MEMORY

Conveyance: Kingfisher Airlines
Location: Approach to New Delhi
Flight attendant: "May I clean your glasses, sir?"

After a seminar in Mumbai, I flew to New Delhi to meet my wife, who was working there with her home-furnishings vendors. It was my first trip on Kingfisher Airlines. As we began our descent, the flight attendant walked down the business-class aisle (about half the aircraft), asking each of us with glasses (most of us) if we wanted those glasses cleaned.

A little thing? Of course, it was important that the plane landed safely and on time . . . but I will remember the glasses-wiping bit until, more or less literally, my last breath!

"Little thing"?
Nope!
Try . . .
"BIG **BIGGER BIGGEST** Thing"!

2. **OWNER ON THE STREET.** Several years ago, my wife and I flew to Chicago for New Year's Eve. We went for the express purpose of having dinner with two good friends. They chose one of this great restaurant city's top restaurants. The meal was fabulous as expected. We stayed until just past midnight. Most diners decided to leave at about the same time. It was a bitter cold Chicago night, with wind coming off the lake. We went out to try the difficult pre-Uber task of hailing a cab. Outside, in that merciless cold, we saw someone in a beautiful light dress running back and forth practically dragging cabs to the curbside. The someone was none other than the restaurant's owner.

Wow.

I'd add that she was always on the short list of most influential foodies in food-mad Chicago. I remember the meal, and I remember the lovely time with our friends and the well-worth-it trip from the East Coast. But mostly I remember the owner on the street passionately pursuing cabs in the bitter cold for her guests.

3. **OVER THE (BRUTAL) HILL.** My wife and I, as I've reported before, spend a bit over two months every North American winter in New Zealand, on Golden Bay at the top of the South Island. We rent a car and, frankly, are too frugal to pay sixty days' worth of the exorbitant Hertz or Avis rates. Hence we use a local company and end up with a manageable tab.

Last year, I drove Susan about twenty-five miles from our tiny cottage to a ferry dock, where she took a short hop to a trailhead and went off for a full day's walk. After dropping her and wandering around a bit, I planned to head for home. I would come back about seven hours later. However, when I got to the car, I couldn't find the key. I searched and searched to no avail. There was no use going home, because we didn't have a spare key.

It was a Sunday, and I decided to call the rental car manager, who we'd gotten to know over the years. Frankly, I had no idea what he could do for me. It wasn't cab country, but maybe I could hitchhike home and then get a neighbor to pick up Susan.

Our rental pal was genuinely sorry I'd gotten myself in a jam. He asked me to hold on for a minute. He came back and said, "Problem solved. I like to take my wife and mother-in-law for a Sunday ride sometimes. I'll come over and bring you a spare key." There is more to the story. He was in fact sixty miles away in the town of Nelson—and between him and me was a brutal hill with, it's said, about two hundred switchbacks. The trip was a major undertaking by any standard. Nonetheless, he and family came over the hill, after an hour-and-a-half slog, and delivered the key. "No worries," he said.

To say that his act of kindness is memorable is totally inadequate. I can only say that I've recommended his company to everyone I can think of, done blog posts on it, and in general tried my best to lionize him. (His drive over the hill has probably even had a tiny impact on New Zealand tourism; I use the story to illustrate to friends what a neighborly attitude we typically find in the land of the kiwi.)

4. **ADVANCED PNEUMATIC ENGINEERING.** My grand-daughter, age four at the time, came with her parents to visit us on the South Coast of Massachusetts. We are about five minutes from Buzzards Bay. Among other things, I got Zoe a cute dragon float to play with at the beach. When it came time to inflate it, I was out of luck. The toy had a weird valve, and my bike pump wouldn't fit. I decided to try the local service station, about ten miles away. Well, their air hose coupling device wouldn't work either. It's a longish story, but the short version is that a station mechanic I knew jury-rigged a fitting, but the job wasn't easy. At one point, there were no fewer than three of them working to inflate Zoe's dragon float. Eventually, the job was done, and back I went to the beach.

I took a picture of the three guys at work on Zoe's float. Among other things, I put the picture on a slide and used it in a speech to car dealers. Also, just a little bit later we had a car problem and should have taken our vehicle to the dealership. Instead, we took it to that local service station for what amounted to an $800 job.

5. **PRIZEWORTHY STONE SCULPTURE.** We put in a new driveway at our Massachusetts residence. There were wetlands involved, a complex and drawn-out town and state approval pro-cess, and by the time all signatures were collected, we had but three weeks to construct a complicated driveway through forest

and rock. The three-weeks-or-else bit came from a permit that established when we had to be finished, based on a looming endangered species migration period.

Susan and I were away in England when most of the hectic road construction was in process. When we got home and traversed the new driveway for the first time, halfway along we literally stopped and gasped. (Accurate word choice, no hyperbole.) The time for the job had been insane based on the project's complexity. For example, along the new roadway, there was a sizable cut in a hillside, perhaps fifty yards long. And there was, another hundred yards along, a significant amount of rock that had to be removed and somehow disposed of. The gasp came from the fact that the new rough hillside cut now featured a sculptural wall worthy of a landscaping prize. The contractor had taken the removed rock farther down the road, moved it to the hillside, and created a work of art. (When various of our friends saw it, it's fair to say that all of them more or less gasped at the result.) We went to thank the contractor, and he was actually upset. He said that because of timing constraints he'd had to do a slapdash job on the stone wall—and would improve it later. He apologized for this incredible piece of unbidden work he had done in very, very short order and with no requested supplement to the fixed-price bid.

Memorable? Gross understatement. This is how a local "driveway contractor" becomes a model of excellence and a priceless community asset.

6. **UNEXPECTED SNOW.** I was off on a trip to God knows where. (I'm always "off on a trip to God knows where.") I had a car and driver pick me up for the seventy-five-mile ride to the Boston airport. I've used the company for years; they specialize

in professionals like me, and the drivers are always dressed in a suit. The driver arrived a bit early, and I in turn was running a bit late. That was very problematic, given that we had just had a surprise dump of about six inches of snow. I finally got ready to roll and headed out the front door. I did a double take. There was the driver, suited up as usual, shoveling the heavy, wet snow on our rather long front walk. He was nonchalant about it and apologized for rummaging in a shed about twenty-five yards away in search of a snow shovel.

Yet another "remember 'til my last breath."

SMALL >>> BIG

QED

All hail . . .

- CLEAN GLASSES
- THE OWNER ON THE STREET
- THE (NASTY) DRIVE OVER THE HILL
- ZOE'S INFLATED BEACH TOY
- THE GREAT STONE SCULPTURE
- THE UNEXPECTEDLY SHOVELED WALKWAY

12.1.7
TGRS/LITTLE >>> BIG: REPLICATION

How do we increase the odds of our team members making gestures like the ones described here? The answer is fourfold:

1. Hire nice/empathetic people whose sensibilities would naturally lead them to do things like those described above.
2. Create a cultural norm of "take the time to be helpful"—to outsiders and teammates alike. Encourage people who go off the clock—support those who do more than chase the last .001 percent of efficiency improvement (i.e., who hustle out to the street in the icy cold to hail cabs for customers).
3. To use a hopelessly hackneyed phrase, "walk the talk" is a prerequisite; if the seniors are consistently seen shoveling the walk or driving on a Sunday across a twisty hill road, emulation will most likely follow.
4. Applause. By hook or by crook, unearth these gestures and privately and publicly recognize them.

12.1.8
"SOURCING" TGRS: GRANITEROCK'S "ALL HANDS" APPROACH

Graniterock of Watsonville, California, is a construction company in the "boring" business of providing road rock, concrete, and asphalt to its clients. Among many other things, Graniterock won a Baldrige Award—the highest national honor for product/ service quality. The basis, says the owner, is the company's "people first" core value.

Some time back, I was invited to give a customer-service seminar for Graniterock. I was prepared to give my standard pitch, but the CEO wanted me, instead, to participate in an open-mic seminar.

Normally, clients do not do much, if any, prep for such an event. Graniterock was the exception. The audience was the entire company, including concrete truck drivers, receptionists, and accountants. They had been asked to prepare by doing the following: For the two weeks prior to the program, they were to formally collect examples of good and not-so-good service in their day-to-day affairs (grocery store, laundry, movie theater, doctor's office, etc.). Those cases would be the data for the ensuing exercise.

In effect, they had accumulated dozens and dozens of examples of TGWs and TGRs. We could then collectively analyze them (e.g., "The person at the checkout acted like an automaton, not even a 'Hello'"). The bottom line was that it was a brilliant event. TGRs to try out at Graniterock and TGWs to avoid came in droves from drivers, receptionists, and first-line and senior managers, all of whom had been given the same assignment.

"Boring" industry.
Great, inclusive approach.
Giant master "to try" list.
Immediate implementation opportunities.

12.1.9
LITTLE >>> BIG: SUMMING UP

Productivity is of the utmost importance to most any firm. Zero doubt of that. On the other hand, cases of "going over the moon" for the customer have the reverberations of a Richter 7.5 earthquake. Recall Vernon Hill's dictum: "Cost cutting is a death spiral. Our whole story is growing revenue." I have observed his Metro Bank employees up close. Their job is to engage the customer (fan-to-be!). And that can take time. And that extra time spent is very okay in the Metro culture.

Likewise, I am a fifty-year client of the giant insurance company USAA. Whenever I have business with them, all of which is done through their single call center at the company's San Antonio headquarters, I am demonstrably struck that the person I'm chatting with acts as if she has all the time in the world for me. Upon questioning her in the midst of our transaction, I was assured that there was no ticking stopwatch next to her desk; she was indeed encouraged to deal at an unhurried pace with my issues. It may sound absurd, but I honestly feel when I hang up that I have a friend in San Antonio—some reaction to an insurance company contact, eh?

You want the driver to shovel a snowy walk or the call-center agent to form a bond with a policyholder? Create a culture where such acts are cherished. It may cost you 1.634 percent on the quarterly productivity scorecard, but I almost guarantee you that the cost will be paid back ten-plus times over with additional revenue and sterling recommendations.

12.1.10

12.1.10.1
TGRS/LITTLE >>> BIG ON STEROIDS

There is a facet of the Little >>> Big story that is worth singling out. It sometimes comes under the heading of "nudgery"; sometimes it is referred to as part of "behavioral economics." Regardless of moniker, the idea is that tiny changes can have enormous impact.

Consider . . .

1. Big carts = **1.5X** = **$$$$$**

   To possibly spur sales of physically bigger items (e.g., microwave ovens), Walmart tests an increase in shopping cart size. (Yawn. Right?)

   Enlarged cart: Physically big item—like those microwave ovens—sales soar **50 percent**. Fifty percent more big items at Walmart = **$$$+++**

2. Glaring Eyes = **-62 percent**

   Bike theft rampant in a European city. Test: Put simple posters above bike rack areas with a pair of glaring eyes; theft down 62 percent in experimental areas.

3. 6.5 feet away = **-63 percent**

   Locate the serving plate 6.5 feet or more from the dining room table after first helpings are doled out. 6.5 feet = Second helpings reduced by 63 percent versus leaving the serving plate on the table.

4. Las Vegas casino driveway: "Slight curve" = **2X** = **$$$**

   "When [designer] Friedman slightly curved the right angle of an entrance corridor to one property, he was 'amazed at the magnitude of change in pedestrian behavior'—the percentage entering increased from one-third to nearly two-thirds."*

   Slightly curved driveway = **2X** patrons = >>**$1 billion** impact.

   (**Little** >>> Big. "Slight" curve? Good God!)

5. Shape alteration = **2X/100 percent**

---

* Source: Natasha Dow Schüll, *Addiction by Design: Machine Gambling in Las Vegas*; an extraordinary book, based on fifteen years of research. I have given away heaven alone knows how many copies; it is a priceless and readable behavioral-sciences/nudgery/Little>>>Big/TGR primer.

Change conference room table shape from oblong to round. Number of comments doubles; number of people commenting approaches 100 percent.

6. +Avatar height = **++Self-Esteem**

"When I work with experimental digital gadgets, I am always reminded of how small changes in the details of a digital design can have profound unforeseen effects on the experiences of the people who are playing with it. . . . For instance, Stanford University researcher Jeremy Bailinson has demonstrated that changing the height of one's avatars in immersive virtual reality transforms self-esteem and social self-perception. . . . It is impossible to work with information technology without also engaging in social engineering."

—Jaron Lanier, *You Are Not a Gadget*

(Frightening: Ease of altering basic personality trait.)

7. Checklist = **11 percent to 0 percent**

Johns Hopkins Hospital ICU/The Power of a "Mere" Checklist:

- Dr. Peter Pronovost, head of the ICU at Johns Hopkins University Hospital, develops a "simple" CHECKLIST to deal with ICU line infections.
- At least one procedural error in a third of IV lines when Pronovost launched the checklist program.
- Significant culture change required for implementation (e.g., nurses given permission/requirement to stop procedure if doc, or anyone else, is not adhering to the checklist).

- Within 1 year, ICU line-infection rate: 11 percent to **ZERO**.

Concerned with high error rates in his Johns Hopkins ICU, Dr. Peter Pronovost, inspired by pilots' checklists, decided to test their use in his own backyard. For cultural reasons (e.g., having nurses stop docs who skip steps)*, implementing this "simple" idea was far easier said than done. It's at first blush a humble notion, but the checklist, applied well beyond ICUs, has amounted to a miracle cure for many patient-safety issues and saved literally thousands of lives.

8. Socks = **+10,000**

   Case: NHS/UK estimates that if, upon admission, every one of its hospital inpatients was automatically issued compression hose to wear, as many as ten thousand lives lost to deep vein thrombosis would be saved each year.

BOTTOM LINE:

- BIGGER SHOPPING CART AT WALMART.
- GLARING EYES POSTER NEAR THE BIKE RACK.
- MOVING THE SERVING PLATE AWAY FROM THE TABLE.
- SLIGHTLY CURVING THE CASINO DRIVEWAY.
- CHANGING FROM RECTANGULAR TO ROUND TABLE.
- ALTERING COMPUTER-GAME AVATAR HEIGHT.

* Primary source: Atul Gawande, "The Checklist," *The New Yorker;* Gawande also wrote a bestselling book on this phenomenon, *The Checklist Manifesto: How to Get Things Right.*

- CHECKLIST IN THE ICU.
- COMPRESSION SOCKS FOR ALL PATIENTS.

Lesson: An infinite (literally) number of low-budget, quickly testable, high-potential ideas are lying about waiting to be discovered and tested if, to use a critical phrase from the innovation chapter, one and all are engaged in constant WTTMSW/"SERIOUS PLAY."

12.1.10.2
TESTING SMALL IDEAS WITH ENORMOUS POTENTIAL BEHAVIORAL IMPACT THROUGH CONTINUOUS "SERIOUS PLAY"

THE PROCESS

- AMENABLE TO RAPID EXPERIMENTATION
- FAILURE IS "FREE" (NO VISIBILITY, NO BAD PR, NO MONEY LOST)
- QUICK IMPLEMENTATION/QUICK ROLLOUT
- AN ATTITUDE (WHOEVER TRIES THE MOST STUFF WINS/ "SERIOUS PLAY") REQUIRED
- A POWER POSITION NOT REQUIRED TO LAUNCH EXPERIMENTS

12.1.10.3
A WORD OF CAUTION

Nudgery can do exceptional things—save lives in the ICU, cut bike theft, and so on. But the fact is that the practice of nudging is anything but innocent. My cautionary term for it is BSBM/ Blatant Subconscious Behavior Manipulation.

For example, virtually everyone on, say, Google's staff is being paid handsome sums to de facto invisibly manipulate people's behavior, and they are getting better and better at it as the power of their tools continues to increase exponentially. At the very least, that should set off high-volume alarm bells.

The most apparently satisfactory answer is transparency. But there is just too much BSBM going on for transparency to be a good defense. Moreover, transparency has become so overused that it is effectively meaningless. And, alas, given the volume of manipulative acts we are subjected to, "forewarned is forearmed" is not much use either—it's laughable, actually. While I'd judge that awareness and vigilance are effectively futile, at the very least we cannot let activity with this much potential for harm pass unmentioned.

Of course, behavioral manipulation is what, say, advertising is and always has been about. But this time, it really *is* different—or has the potential to be. In the age of big data and algorithm power, the manipulation becomes almost infinitely fine-grained, invisible, and—no small thing—astoundingly individualized. Inadvertent damage is almost certain.

This note is to myself as much as you—I get jazzed by the cool examples such as the bigger shopping cart or curved driveway. What fun! But then I need to remind myself—and, yes, you— that there is more to it than meets the eye.

12.1.11
SUMMARY/TGRS

TEST 'EM.
FAST.
FIX 'EM.
FAST.
TEST 'EM.
AGAIN.
FAST.
MANAGE 'EM.
MEASURE 'EM.
START.
TODAY.

IN CLOSING:

An ongoing "TGR Enhancement Process" is a STRATEGIC ASSET.

The process ought to be EXPLICIT & FORMAL & MEASURED & REWARDED.

12.2 THE SERVICES ADDED NARRATIVE

IT HELPS TO BE AS HELPFUL AS YOU CAN BE: SERVICES (OF EVERY CONCEIVABLE FLAVOR) ADDED

12.2.1
SERVICES ADDED: AVOIDING COMMODITY HELL

You are headed for commodity hell if you don't have services.
—Lou Gerstner, former CEO, IBM

As noted in chapter 3, Gerstner took over a sickly IBM in the early 1990s and rejuvenated the company with a services-added strategy. In particular, he took a tiny adjunct client-support unit and turned it into a $50 billion business . . .

IBM Global Services.

IBM's aims were encompassing. As *Bloomberg Businessweek* reported at the time, "Never mind computers and tech services. IBM's radical new focus is on revamping customers' operations—and running them."

BOTTOM LINE: IB**M/**International Business **Machines** became

I**B**M/International **Business** Machines.

At one level, the story here couldn't be simpler: The more helpful you are to the customer (depth and breadth of the relationship and services rendered), the more revenue you can generate, and the likelier you are to hold on to the business. With that in mind, I got out my editing pen and took the original businesslike title of this section, "Services of Every Conceivable Flavor Added," and made it the subhead. Then added (at the top):

IT HELPS TO BE AS HELPFUL AS YOU CAN BE.

That's the point. Given the Web, artificial intelligence, globalization, and the like, we need to scramble to add more and more (and more) value. Consider the first two subsections of this chapter: scintillating, emotionally compelling design; adding ever-more memorable Things Gone Right.

That is . . .

"Soft" stuff.
Human stuff.

Now this section:

BE MORE HELPFUL.
DAMN IT.
(OR ELSE.)

12.2.2
THE PASSING OF LUMPY OBJECT (AIRCRAFT ENGINES) PRIMACY

I do not think I'm exaggerating when I say I did a classic double take after reading this sentence in *The Economist*:

Rolls-Royce now earns MORE from tasks such as managing clients' overall procurement strategies and maintaining aerospace engines it sells than it does from making them.

Thus, the quintessential lumpy object producer, akin to yester-year's IBM, principally becomes a services-added company that also happens to make lumpy objects.

In particular, note **"overall procurement strategies."** It's not just a matter of maintaining the lumps you sell; it's becoming a central strategic player in the client's full-bore business activities.

12.2.3

12.2.3.1
UPS TO UPS (EMPHASIS UPENDED: PACKAGES TO SERVICES)

Big Brown's New Bag: UPS Aims to Be the Traffic Manager for Corporate America —*Bloomberg Businessweek* headline

It's all about solutions. We talk with customers about how to run better, stronger, cheaper supply chains. We have 1,000 engineers who work with customers.
—Bob Stoffel, UPS senior exec

UPS means complex services; in fact, the company has service-marked:

UPS = United Problem Solvers.

From swarms of brown trucks tossin' packages (lumps) onto the porch to—at the apex of the firm's contemporary work—enterprise-wide logistics-systems overlords and full-fledged strategic partners with giant companies.

Multibillion-Dollar Integrated Supply Chain Solutions

Night versus day!

12.2.3.2
MATCHLESS DEMO/SPUR TO ACTION

Burn into your cranium the UPS example. It is a perfect case of an excellent organization expanding and redefining its fundamental purpose *and* way of being. And switching from a brute-force, one-way business into a cooperative, coinventing full-services-business-and-profit-enhancing-partner with the client. At the highest level of analysis: trucking company to intellectual property–based firm.

Yes, UPS is doubtless a jillion times bigger than your unit or company. But that switch from "hard stuff"–driven enterprise into "soft stuff"–IP-driven-integrated-services enterprise is an invaluable and clear-cut lesson for most of us (e.g., me: significantly shifting emphasis from formal speeches and books to Web-driven activities).

12.2.4
"GEEKS" = STRATEGIC REPOSITIONING

1. LAN Installation Co. (3 percent local market share)
2. Renamed Geek Squad (local market share soars to 30 percent with name change)
3. Geek Squad acquired by one of its local clients, Best Buy
4. Geek Squad becomes the centerpiece of Best Buy's strategic positioning

The local LAN (Local Area Network) Installation Co. had a 3 percent market share in Greater Minneapolis. Helped by the "experience marketing" gurus Joe Pine and Jim Gilmore, LAN changed its name to the more personable Geek Squad and watched local market share soar by a factor of ten.

The reincarnated Geeks also began to do some work for neighboring Minneapolis-based electronics retailer Best Buy. Eventually, giant Best Buy bought the Geek Squad and made the Geek Squad's "customer success" (i.e., solutions to customers' electronics problems) philosophy the epicenter of Best Buy's overall market positioning. The Geek Squad helped put Best Buy competitor Circuit City out of business. Faced with fearsome Web-sales competition, Circuit City *cut* costs and floor staff. Best Buy took the opposite path, went on a services-added binge, and has so far lived to tell the tale.

12.2.5
IDEO'S PROGRESSION

Product design *to* . . .
Product design training *to* . . .

Enterprise Innovation Culture Training/ Consulting

Twenty years ago, IDEO sat atop or near the top of the list of product design firms. Their creativity was so high that clients begged them to teach "the IDEO Way" of design. IDEO did just that. But as their clients viewed IDEO's continuing string of successes and ever-higher profile, they became interested in yet a higher order issue—IDEO's fundamental approach to innovating. Next thing you knew, IDEO was doing systemic, strategic, culture change work with giant enterprises on the overall process of innovation.

Climb that services-added ladder: product designer to strategic innovation partner.

The sky is the limit.

12.2.6 CAUTIONARY NOTE

SHIFTING TO A RADICAL SERVICES-ADDED FOCUS MEANS FIRST AND FOREMOST A—AND HERE WE GO AGAIN—RADICAL INTERNAL CULTURAL SHIFT. "BOX MAKING" AND IP-DRIVEN "INTEGRATED STRATEGIC SERVICE PARTNERS" ARE, TO SAY THE LEAST, TWO DIFFERENT KETTLES OF FISH—SWIMMING IN TWO DIFFERENT OCEANS. MANY A WELL-INTENDED STRATEGIC SHIFT TO SERVICES HAS COME A CROPPER.

12.2.7
SERVICES ADDED: WHITHER "DISTRIBUTORS" . . .

"Distributors" = "Middlemen"?

DONE FOR.
OVER.
KAPUT.

It simply won't work anymore; the Web-word is *direct*, and the middleman becomes an expensive and delay-inducing anachronism.

Unless . . .

Alternative "distributors" role, fit for 2018: **"Value-Added Client Service Maestros"** (e.g., systems integrator, subcontractor manager, strategic adviser, employee trainer, full-scale partner—i.e., a de facto general services store—ready to do any damn thing the client would like to have done).

A NEW/EXPANDED/ENCOMPASSING ROLE FOR "MY" DISTRIBUTORS

I spoke in early 2016 to industrial equipment distributors. They were subject to merciless attack on all fronts. In particular, via the Web's ever (exponentially) growing presence, these middlemen were increasingly being bypassed and pinched by both ends of the chain: (1) equipment manufacturers going directly to the end user, and (2) end users bypassing the distributor to seek out the producers on their own.

I trotted out the likes of the UPS model—where the (package) distributor radically redefines its role to be a full-service systems integrator/manager/strategic partner for major clients. The distributor (UPS in this instance) unabashedly aims to be the tail that wags the (client) dog—and the camel with its nose and every other body part (waaay) inside the tent, bringing to bear its encompassing industry expertise and taking on more and more of the client's previously internal activities.

Here, then, is the case I made:

The (imaginative/determined/effective) distributor (my audience member), because of its breadth of knowledge (numerous longtime customers on both ends of the sale and purchase process) and mastery of the entire supply chain, is particularly well positioned to perform encompassing service activities for its clients. Though it may sound jargony, the trick is going from basic, readily definable buy-and-sell services to full-scale business partner through the creation of integrated service packages, which assist in strategically realigning and even reinventing the client's business. This was the bold IBM Global Services approach: "We will (de facto, and often de jure) run your business for you" was the implicit, or pretty damned explicit, message, which resulted in the creation of that enterprise within an enterprise with, eventually, revenue of $50 billion.

The (former) distributor in fact has an extraordinary potential advantage in expanding relationships. Most of its clients are not giants, and their reach is therefore limited, as is the likely sophistication (lack thereof) of their staff. Our distributor-turned-full-service-business partner should readily be able to bring to the party a broad variety of experiences from dozens upon dozens of settings, which can be, when well used, invaluable to any given customer/client.

I felt I had stuck my neck further out than was justified with my idea of transforming a "mere" handler of goods/middleman into a first-rate client-partnering professional services firm. Needless to say, I was delighted when the association executive director gave me feedback, about three months later, that the presentation had been very well received and that he in fact, from the association's oversight perch, was organizing workshops aimed at understanding and codifying sophisticated value-added opportunities for his member distributors. He added, not surprisingly, "As usual, the rich get richer—our best distributors were already heading down the playing field you described, but they are the ones you seem to have spurred to even further action. A couple are experimenting with a broader and deeper set of offerings aimed at increasing linkages with their best clients."

12.2.8
TASKRABBIT: THE UBER OF EVERYTHING

Perhaps the purest model of "services unlimited" is TaskRabbit; its vetted part-timers will more or less do any chore for any customer.

Here are a few TaskRabbit facts as of early 2017:

- The company was launched in Boston as RunMyErrand in 2008 and changed its name to TaskRabbit and moved to San Francisco in 2010.
- TaskRabbit has raised $50 million in venture funding since its founding.
- "Taskers" average $35 per hour.
- TaskRabbit launched its first overseas service in 2013 in London.
- TaskRabbit, as I write, is profitable in each of the eighteen cities in which it offers services.
- The Verge, a technology news service, called TaskRabbit the "Uber of everything."
- *Fast Company*, in a cover story, gave TaskRabbit a slot on its list of "World's Most Innovative Companies of 2017."

The report here is indeed brief, but the company certainly deserves an entry in this section on imagination-in-services added. Moreover, the spirit of TaskRabbit can be translated into any and every enterprise, from 1 to 100,001 employees.

12.2.9
THE UNLIMITED REACH OF THE PROFESSIONAL SERVICE FIRM MODEL

It *is* an age of intellectual capital—or bust.
   It *is* an age of project-centric fluid organizations—or bust.

Good news . . .

To join the parade, the wheel need not be reinvented (for the likes of our Rolls-Royce or UPS friends).

There is a tested set of role models.

12.2.9.1
THE WAY OF THE PSF/PROFESSIONAL SERVICE FIRM

There's a large set of firms of all sizes (up to several hundred thousand employees) that have played, since their founding (e.g., my former employer McKinsey & Co., 1926), in the game called:

INTELLECTUAL CAPITAL IS ALL.

   (Far beyond aircraft engines and big brown delivery trucks.)

PROJECTS, PROJECTS, NOTHING BUT PROJECTS.

   (*Everybody* is working on projects *all* the time.)

SHAPE-SHIFTING IS THE NORM.

   (The organization never has the same shape two days running.)

TALENT IS THE WHOLE BALL GAME.

("People first" is not a slogan; it's a life-or-death "whole ball game" proposition.)

CLIENT ENGAGEMENT IS THE WAY OF BEING.

Professionals live for their clients, eat with their clients, and are intimately (and often profitably!) entangled with their clients.

I've been arguing the PSF case since the early '90s. As outsourcing started to pick up speed and then artificial intelligence began to spread its wings, it was clear that the future of the bureaucratic "department" as it had been since time immemorial was shaky. After all, what did we most often call our myriad of departments? The likes of "cost centers," "bureaucratic impediments," and so on.

Sure, they did work that needed to be done, but they fell under the heading of "necessary evil" that drags down the P&L.

By the PSF case, I meant that I could imagine that department/cost center/impediment becoming a hotbed of ideas that would propel the *entire* enterprise toward a rosier future.

In my model, *every* internal "department" would be transformed into a full-fledged PSF/business!

And, by extension, the corporation as a whole would become no less than an . . .

IP-Intensive Innovation- and Growth-Focused Mega-PSF.

(Wretchedly jargony but directionally accurate.)

12.2.9.2

CORPORATE VALUE-ADDED BONANZA: UBIQUITOUS INTERNAL PSF TRANSFORMATION

Here's the way the story might unfold:

The training subdepartment, for example, is reincarnated as Training Inc. A fourteen-person unit/cost center becomes a full-fledged professional service firm embedded (at least for now) in a fifty-person HR department in a $200 million business unit in, perhaps, a $3 billion corporation. That reincarnated cost center, now Training Inc., aims to be best of breed—not the best department in the division or firm but the best damn training organization in, say, the entire industry!

Its product (services packages) would exude excellence and "Wow!" Magazines would feature it. Its IP would grow like Topsy and achieve renown! Training Inc. would add immense value to the corporation as a whole by upgrading the quality of every member of the staff and pursue outside work as well.

The above, taken as a whole, is asking for a lot and would hardly be the norm. But you doubtless get the idea: The former department (and its fellow departments) would be viewed as corporate assets (rather than liabilities) and engines of progress to be cherished and developed and integrated into the overall enterprise strategy, not cost centers to be outsourced (or replaced by high-speed algorithms) as soon as is humanly possible.

TRAINING INC.: MANTRA

We *are* Training Inc.

This is *our* house.

It is *our* life.

We are in charge.

We are engine number one of enterprise value-added.

Excellence is in *our* hands . . . to choose . . . or lose.

BOTTOM LINE: Training Inc. and its peers (former bureaucrat-infested, cost-absorbing, value-destroying departments) become THE growth and development and strategic positioning engine of the entire business unit.

12.2.9.3
CASE STUDY/PSF TRANSFORMATION: TREK CREDIT DEPARTMENT

Trek (high-end bicycles) CEO John Burke offered this case study of departmental transformation ("cost center" to engine of overall corporate value-added) within his company:

WAS	IS
Credit Department	Financial Services Unit
Hammer on dealers until they pay	Make dealers successful so they CAN pay
Accounts receivable sold to outside commercial company	Trek is the risk-bearing commercial company

Oversee peak accounts receivable of $70 million	Oversee peak accounts receivable of $160 million
Identify risky dealers	Identify dealer opportunities
Cost Center (-)	Profit Center (+)
No products	Products: Consulting, MC/Visa, stored value of gift cards, gift card peripherals, etc., etc.

12.2.9.4
INTERNAL PSF FRAMEWORK: DO OR DIE

YES, YOU CAN:

The question arises: But can we do all this when wrapped within in a midsize division of a huge company?

My answer: Yes.

My second answer: You have no choice!

Fact is, you are already a PSF. Every organizational unit on earth serves customers. Serving another department is as much serving a customer as would be the case if the customer were an outside entity.

And every one of your activities is or can be reinvented and repackaged as a value-adding (would-be "Wow!") project.

What I'm suggesting, then, is that you step up your game dramatically and act like the value-adding superstars you know down deep you can be.

As to the *die* part of "do or die" in the section title, recall from chapter 6 these words of former U.S. secretary of labor Robert Reich:

If you think being a "professional" makes your job safe, think again.

Think again indeed.

12.3 THE SOCIAL BUSINESS NARRATIVE

SOCIAL BUSINESS: WHO? EVERYONE! NO HALFWAY!

12.3.1
SOCIAL BUSINESS: THE 20/5 RULE++

Entrepreneur and respected customer service campaigner John DiJulius, in his book *The Customer Service Revolution: Overthrow Conventional Business, Inspire Employees, and Change the World,* earns the leadoff slot in this discussion of our third value-added strategy:

What used to be "word of mouth" is now "word of mouse." You are either creating brand ambassadors or brand terrorists.

The customer is in complete control of communication.

It takes 20 years to build a reputation and five minutes to ruin it.

[Customers] expect information, answers, products, responses, and resolutions sooner than ASAP.

The language is strong.

And merited.

DiJulius describes a new world order in which *responsiveness* takes on an entirely new meaning. In which the word *instant* is not an exaggeration. In which, when referring to reputation, *precarious* is a 60/60/24/7/365 state of affairs.

That, in turn, suggests, for one big thing, a (very) revved-up definition of employee engagement. Recall the statement by ex–Burger King CEO Barry Gibbons in chapter 2; he said he would only succeed if every one of his 250,000 employees was "in the brand."

12.3.2
SOCIAL BUSINESS: THE SEVEN CHARACTERISTICS OF THE SOCIAL EMPLOYEE

Effectively operationalizing Mr. Gibbons's one and all "in the brand," Cheryl and Mark Burgess, in *The Social Employee*, insist that *every* employee—now a social employee—should (must!) necessarily take on a new, fully engaged role.

From the book:

THE SEVEN CHARACTERISTICS OF THE SOCIAL EMPLOYEE

1. Engaged
2. Expects integration of the personal and professional
3. Buys into the brand's story
4. Born collaborator
5. Listens
6. Customer-centric
7. Empowered change agent

That is a very tall order. But it is not clear that you or I, in a firm or unit of any size, including a one-woman band, have a choice in a world where it's no stretch to claim that a hard-earned reputation can indeed be destroyed in a matter of minutes.

The most important of the seven characteristics, as I see it, is the last one. Employees, including the newest kids on the block, must have the leeway to respond to untoward events without waiting for the approval of their overlords.

12.3.3
SOCIAL BUSINESS: A SINGLE TWEET TOPS A SUPER BOWL AD

Peter Aceto is the former CEO of Tangerine, a very successful Canadian company that aims to change the world of finance through social media. The startling quote below from Mr. Aceto appears in *A World Gone Social: How Companies Must Adapt to Survive*, by Ted Coine and Mark Babbit:

I would rather engage in a Twitter conversation with a single customer than see our

company attempt to attract the attention of millions in a coveted Super Bowl commercial. Why? Because having people discuss your brand directly with you, actually connecting one to one, is far more valuable, not to mention far cheaper!

Consumers want to discuss what they like, the companies they support, and the organizations and leaders they represent. They want a community. They want to be heard.

Between using this quote in speech after speech and writing this book, I'd guess I've read Aceto's words more than fifty times. And every time I read them, I am startled anew. Yet I believe, especially after reading Aceto's own book, *Weology: How Everybody Wins When We Comes Before Me*, his remark accurately reflects today's emergent reality.

Even if you can imagine your way into the CEO role but cannot imagine making a statement like this, do consider it a marker of the times. It cannot and should not and must not be labeled "extremist."

One more obvious takeaway: **THE CEO TWEETS.**

And you . . .

(More on the topic in our leadership chapter.)

("And you" refers to the chief of a one-person business as much as to the CEO of a big firm.)

12.3.4
SOCIAL BUSINESS: CUSTOMERS TAKE THE LEAD

In *Social Business by Design: Transformative Social Media Strategies for the Connected Company*, Dion Hinchcliffe and Peter Kim write:

Customer engagement is moving from relatively isolated market transactions to deeply connected and sustained social relationships. This basic change in how we do business will make an impact on just about everything we do.

DEEP CUSTOMER ENGAGEMENT.

One more time: Forget 24/7.

Substitute: **60/60/24/7/365**.

Remember: Five *minutes* to destroy twenty *years* of backbreaking effort.

12.3.5

12.3.5.1
SOCIAL BUSINESS: RETURN ON INFLUENCE

From Mark Schaeffer's *Return on Influence: The Revolutionary Power of Klout, Social Scoring, and Influence Marketing*:

When Virgin America opened its Toronto route, it asked Klout to find a small group of influencers to receive a free flight in hopes that they'd effectively spread the word. . . . After the initial 120 participants and an additional 144 engaged

influencers had been accrued, the word-of-mouth power kicked in as those highly social individuals generated more than 4,600 tweets about the new route. That led to more than 7.4 million impressions and coverage in top blogs and news outlets such as the *LA Times* and CNN. . . .

Social scoring is creating new classes of haves and have-nots, social media elites and losers, frenzied attempts to crash the upper class, and deepening resentments.

Social scoring is also the centerpiece of an extraordinary marketing movement. For the first time, companies can, with growing confidence, identify, quantify, and nurture valuable word-of-mouth influencers who can uniquely drive demand for their products.

I think this analysis speaks for itself—and speaks a thousand, thousand words. However, as is so often the case, it suggests much more than ginning up a social media initiative. It describes a way of life (that old bugbear, culture) infused with an all-hands (recall *The Social Employee*) OBSESSION with social connection.

12.3.5.2
SOCIAL BUSINESS: WE *ALL* NEED AN AMY HOWELL/ EPIDEMIC IGNITION IS HER SHTICK

Again, from *Return on Influence*:

Amy Howell [social marketer extraordinaire, founder of Howell Marketing] ignites epidemics. In a good way, of course. Epidemics of excitement. Epidemics of business connections. Epidemics of influence.

My stepson is following a career in social media marketing. It began with a several-year stint at a sizable Manhattan agency, The 88, where his clients included the likes of Coca-Cola. The lure of the mountains has led him to Denver. His gigs there to date, including full-time stints as director of social media, have included several small firms—restaurants and the like. The point being that the intensive exploitation of social media is not the exclusive provenance of large firms. Epidemic ignition, à la Amy Howell above, is everybody's business in 2018.

12.3.6
SOCIAL BUSINESS: LOCATION/SIZE INDEPENDENT

Today, despite the fact that we're just a little swimming pool company in Virginia, we have the most trafficked swimming pool website in the world. Five years ago, if you'd asked me and my business partners what we do, the answer would have been simple, "We build in-ground fiberglass swimming pools." Now we say, "We are the best teachers . . . in the world . . . on the subject of fiberglass swimming pools, and we also happen to build them."

**—Marcus Sheridan, founder, River Pools
and Spas, Warsaw, Virginia, quoted in Jay Baer,
*Youtility: Why Smart Marketing Is About Help, Not Hype***

The protagonist, River Pools and Spas, is a small-ish ($5 million in revenue) company in a nonexotic industry in an out-of-the-way corner of the world.

Did what?

They became, in effect, the . . . **#1 World Power Player** in their industry.

BOTTOM LINE:

- Warsaw, Virginia
- Swimming pools
- $5 million revenue
- BEST-IN-WORLD
- Social media superpower

12.3.7
SOCIAL BUSINESS: ZMOT

84 PERCENT OF THE TIME THE PURCHASING DECISION IS MADE BEFORE THE TRADITIONAL MARKETING PROCESS EVEN COMES INTO PLAY.

WELCOME TO THE ERA OF ZMOT: THE "ZERO MOMENT OF TRUTH."

Over time, the idea that we need this or that (perhaps a more powerful vacuum cleaner) percolates and becomes more real. And, as our senses become attuned (to those vacuums), we look at ads in the paper or on TV. Now, on an unfilled Saturday afternoon, maybe it's time for the ten-minute trip to the mall. Let's get serious about this new vacuum.

That was yesterday.

This is today.

The idea of needing a vacuum crosses our mind. We do what

we always do (these days). We grab our iPad or iPhone or the like and immediately start researching vacuums. Because big data perfectly informs the online process, we are quickly sent to exactly the right place and exposed to teasers that were tailor-made for Tom Peters or Angela Smith based on our last five years' shopping activities, including credit card data. Odds are high that in a proverbial flash, we've jumped to the purchase moment—and, in another literal flash, Amazon Prime has got the drone warming up.

The sale is made before the traditional selling process even starts—frankly, before the idea has in any way congealed in our minds, and maybe even (increasingly) before we had the idea.

One term for the likes of this is ZMOT.

ZERO MOMENT OF TRUTH.

Here's Jay Baer's description in *Youtility*:

You know what a "moment of truth" is. It's when a prospective customer decides either to take the next step in the purchase funnel, or to exit and seek other options. . . .

But what is a "zero moment of truth"? Many behaviors can serve as a zero moment of truth, but what binds them together is that the purchase is being researched and considered before the prospect even enters the classic sales funnel. In its research, Google found that 84 percent of shoppers said the new mental model, ZMOT, shapes their decisions. . . .

(Also see www.zeromomentoftruth.com for ZMOT in book-length format.)

Query: Is your enterprise (of any size) engaged online to the extent that you can fully participate in the . . . Great Battle of ZMOT?

12.3.8
SOCIAL BUSINESS: BOTTOM LINE I/EVERYONE

Who should be social media fanatics: **EVERYONE.**
Who needs a social media director: **EVERYONE.**
No hype in those assertions: **EVERYONE = EVERYONE.**

(**Case Study/Social Media and Me:** Back in 2004, I said, "What the hell; better try this," and launched my blog. Great fun—and the blog made it onto several "Top 500" lists for the entire Web. I started tweeting with a vengeance five years ago. Fifty thousand or so tweets later, my rank on an algorithmically determined list of "Thought Leaders 2014: Global Top 100 Influencers," published by the Swiss think tank Gottlieb Duttweiler Institute and MIT, was behind the pope but ahead of the likes of Elon Musk. That's downright silly, and this note is *not* intended as braggadocio. It *is*, however, compelling testimony concerning one soul [me] embracing social media with open arms and being stunned by the result.)

12.3.9

12.3.9.1
SOCIAL BUSINESS: BOTTOM LINE II/SOCIAL SURVIVAL MANIFESTO

Social media guru Tom Liacas's "Social Survival Manifesto" (also see www.socialdisruptions.com):

1. **Hiding is not an option.**
2. Face it, you are outnumbered.
3. **You no longer control the message.**
4. Try acting like . . . a human being.
5. **Learn to listen, or else.**
      (REALLY listening to others is a must.)
6. Admit that you don't have all the answers.
7. Speak plainly and seek to inform.
8. Quit being a monolith. (Your employees, speaking online as individuals, are a crucial resource . . . can be managed through frameworks that ENCOURAGE participation.)
9. Try being less evil.
10. Pay it forward, now. (Internet culture largely built on the principal of the gift economy . . . give value away to your online communities.)

Comment: I wouldn't change a word.

12.3.9.2
SOCIAL BUSINESS: BOTTOM LINE III/*11 RULES FOR CREATING VALUE IN THE SOCIAL ERA*

From Nilofer Merchant's book, *11 Rules for Creating Value in the Social Era*:

1. **Connections create value.**
2. Power in community.
3. **Collaboration > Control.**
4. Celebrate *onlyness*. (Uniqueness of every person; take advantage thereof.)
5. Allow all talent. (Forget titles and labels; all are players.)
6. **Consumers become co-creators.**
7. Mistakes can build trust.
8. Learn. Unlearn. (Repeat.)
9. Bank on openness.
10. Social purpose unleashes ownership.
11. There are no answers.

Comment: Ditto from above: I wouldn't change a word.

(One of the reasons for presenting the three lists in this section is to emphasize their similarity. Though implementation in general badly lags what's needed, there is substantial agreement about what should be in the guide book.)

12.3.10
SOCIAL BUSINESS: MY "BIG FIVE"

- FIVE MINUTES TO LOSE A REPUTATION THAT TOOK TWENTY YEARS TO BUILD
- 100 PERCENT OF EMPLOYEES IN THE BRAND WITH THE AUTHORITY TO ACT INDEPENDENTLY
- SINGLE TWITTER EXCHANGE > SUPER BOWL AD
- SMALL TOWN/SMALL COMPANY/BEST IN WORLD VIA SOCIAL MEDIA PRESENCE
- ZMOT/ZERO MOMENT OF TRUTH

12.3.11
FAR FROM INNOCENT: "SOCIAL" KNOWS ALL/ WELCOME TO THE AGE OF "AUGMENTED MEMORY" (ETC., ETC.)

You can run tests on your e-mails for the last year for key-stroke data (how hard you hit the keys, serving as a proxy for anger/stress) and see what times of the day or week you tend to be emotional and how that effects people's responses to your messages. . . . You can cross-reference your GPS data with your e-mails . . . using sentiment analysis (technology that identifies certain words that infer positive, negative or neutral language patterns) to identify the places where you are most productive.

—John Havens, *Hacking Happiness*

The "social" "game"—**IT MOST DECIDEDLY AIN'T A GAME**—has barely begun.

These are power tools.

Dewy-eyed cheerleading is inappropriate.

Wariness is called for.

12.4 THE BIG DATA NARRATIVE

BIG DATA MAMMOTH OPPORTUNITIES, UNDEREXAMINED DOWNSIDES

12.4.1
CAESARS' PRIORITIES

Caesars Entertainment has bet their future on harvesting personal data rather than developing the fanciest properties.

—Adam Tanner, *What Stays in Vegas:*
The World of Personal Data—Lifeblood of
Big Business—and the End of Privacy
as We Know It (also see, previously cited,
Natasha Dow Schüll's *Addiction by*
Design: Machine Gambling in Las Vegas)

This section on Big Data is short. But I hope reasonably sweet. At some level, all you need to know is included in the quote above.

MESSAGE 2018 (courtesy of Caesars):

Forget . . . the real estate!
Invest . . . in the data!

A multi-billion dollar enterprise—best known for its lavish brick-and-mortar gambling palaces—concludes that those collections of bricks and mortar will effectively be supplanted by the very rapid collection and mastication of 1s and 0s: That is, supplanted by hyper-fast, hyper-high volume data processing overseen by unimaginably complex algorithms (which are quickly becoming self-learning algorithms); the thoroughly digested mountains of data will microscopically probe clients' psyches, determine smells and colors that keep those clients pinned to the machines (machines now account for the bulk of casino profits) as long as possible—and all this will drive and ultimately determine the P&L and the future of this giant concern.

That is a mouthful.

But how exactly does it apply to you and me when we are away from Las Vegas?

Our tastes and preferences are becoming ever better known to all with whom we come in contact via our computers and, especially, our mobile devices—and via our thermostats and our cars and our refrigerators and our physical movements, one step at a time, wherever we happen to be.

And the cast of our eyes and the gestures we make at work (or play) are also microscopically examined by our employers—see my riff on HR software in chapter 5.

Some of this will improve our lives (e.g., better medical diagnoses).

And some of it will be destructive—being denied some variety of insurance coverage because of some confluence of forgotten events in our distant past.

And, in 2018, we are only about ten yards down the hundred-yard field.

So . . .

12.4.2
PERSADO'S RESPONSE RATE

BIG DATA: PERSADO
(PERSADO PERSUASION AUTOMATION [INC.])

COPYWRITER VERSUS ALGORITHM:
Adapted from *The Wall Street Journal*, "It's Finally Time to Take AI Seriously":

1. COPYWRITER: An industry-experienced human copy-writer develops an ad for a cruise-line special offer:
   Up to $250 to Spend on
   All Ships to All Destinations.
   2 Days Left
   The copywriter's ad bags a **1.3 percent** customer response rate.
2. ALGORITHM: Persado AI is based on big data analysis of the most likely candidates for a cruise experience. The algorithm, per its creators, focuses on "emotion words, product characteristics, a 'call to action,' and the position of text and images."

Persado's algorithmically determined ad:
No kidding! You Qualify to
Experience an Incredible
Vacation With Us :-)

Persado Persuasion Automation's ad results in a **4.1 percent** response rate.

Algo versus Human response yield: 4.1 percent versus 1.3 percent = 3X = $$$$$.

A creative person is good but random. We've taken the randomness out by building an [AI-driven] ontology of language.
—Lawrence Whittle, head of sales, Persado

Good-bye copywriters?
One suspects that the great ones will most likely thrive.
But the other 70 to 90 percent????

Read! Study! Cautionary Tales!

Weapons of Math Destruction: How Big Data Increases Inequality and Threatens Democracy by Cathy O'Neil

Dataclysm: Who We Are (When We Think No One's Looking) by Christian Rudder

Ethical IT Innovation: A Value-Based System Design Approach by Sarah Spiekermann

12.5 THE IoT NARRATIVE

IOT/INTERNET OF THINGS, IoE/INTERNET OF EVERYTHING: A FIRST-ORDER GAME CHANGER

EVERYTHING TALKING TO EVERYTHING ELSE EVERYWHERE ALL THE TIME

It's entirely possible that the emerging Internet of Things will be the biggest tech "disruption" of them all!

12.5.1
IoT COMES TO HEARTH AND HOME: CREATING THE CONSCIOUS HOME

From Steven Levy, in *Wired*, "Where There's Smoke . . .":

The algorithms created by Nest's machine-learning experts— and the troves of data generated by those algorithms—are just as important as the sleek materials carefully selected by its industrial designers. By tracking its users and subtly influencing their behaviors, Nest Learning Thermostat transcends its pedestrian product category. . . .

Nest has similar hopes for what has always been a prosaic device, the smoke alarm. Yes, the Nest Protect does what every similar device does—goes off when smoke or CO reaches dangerous levels—but it does much more, by using sensors to distinguish between smoke and steam, Internet connectivity to tell you where the danger is, a

calculated tone of voice to convey a personality, and warm lighting to guide you in the darkness.

In other words, Nest isn't only about beautifying the thermostat or adding features to the lowly smoke detector. "We're about creating the conscious home," [Nest CEO Tony] Fadell says. . . . Left unsaid is a grander vision, with even bigger implications, many devices sensing the environment, talking to one another, and doing our bidding unprompted.

("GET IT OFF MY CHEST" RANT: I do not believe that in any way, shape, or form I qualify as a Luddite. I tweet and I blog like a maniac, and I am an iPhone addict by any measure, even compared to those who are half my age. When I am on a two-day business trip, I generally carry nine electronic devices—count 'em; that is not an exaggeration.

On the other hand: **I will not use Nest products.** A thermostat given to me by a high-powered techie friend sits untouched in its box in the corner of my basement. I genuinely believe I merit a perfect ten, or close to it, on the "nothing to hide" scale. But I'll be damned if I want my devices—from Nest or the refrigerator company or my robotic vacuum cleaner or the smart TV maker—chatting about my life with the world at large. I love my *unconscious* home.

Stuff it, Tony!

And, yes, I know it's a losing battle.)

12.5.2
IoT/SENSOR PILLS: "YO, DOC, TOMMY DIDN'T TAKE HIS NIGHTTIME SOTALOL"

Robert Scoble and Shel Israel, from *Age of Context: Mobile, Sensors, Data, and the Future of Privacy*:

Proteus Digital Health is one of several pioneers in sensor-based health technology. They make a silicon chip the size of a grain of sand that is embedded into a safely digested pill that is swallowed. When the chip mixes with stomach acids, the processor is powered by the body's electricity and transmits data to a patch worn on the skin. That patch, in turn, transmits data via Bluetooth to a mobile app, which then transmits the data to a central database where a health technician can verify if a patient has taken her or his medications. This is a bigger deal than it may seem. In 2012, it was estimated that people not taking their prescribed medications cost $258 billion in emergency room visits, hospitalization, and doctor visits. An average of 130,000 Americans die each year because they don't follow their prescription regimens closely enough.

It's "only" 2018. The starter's gun was just fired. The Everything-to-Everything-Else Derby is under way (e.g., the Proteus tool recently received FDA approval).

Translation for you in your twenty-five-person HR shop:

Do you have an IoT adviser?

Do you have a staff techie who is keeping up with the latest move in IoT world?

This is *not* a continuation of my Nest rant above: Saving some fraction of 130,000 lost lives is hardly a small thing. But, as always today, there is an "on the other hand." On the other hand, what if I lose my health insurance coverage because Proteus data informs my insurer that I am a person who consistently forgets to take my pills? Not idle speculation. Similar data collection is definitely leading to, for instance, cancellation of auto insurance.

12.5.3
IoT: WELCOME TO BOSTON, MR. IMMELT

I live near Boston. That's the Boston that in 2016 became the corporate headquarters for America's iconic company, General Electric. Why? GE urgently needs to recruit a multiregimental army of software superstars and attempt to inject a start-up's mind-set into a giant bureaucracy. Alas, Fairfield, Connecticut, did not fill the technical or psychological bill. Boston, on the other hand, is home to a peerless population of universities such as tech superstar MIT and home to a growing population of business incubators. Some suggest that its tech-energy score approaches that of Silicon Valley.

The need for all this and the associated urgency? Former GE CEO Jeff Immelt effectively, and controversially, "bet the company" on the **IoT**. Making the giant firm's array of industrial products smarter and smarter and connected to all the world is seen as the future. (The process is indeed under way. In a Pacific Ocean plane crash in 2016, the best data on the location of the crash came not from navigation systems, but from the aircraft's GE engines; those engines were, for performance reasons, in constant communication with systems in the GE aircraft engine group's infrastructure.)

12.5.4
THE MANY FLAVORS OF IoT

IoE/The **Internet of** *Everything*
M2M/machine-to-machine
Ubiquitous computing
Embedded computing
Pervasive computing
Industrial Internet

Here are a few numbers that illustrate the enormity of IoT-world (Primary source: "The Big Switch," *Capital Insights*):

- "More than 50 BILLION connected devices by 2020"—Ericsson
- Estimated 212 BILLION connected devices by 2020—IDC
- Estimated IoT market size, next decade: $14.4 trillion
- "By 2025 IoT could be applicable to $82 trillion of output or approximately one half the global economy"—GE
- 100 TRILLION sensors by 2030—Michael Patrick Lynch, *The Internet of Us*

The IoT—coming at us like an express train—may change more or less everything for everybody over the next fifteen years.

 My usual Piece of Advice #1 for one and all: Study as if your professional life depends on it.

 It does.

UNDERSERVED MARKETS I

12.6 THE WOMEN'S MARKET NARRATIVE

WOMEN AS (OVERWHELMINGLY) PREDOMINANT CUSTOMER FOR EVERYTHING

MY EDUCATION

Heather Shea Schultz called me while I was on the road. She was the CEO of my Palo Alto–based training and consulting company. Heather said she'd organized a meeting to enlighten me on women's issues. (Presumably, she thought I had a deficit that needed addressing.) She pretty much ordered me to attend—and respecting her (and her tenacity) as I did, I dutifully agreed to show up.

The group she'd assembled and I met in Boston.

My life was never again the same.
(That is not an exaggeration.)

At the appointed moment, I walked into the conference room at Wordworks, a superb editorial-talent organization run by my longtime colleague Donna Carpenter LeBaron. About fifteen women were having coffee and conversing.

Heather introduced me around, and I was, frankly, overwhelmed. One of the women owned a wildly successful home furnishings company. There was an Indy race car driver, the first woman to race at Indy as I recall. And a senior Disney executive. A college president. And on it went.

Heather called us together and said something like the following: "Tom has become one of the most prominent people in the business world, and he is a very okay guy. He believes in dramatically increasing the proportion of women in leadership roles and so on. And he appointed me to lead his training company—the appointment, moreover, was made while I was on maternity leave; points for that. As well as a colleague, he is also a friend; hence, I feel comfortable saying in the de facto privacy of this room that, like most of his species, he is more or less clueless about what it's like to be a woman in business—both in our professional roles and as consumers. And you all have agreed to join me in providing him with a speed-learning experience."

These were powerful women, and they were unemotional as they recounted tale after tale of misunderstandings and indirect (and sometimes direct) snubs, from the boardroom to the car dealer's showroom and the doctor's examining room.

Thus, in 1996, began my now twenty-two-year-old "women's campaign."

Let me be clear: I am obsessively devoted to business excellence. And I believe in markets—that is, "Tom's women's thing," as some have called it, is professionally animated by bottom-line pragmatism:

1. Women are the premier purchasers of more or less everything, and while most businesses acknowledge that at some level, it is the rare business, still, in 2018, that makes an all-out effort to serve the woman consumer in terms of "the works": product design, marketing, delivery—and, in fact, overall enterprise strategy.

2. More women in leadership roles = More money on the
   bottom line. (By a wide margin. Evidence galore—e.g.,
   see chapter 15.)

To state the obvious, or what should be obvious, the two halves of the puzzle interlock perfectly: If you want to take full advantage of women as the predominant purchasers of everything, consumer and commercial, then women must be fully represented at all levels of the organization, especially in senior management and as members of the board of directors.

12.6.1
WOMEN'S MARKET: GLOBALLY DOMINANT

Headline from *The Economist*:

Forget CHINA, INDIA and the INTERNET: Economic Growth Is Driven by WOMEN

(Note: *The Economist* is not given to hyperbole.)

From Michael Silverstein and Kate Sayre, "The Female Economy," *Harvard Business Review*:

Women now drive the global economy. Globally, they control about $20 trillion in consumer spending, and that figure could climb as high as $28 TRILLION in the next five years. Their $13 trillion in total yearly earnings could reach $18 trillion in the same period. In aggregate, women represent a growth market bigger than China and India combined—

more than twice as big, in fact. Given those numbers, it would be foolish to ignore or underestimate the female consumer. And yet many companies do just that, even ones that are confident that they have a winning strategy when it comes to women.

To put this staggering data into equation form:

$$W = >2 \times (C + I) = \$28T$$

Women's Market Size = More Than Two Times China Plus India Combined = $28 Trillion

WOMENOMICS

One thing is certain: Women's rise to power, which is linked to the increase in wealth per capita, is happening in all domains and at all levels of society. . . . This is just the beginning. The phenomenon will only grow as girls prove to be more successful than boys in the school system. For a number of observers, we have already entered the age of "womenomics," the economy as thought out and practiced by a woman.

—Aude Zieseniss de Thuin, founder, Women's Forum for the Economy and Society (from the *Financial Times*)

This brief set of quotes hardly tells the whole story of women's market power. They are, however, indicative of the enormity of the phenomenon and hence the enormity of the opportunity represented thereby.

12.6.2
UNITED STATES/WOMEN AS DECISION-MAKERS

Women are THE majority market.
—Fara Warner, *The Power of the Purse*

From various sources:

Home furnishings . . . 94 percent

Vacations . . . 92 percent

Houses . . . 91 percent

Consumer electronics . . . 51 percent (66 percent home computing devices)

Cars . . . 68 percent (significantly influence buying decision . . . 90 percent)

All consumer purchases . . . 83 percent

Bank account, choice of provider . . . 89 percent

Household investment decisions . . . 67 percent

Small business loans/small business start-ups . . . 70 percent

Health care (all aspects of decision-making) . . . 80 percent

AND: In the United States, women hold over 50 percent of managerial positions overall, including over 50 percent of purchasing officer positions. Hence, women also make the majority of *commercial* (as well as consumer) purchasing decisions.

Add it up:

Women: #1 consumer purchases.
Women: #1 commercial purchases
= Women buy EVERYTHING

Hard.
Cold.
Data.

Subtext of this is: "It ain't even close." The message is not: "The women's market is too big to be ignored." Or some such. The message is, to repeat myself: "WOMEN BUY EVERYTHING."

Therefore:

Do your strategy, culture, and staff composition square with the data above?

12.6.3
DISTINCT GENDER PROCLIVITIES: SALES/AFTER-SALES PROCESSES

A few snapshots as to how this data translates to processes observed in the marketplace:

The MOST SIGNIFICANT VARIABLE in EVERY sales situation is the GENDER of the buyer, and more importantly, how the salesperson communicates to the buyer's gender.
—Jeffery Tobias Halter, *Selling to Men, Selling to Women*

I have indeed spent twenty-plus years studying the phenomena associated with the data just presented and about to be presented. In my home office, there are two shelves filled to the brim with books—political science, history, economics, marketing, sociology, psychology—that describe and analyze everything from women's social justice movements around the world dating back to the 1700s to male-female brain structure differences to business and marketing processes associated with gender differences.

All of which is to say that the statements presented here, necessarily limited by space, are hardly anecdotal—though if there were more space, there is little that I would enjoy more than sharing the stories that I've collected from women—both frustrated and amused—over those two decades.

There are a million male/female jokes, which range from funny to stupid to rude and crude. *There are no jokes here.* The discussion is, however, about stupidity—businesses' continuing stupidity in approaching the largest of all markets.

PURCHASING PROCESS: MALE/FEMALE DIFFERENCES

The female editor in chief of the United Kingdom's Redwood Publications attended a London conference where I spoke. In a conversation about male/female differences after the talk, she observed:

Editorial content—men prefer: **tables, rankings.**
Editorial content—women prefer: **"narratives" that cohere and stir the imagination.**

By and large, she said, men are attracted to an emotionless marketing pitch. They want hard-nosed comparison of product characteristics. Women, on the other hand, are by and large more interested in stories about the product in use, its benefits and drawbacks.

(In the paragraph above, I used the term **by and large** *twice. It is implied in every example in this section of the book. There are significant variations in female or male behavior. What is reported here is, if you will, the modal behavior in a bell-curve representation of data.)*

For fifteen years, my wife operated a home accessories company—Susan Sargent Designs. One of her product lines was furniture, which she presented, among other places, at the High Point, North Carolina, market. She reported:

Male buyers would look at a dining room table and typically comment on something like what sort of a lathe had been used to turn the table legs. Women buyers would imagine the table in their customer's dining room and talk about that. This was the way it played out, virtually without exception.

Well, I stick with my *by and large* above—but my own repeated High Point observations did square with Susan's—ZERO variation.

More, and confirmation of the same idea, from Jeffery Tobias Halter in *Selling to Men, Selling to Women*:

Selling to men: **the transactional model**
Selling to women: **the relational model**

And a ditto from women's marketing guru Faith Popcorn in *EVE-olution*:

Women don't "buy" brands. They "join" them.

Stanford professor Judy Rosener, in *America's Competitive Secret: Women Managers*, offers this parallel description:

Women speak and hear a language of connection and intimacy, and men speak and hear a language of status and independence. Men communicate to obtain information, establish their status, and show independence. Women communicate to create relationships, encourage interaction, and exchange feelings.

One last example of the women's proclivity for connection—this from a conversation I had after a speech to a women's group:

A Manhattan-based financial advisory services CEO reported that about five years before he had purposefully reoriented his practice toward women's concerns. Among other startling and, he said, unexpected differences that emerged was that his average male client recommends him to 2.6 others; his average female client recommends him to 21 others.

2.6 versus 21.
Wow.

Read! Study!

Marketing to Women: How to Increase Your Share of the World's Largest Market by Marti Barletta

The Power of the Purse: How Smart Businesses Are Adapting to the World's Most Important Consumers— Women by Fara Warner

Why She Buys: The New Strategy for Reaching the World's Most Powerful Consumers by Bridget Brennan (Keyword: World—this applies literally everywhere.)

What Women Want: The Global Market Turns Female Friendly by Paco Underhill

The Soccer Mom Myth: Today's Female Consumer, Who She Really Is, Why She Really Buys by Michele Miller and Holly Buchanan

Influence: How Women's Soaring Economic Power Will Transform Our World for the Better by Maddy Dychtwald

The Female Brain by Louann Brizendine, M.D.

12.6.4
CAN YOU PASS THE "SQUINT TEST"?

One indicator of readiness to embrace this colossal women's market opportunity comes from conducting what I call a "Squint Test":

1. Look at a photograph of your exec team.
2. Squint.

3. Does the composition of the team look more or less like
   the composition of the market you aim to serve?

For example:

**If women buy 70 percent of your goods and ser-
vices (consumer and/or commercial), does the
squint reveal a heavily female-laden top team?**

This is not in any way, shape, or form about "quotas."

It is about good sense and the capitalistic pursuit of profit
maximization.

12.6.5
OPPORTUNITY KNOCKS, BUT IT'S NOT ALL THAT EASY TO OPEN THE DOOR

This section is *not* about "selling to women." It *is* about understanding the enormity of the women's market opportunity and
responding to that opportunity. Responding effectively in fact
translates into no less than a stem-to-stern strategic reorientation
of the enterprise. Marketing and selling is the tail of the dog—
and it does not wag the dog.

Far more important than selling and marketing are the attributes of product or service itself.

For example, according to the advisory services firm CEO
quoted above, the concerns women have about their financial
future are "different in kind, not different in degree." The men
were more inclined to want to "play the market" as if it were a

game. The women, he said, were overwhelmingly more interested in long-term personal and family security—investing was anything but a game to them. Therefore, his basic financial management product portfolio needed to be very different to cater to women's goals.

BOTTOM LINE: **The company that wishes to take full advantage of the opportunity outlined in this section must begin its journey with a stem-to-stern examination of every nook and cranny of the organization.**

A HOW-<u>NOT</u>-TO GUIDE: **Taking advantage of this enormous underserved market is *not* about a "2018 women's initiative" or a "marketing to women" campaign.**
It *is*—if you are serious—about wholesale enterprise realignment.
Period.

12.6.6 MARKET POWER: COMING ($$$$$) ATTRACTIONS

$22 Trillion in Assets Will Shift to Women by 2020

Source: *The Street* and *Investment News* (full title of the article: "$22 Trillion in Assets Will Shift to Women by 2020: Why Men Need to Watch Out").

Principal causes for the staggering wealth transfer: (1) enormous aging family population (boomers plus) in which men die first; (2) women's significant advances in the workplace.

UNDERSERVED MARKETS II

12.7 THE AGING/OLDIES MARKET NARRATIVE

THE ENORMOUS AGING MARKET: OLDIES ARE BEAUTIFUL WITH LOTS OF YEARS TO GO . . . AND ALL THE MONEY

Women's purchasing power—at home and worldwide—is stupendous. And while most would acknowledge that, all too few take the plunge—and launch the wholesale enterprise renovation needed to fully exploit this, yes, stupendous opportunity.

There is a second (**wildly**) underserved market. It, too, is "stupendous" in size. In this case, however, most firms seem clueless—or, WORSE, even seem to turn their back on the opportunity.

12.7.1 EVERY EIGHT SECONDS

AARP, referring to what it calls the "silver Tsunami," offered these overpowering statistics:

1. U.S./Population **over . . . 50: 109,000,000**
   Next ten years: Age 50+: +19,000,000; ages 18–49: +6,000,000

2. Percent of total spending by "over 50s": **50 percent**
Percent of marketing budgets aimed at "over 50s": **10 percent**
3. U.S.: **1 BOOMER** (born between 1946 and 1964) **will turn AGE 65 every 8 SECONDS through 2029.**

12.7.2
THE NEW CUSTOMER MAJORITY

David Wolfe and Robert Snyder, in their book *Ageless Marketing*, translate the information above into a concise statement about the aging market:

Age **forty-four** to **sixty-five**, they say, is the . . .

NEW CUSTOMER MAJORITY

Ken Dychtwald, the rare marketing guru who pays attention to the aging market opportunity, says in *Age Power: How the 21st Century Will Be Ruled by the New Old*:

"Age Power" will rule the 21st century, and we are woefully unprepared.

We are in general unprepared, with fundamental repercussions in many arenas (e.g., health care in particular). When it comes to businesses, though, I'd say we are unprepared *and* have (for reasons unclear) paid virtually no attention to that forty-four to sixty-five age group Wolfe and Snyder discuss.

12.7.3
50@50

On rare occasions, one comes across a remark—a single sentence—that completely reframes your worldview. What Bill Novelli, former AARP chief, says below, from his book *50+: Igniting a Revolution to Reinvent America*, was for me one of those times:

PEOPLE TURNING 50 TODAY HAVE MORE THAN HALF OF THEIR ADULT LIFE AHEAD OF THEM.

Fifty years of age.
Only . . . HALF DONE.
Businesses: LISTENING?

HALF DONE AT FIFTY: 7/13

From Marti Barletta in *PrimeTime Women*:

Average number of cars purchased per [U.S.] household, "lifetime": 13
    Average number of cars bought per household after the "head of household" is age fifty or above: 7

(Anybody in Detroit listening? Not as far as I can determine.)

RELATED: 55–64 versus 25–34

More from *PrimeTime Women:*

New cars and trucks: 20 percent more spending by 55–64s than by 25–34s

Meals at full-service restaurants: +29 percent

Airfare: +38 percent

Sports equipment: +58 percent

Motorized recreational vehicles: +103 percent

Wine: +113 percent

Maintenance, repairs, and home insurance: +127 percent

Vacation homes: +258 percent

Housekeeping and yard services: +250 percent

(Honestly, need I comment?)

12.7.4
AGING MARKET/WEALTH: 47×

From Pew Research:

In 2009, households headed by adults ages 65 and older . . . had 47 times . . . as much net wealth as the typical household headed by someone under 35 years of age. In 1984, this had been a less lopsided 10-to-1 ratio.

12.7.5

AGING MARKET: NOT "BEST OPPORTUNITY"; TRY "*ONLY* OPPORTUNITY"

The New Customer Majority is the . . . ONLY . . . adult market with realistic prospects for significant sales growth in dozens of product lines for thousands of companies.

—David Wolfe and Robert Snyder, *Ageless Marketing*

12.7.6

"THEY" JUST DON'T "GET IT"

Marketers' attempts at reaching those over 50 have been miserably unsuccessful. No market's motivations and needs are so poorly understood.

—Peter Francese, founding publisher,
American Demographics

Marti Barletta, *PrimeTime Women:*

One particularly puzzling category of youth-obsession is the highly coveted target of men 18–34, and it's always referred to as "highly coveted category." Marketers have been distracted by men age 18–34 because they are getting harder to reach. So what? Who wants to reach them? Beyond fast food and beer, they don't buy much of anything. . . . The theory is that if you "get them while they're young, they're yours for life." What nonsense!

Fifty-four years of age has been the highest cutoff point for any marketing initiative I've ever been involved in. Which is pretty weird when you consider age 50 is right about when people who have worked all their lives start to have some money to spend. And the time to spend it.

Older people have an image problem. As a culture, we're conditioned toward youth. . . . When we think of youth, we think "energetic and colorful"; when we think of middle age or "mature," we think "tired and washed out," and when we think of "old" or "senior," we think either "exhausted and gray" or, more likely, we just don't think. . . . The financial numbers are absolutely inarguable—the Mature Market has the money. Yet advertisers remain astonishingly indifferent to them.

12.7.7
A LITTLE (MORE) ICING ON THE OLD FOLKS' CAKE

Forrester Research: **"[Age fifty-five-plus] are more active in online finance, shopping and entertainment than those under 55."**

Kauffman Foundation: **U.S. 1996–2007: Highest rate entrepreneurial/start-up activity was ages fifty-five to sixty-four. (Lowest rate: ages twenty to thirty-four.)**

12.7.8
CONCLUDING NOTE: NOT AN "INITIATIVE"

I have offered very little commentary in this section. This, I believe, is one of those times when the collective statistics really do speak for themselves.

Or, perhaps more accurately: These stats outline in incontrovertible terms an incredibly large opportunity in an incredibly large, incredibly underserved market.

Sooooo?

Please get off your bloody millennials high horse and get on the horse that will take you straight to the bank. I and mine—we oldies—have the money [**47 times**] *and* have the time [**50@50**] to spend it.

NOTE/NOT AN "INITIATIVE": As I said in the last section, referring to the enormity of women's purchasing power, seriously attempting to take advantage of an opportunity of this size requires far more than the "2018 Old Folks Initiative." It requires a stem-to-stern assessment of organizational skills and assets and culture that could be brought to bear on the oldies' (trillions upon trillions of dollars) of marketplace spending power.

(HMMM. I THINK IT IS LIKELY [CERTAIN?] THAT THIS IS THE GREATEST MARKETPLACE OPPORTUNITY CONSIDERED IN THIS BOOK.
AND THE WONDERFUL NEWS IS THAT MOST OF YOUR COMPETITORS ARE IDIOTS ON THIS TOPIC. PRESUMABLY YOU ARE NOT. RIGHT?)

12.8 THE VALUE-ADDED ASSET #1 NARRATIVE

THE "BIG DUH": OUR PEOPLE/FULLY ENGAGED/INNOVATORS ALL: #1 VALUE-ADDED DRIVER!

It would be inappropriate to conclude this chapter without mentioning the obvious. Our topic is value-added strategies—and I believe that the eight that we have just examined (and a ninth in chapter 11), while hardly an exhaustive set, do offer, in each instance, an enormous opportunity. However, none of these opportunities can in any way, shape, or form be realized unless we take the lessons of chapter 5 very seriously.

That is, unless we . . .

Put People (REALLY) First.

For example (recall) . . .

- Hire nice people, hire for "listening, caring, smiling, saying 'Thank you,' and being warm"—and character.
- Make training "Investment #1," and create training courses that routinely merit supercalifragilisticexpialidocious.
- Ask all of our leaders to be, in effect, dream managers committed to helping every employee grow in a way that will make her or him a lifelong learner, more valuable on the labor market when she or he leaves than when she or he arrived.

- Aim to be a "best place to work"—as we saw, that aspiration is achievable in groceries and hospitality and on tea plantations, not just in Google-world or Facebook-world.

My favorite expressions of all this were from entrepreneur and customer-service guru John DiJulius:

Your customers will never be any happier than your employees.

And from Zingerman's (food service) Ari Weinzweig:

If you want staff to give great service, give great service to staff.

I repeat:

NONE OF THE VALUE-ADDED OPPORTUNITIES COVERED IN THIS AND THE PRIOR CHAPTER WILL EVEN APPROACH TAKE-OFF SPEED UNLESS WE POUR HEART, SOUL, AND WALLET INTO DEVELOPING A PEERLESS, TURNED-ON, PERSONAL-GROWTH-OBSESSED WORKFORCE.

LEADERSHIP EXCELLENCE

13 LISTENING, THE BEDROCK OF LEADERSHIP EXCELLENCE

MY STORY

THIS IS A STORY ABOUT A BEAUTIFUL WOMAN, A DINNER IN PARIS, AND THE EVENING I KEPT MY MOUTH SHUT.

I was on my way from two all-day seminars in London to an all-day seminar in Munich and had a day in between. I decided on the spur of the moment to make a stop in Paris, a city I love. Moreover, I had a friend who lived an hour outside the city, who I hadn't seen since my Stanford days, a decade before (she had been a teaching assistant while pursuing her Ph.D.). I told her I was coming through and asked her if she was free and, if so, would she consider hopping a train to the city in return for a meal at the restaurant of her choosing.

She said she'd enjoy a visit and picked a lovely little restaurant for our long-overdue rendezvous. It was great to see her. But, alas,

I was no charming social butterfly that evening; I was brutally exhausted and heading for more exhaustion.

Delighted though I was with her company, I needed a strategy to make it through the dinner that minimized exercising my conversational skills. So after a bit of catching up, I pretty much said, "Janet, we've known each other for years, but in fact I think I barely know you. How about the 'Story of Janet,' starting more or less at conception?" In effect, I then sat back and listened, with only an "Um" or "Amazing" thrown in from time to time. Her saga *was* incredible, roots in an isolated town in Canada, breaking out via a series of unlikely events, and so on, and it ended with musings about her current job and fascinating work at an international research institute focused on the future of work.

It was pleasurable, and I learned so damn many things about so damn many things that my head was swimming for days. Though I was indeed fond of her, this is no romantic tale, and after dinner, I taxied to my hotel, where I would be picked up at 4:00 a.m. to begin my next act, and she went off to a good friend's pad in the City of Light.

I did hear from her a few days later, and in addition to pleasantries, she commented effusively that I might be the best listener she's ever known.

Sorry to say, she's dead wrong. I'm usually full ADD, a shitty listener, and a serial interrupter. But her comment got me thinking about people, in particular leaders, I especially admired. I realized that pretty much uniformly the best of the best *are* extraordinary listeners. With apparent ease and many head nods, they drag things out of you—facts, observations, opinions, confessions—that you barely knew existed. For example, one of my local friends is a retired financial services CEO; every time I get home from a dinner and conversation with him, I realize anew that "we" talked for an hour—and he said barely a word. It's not that I rambled on like a blathering idiot (I hope!), but that he asked fascinating and probing questions and follow-up questions and then more questions as we dove into this or that generally serious topic and that he then went silent and let me speak my piece. I shared my observation with his wife, and she laughed aloud and said, "You've tripped over David's big success secret. He *is* a listener extraordinaire."

Bravo to him!

(Listening deservedly earns the top slot in this leadership section and decidedly merits a standalone chapter. We doubtless all agree about the importance of listening but rarely behave accordingly. We probably think we're pretty good at it, but with all due respect, in five out of six cases, we are likely delusional. Hence, unlike my banker friend who is a listener extraordinaire, we throw away a golden opportunity to enhance our leadership effectiveness. Please think about that as you peruse the chapter.)

THE LISTENING EXCELLENCE NARRATIVE

13.1 LISTENING

The best way to persuade someone is with your ears, by listening to them.

—Former U.S. secretary of state Dean Rusk

A great one-liner.

More important: **quite possibly (or most certainly) a life-altering idea.**

13.2 LISTENING = "FIERCE" ATTENTION
LISTENING-IS-STRATEGY

It's amazing how this seemingly small thing—simply paying fierce attention to another, really asking, really listening, even during a brief conversation—can evoke such a wholehearted response.

—Susan Scott, *Fierce Conversations:*
Achieving Success at Work and in Life,
One Conversation at a Time

Attention is one thing. FIERCE attention resides on a different planet. Fierce attention is a degree of attentiveness that is palpable, that makes you (the one responding to the comment or question) feel fully engaged and at the center of the universe and feel as if you'd damn well better say something useful and coherent. You could readily say that this entire chapter is about the difference between *attention* and *FIERCE Attention*.

The adjective—**FIERCE**—says it all.

Ms. Scott's book is a masterpiece, and the book implies that a topic like listening/conversation can be assessed at length. Listening can be a subject of deep professional study; yes, as "studiable" as, say, accounting or neurosurgery!

Listening IS Strategy.

And turning everyone into a full-fledged *"listening professional"* is an entirely plausible notion.

If *fierce* is a key word here, so, too, is *professional*. The point is not to *listen* or even to *get better at listening*. The point is to unabashedly make listening (*fierce* listening) the centerpiece of your existence—to make it no less than your strategic strength/strategic differentiator number one.

It is so easy to write the words above and so very, very difficult to bring them to life. The idea of listening as a topic of formal study, of listening as a profession or calling is far from commonplace. I'll bet not one in a hundred—in a thousand?—readers has studied a *textbook* on listening or taken a *training course* exclusively devoted to listening. I am hoping that this chapter—positioned as the number-one leadership key—will at least give you pause. That you will ponder the idea that animates the chapter, talk about it with colleagues. And then maybe, just maybe, move in the direction suggested here.

13.3 THE EIGHTEEN-SECONDS SYNDROME

Jerome Groopman, a physician and Harvard med school professor, wrote *How Doctors Think*. He asserts that the key to collecting useful information and solving the patient's health puzzle is to let the patient say her or his piece. Yet Groopman cites research that paints a rather sorry picture.

Namely:

The doctor interrupts the patient presenting her symptoms after . . .
EIGHTEEN SECONDS.

Over to you, dear reader: Are *you* an eighteen-second interrupter?

The average doc, presumably, is like you or me—a pro who knows what he or she is talking about. Hence, you (patient) launch into your tale that brought you to the examining room, and in a flash our medico has scoped the situation—and without missing a beat injects his or her ten (or twenty-five or fifty) cents' worth.

Case closed.

Write the prescription.

"Next . . ."

Well, the odds are actually surprisingly high that the doc has *not* properly scoped the problem. And even if she or he has more or less figured things out correctly, she or he surely has not made the patient feel at the center of the process. The doctor has in fact in a beat marginalized the patient. It's *my* game (doctor), not *your* game (patient).

Which is to say, we miss the whole damn point, which is . . .

1. engagement and co-ownership of the issue.
2. extracting useful information, which usually comes not in a flash but from an erratic back-and-forth process that allows a reasonably coherent story and a batch of new data to eventually emerge.

First step in your recovery from the eighteen-second syndrome?

Own up to the hard/harsh fact that you most likely *are* one of the army of eighteen-second interrupters—and, perhaps, with a nudge from this chapter, you can, through hard and continuous study and practice and acceptance of feedback, do something about your "habit interuptis"—and in the process turn a glaring weakness into no less than a towering strength.

(I always begin my discussion of this topic with a slide that features the eighteen-second quote. And when I make a comment about, "Are you an eighteen-second manager?" I invariably get a big laugh—you know, the kind that communicates, "You got me on that one, brother." It is *the* perfect intro to the topic, and the guilty clearly outnumber the innocent, starting, to be sure, with me!)

(FYI: My goal is not to single out M.D.s for exhibiting this shortcoming. Though they happen to be the subject of the research finding Dr. Groopman offers us, my intent is to quickly spread the accusation to all the rest of us.)

13.4 THE ENCOMPASSING POWER OF LISTENING

AN *OBSESSION* WITH LISTENING IS . . . THE ULTIMATE MARK OF RESPECT:

. . . the heart and soul of engagement and thoughtfulness.
. . . the basis for collaboration and partnership and community.
. . . a developable individual skill. (Though women are, in general, notably better at it than men.)

... the core of effective cross-functional communication. (Which is in turn Attribute #1 of organization effectiveness.)

... the key to making the sale.

... the key to keeping the customer's business.

... the linchpin of memorable service.

... the core of taking diverse opinions aboard.

... profitable. (The ROI from listening is arguably higher than from any other single activity.)

... the bedrock that underpins a commitment to EXCELLENCE.

The list of benefits of an obsession with listening may feel like a laundry list dashed off in a flash. But I would urge you to go through the items one at a time and draw your own conclusions. "Ultimate mark of respect? Hmmm. **OF COURSE**." "Key to making the sale? Hmmm. **OF COURSE**." "Linchpin of memorable service? Hmmm. **OF COURSE**." I think the odds are high that's the way it'll go. And at the end of the exercise, you will perhaps begin to consider that listening *is* a crucial activity and opportunity that deserves your (and your organization's) *systematic* attention as a *strategic* skill to be developed in one and all.

13.5 LISTENING IS RESPECT

It was much later that I realized Dad's secret. He gained respect by giving it. He talked and listened to the fourth-grade kids in Spring Valley who shined shoes the same way he talked and listened to a bishop or a college president.

He was seriously interested in who you were and what you had to say. —Sara Lawrence-Lightfoot, *Respect*

I wasn't bowled over by his intelligence. . . . What impressed me was that when he asked a question, he waited for an answer. He not only listened . . . he made me feel like I was the only person in the room.

—An attorney recounting his first meeting with renowned attorney David Boies, from Marshall Goldsmith, "The Skill That Separates," *Fast Company*

You doubtless have met a few standouts like the two described immediately above. The force field that individuals like this aim directly at you almost makes you step backward. I cannot suggest, "Be like this"—talk about useless. I am instead simply reminding you of the power of listening (**FIERCE** listening) and urging you one more time to make the idea and practice of listening into an enterprise-wide, as well as personal, strategic objective.

13.6 AGGRESSIVE LISTENING

Mike Abrashoff was captain of the guided-missile cruiser USS *Benfold* and is author of the book *It's Your Ship: Management Techniques from the Best Damn Ship in the Navy.* His ship was given the U.S. Navy's highest performance evaluations—a last-to-first tale. He is now, among other things, a highly sought-after management speaker.

Abrashoff shares with us the start of his journey toward effective leadership-through-listening:

> **My education in leadership began in Washington when I was an assistant to Defense Secretary William Perry. He was universally loved and admired by heads of state . . . and our own and allied troops. A lot of that was because of the way he listened. Each person who talked to him had his complete, undivided attention. Everyone blossomed in his presence, because he was so respectful, and I realized I wanted to affect people the same way.**
>
> **Perry became my role model but that was not enough. Something bigger had to happen, and it did. It was painful to realize how often I just pretended to hear people. How many times had I barely glanced up from my work when a subordinate came into my office? I wasn't paying attention; I was marking time until it was my turn to give orders. That revelation led me to a new personal goal. I vowed to treat every encounter with every person on *Benfold* as the most important thing at that moment. It wasn't easy, but my crew's enthusiasm and ideas kept me going.**
>
> **It didn't take me long to realize that my young crew was smart, talented and full of good ideas that usually came to nothing because no one in charge had ever listened to them. . . .**
>
> **I DECIDED THAT MY JOB WAS TO LISTEN AGGRESSIVELY.**

Command a warship effectively? A warship is a setting in which the officers talk and the sailors learn but one thing: "Shut up and do as you're told."

Right?

Captain Abrashoff tells us: **WRONG!**

13.7 LISTENING IS AN *ACTION* WORD

Language to deliberately consider:

FIERCE listening.
AGGRESSIVE listening.

These two words are extraordinarily important. Each is an *action* word. One tends to think of listening as a passive activity.

WRONG.

WRONG.

WRONG.

Listening is 100 percent about engaging; it is in fact the most emotionally intense of human activities.

LISTENING = **ACTIVE!/ACTION!**

I firmly believe that if, after a half-hour conversation, you are not exhausted, you were not seriously/fiercely/aggressively attentive.

13.8 LISTENING: CORE VALUE #1

#1 = #1

Suggested Core Value #1:

We are Effective Listeners—We Treat Listening EXCELLENCE as the Centerpiece of our Commitment to Respect and Engagement and Community and Growth.

There are numerous legitimate candidates for the number-one slot in your set of core values, but if you buy into the commentary in this chapter, then listening is a good choice for that top slot, eh?

This is a stretch.

Or is it?

(Please ponder.)

13.9

13.9.1
SIR RICHARD SAYS: "PART 1: LISTEN"

Fully ONE-THIRD of Richard Branson's most recent book, *The Virgin Way: How to Listen, Learn, Laugh, and Lead*, is devoted to listening. ("The key to every one of our [eight] leadership attributes was the vital importance of a leader's ability to listen.")

This stunned me. I've surely read hundreds of books on leadership. Listening was doubtless alluded to. But this!

Repeat:

ONE-THIRD OF THE ENTIRE BOOK.

OVER ONE HUNDRED PAGES.

THE FIRST HUNDRED-PLUS PAGES.

LISTENING.

PER SE.

13.9.2
MULTIPLIER: TAKE NOTE(S)

Branson is also an avid (fanatic!) notetaker. He has accumulated hundreds of notebooks over the years. Note-taking, he says, is _the_ key to effective listening.

Among other things, note-taking forces you to pay attention. It also signals the other party that you are serious, that you take her or him seriously. Your implicit message is:

"You have things to say that are of value to me, things that provide me new data, things that signal the state-of-the-organization. For the duration of our time together, you are the most important person in my life."

(BONUS: Note-taking also forcibly keeps you from spending your listening time preparing your clever, self-serving retort. This is not a guru's throwaway line. Solid research confirms that the centerpiece of most people's listening practice is preparing their next [doubtless brilliant] interjection.)

13.10 COMMENTARY FROM TWITTER

Tweets on Listening/@tom_peters:

I always write "LISTEN" on the back of my hand before a meeting.

(I've started doing this—it helps. And it's been one of the most re-tweeted remarks in my Twitter feed. **TRY IT!**)

If you are "listening" and in your mind preparing your response, then, duh, you *aren't* listening!

People are onto you! They are able in a flash to discern that even though you asked a question you are not tuned in to their response.

If you ask a question and don't ask two or three follow-up questions, odds are you weren't listening to the answer.

I grew up near railroad crossings. As kids, we had drummed into us, "STOP. LOOK. LISTEN." Bosses should religiously heed this advice!

Listening is a purposeful act requiring effort and 100 percent attention. There's nothing casual or automatic about it.

Listening is expensive (in time consumed). It's just that the alternative is far more expensive.

Mikael Pawlo tweet: **"Nothing beats eye-to-eye or ear-to-ear.** Asking questions and listening with a smile is raw power."

"Raw power"—thank you, Mikael.

13.11 THE GOOD LISTENER'S RULES (A SAMPLER)

Herewith:

- A good listener exists totally for the given conversation. There is nothing else on earth of any importance to me for these (five, ten, thirty) minutes.
- To borrow from Susan Scott again:
  Listening success = FIERCE ATTENTIVENESS.
- Keeps her or his f-ing mouth shut.
- A good listener gives the other person time to stumble toward clarity without interruption. (A ten- or twenty-second pause, a forty-five-second pause, when someone is thinking before talking is *not* an invitation to interrupt. DAMN IT.)
- A good listener NEVER finishes.
- A good listener becomes INVISIBLE; makes the respondent the centerpiece.

(My friend Dennis Littky, founder of Big Picture Learning, had an interesting habit, which we caught on film for a PBS show on leadership. He would enter, say, a tenth-grade classroom and go up to a student's desk to chat. [Dennis was the principal of Thayer High School in Winchester, New Hampshire, at the time.] When he got to the desk, he would reflexively get down on his knees so that he was looking up at the student. Talk about a change in the standard dynamic!)

- A good listener does not EVER take a call, even from her or his boss.
- A good listener takes EXTENSIVE notes.
- A good listener CALLS (better than e-mails, damn it) a couple of hours later to thank the other for her or his time.
- A good listener calls the next day with a couple of follow-up queries.
- A good listener does NOT pontificate!

Remember: IF YOU AIN'T EXHAUSTED (AFTER A SERIOUS CONVERSATION), THEN YOU WEREN'T REALLY LISTENING.

13.12 LISTENING: LAST WORDS

Never miss a good chance to shut up.   —Will Rogers

14 FRONTLINE LEADERSHIP EXCELLENCE, THE MOST UNDERVALUED ASSET

MY STORY

"YOU *WILL* DEFER TO THE CHIEFS!"

Back to those formative U.S. Navy days. Upon arrival in Vietnam, my battalion had convoyed to our camp at Red Beach, outside of Danang. Of the officer complement of about thirty, six of us were ensigns, the lowest-ranking commissioned officers ("O-1s" in military lingo). Our crusty commanding officer, the star of the opening story in chapter 1 on "Execution," made it clear to us that we were starting off as second-class citizens, regardless of that fresh shiny gold bar on our collars that signified officer status.

At one point early in his on-the-beach initiation speech, he said as I recall (and I think it's pretty accurate—I can still hear him), "There is a key to your success, and it is a key to which I will brook no exceptions. You will—that is, *will*—take your cues from your chiefs." (Chiefs—chief petty officers—are the navy's highest-ranking enlisted men; they are the old pros who have seen it all, including a parade of clueless young officers.) He continued, "They know their business, and they wouldn't be where they are in my command unless they had won the respect of their sailors. Fact is, boys, they run this show."

The chiefs are the leaders who supervise the work of the ship—or, in my case described here, the work of U.S. Naval Mobile Construction Battalion 9. The chiefs run the navy, and the sergeants run the army. And in private enterprise, the first-line supervisors/bosses serve the same role. The first-line bosses are the ones with direct contact with those who do the actual work. What role—and role holders—could be more important in U.S. Naval Mobile Construction Battalion 9 or in the Honda dealership in your town? Answer: NONE. The chiefs/sergeants/first-line bosses connect the aspirations of the business to the people who do the work. The chiefs/sergeants/first-line bosses animate and exemplify the culture of the organization. Implicit in these last two sentences is "for good or for ill." Per my way of thinking, the full set of first-line chiefs/bosses/leaders are no less than Asset #1 on the organization's balance sheet.

This is a short chapter, but it is a topic clearly worthy of a chapter. Most all would agree that the first-line boss's role is important. But damn few see the virtually limitless value of their full cadre of first-line leaders. I hope these next few pages will be the impetus for a rethink.

(I listened to my commanding officer. And I took him damn seriously. It changed my life. I made it clear to my chief, Master Chief Olsen, that I agreed that I was basically clueless and needed all the advice and mentoring he'd be willing to give. We became fast friends, and through him I wormed my way into the chiefs' world, learned

at the speed of light, had a superb deployment, and went forward from there in the navy and beyond. Some of my ensign peers were a bit too aware of that little gold bar on their collars, were standoffish with their chiefs—and learned less and got less done than I did—and earned the ire of Captain Dick Anderson, our commanding officer. The final upshot of the little saga here is, in fact, this chapter in my book.)

THE FIRST-LINE CHIEFS NARRATIVE

14.1 FIRST-LINE CHIEFS ARE KEY #1 TO ORGANIZATIONAL EFFECTIVENESS, AND WE INVARIABLY (WAAAAY) UNDERPLAY THEIR COLLECTIVE IMPORTANCE

FACT: If the regimental commander lost most of his second lieutenants and first lieutenants and captains and majors, it would be a tragedy. If he lost his sergeants, it would be a catastrophe.

FACT: The army and the navy are fully aware that success on the battlefield is dependent to an overwhelming degree on its sergeants and chief petty officers—that is, its population of frontline managers.

Does industry have the same awareness?

My answer: **NO!**

Do enterprises think that getting the right person to fill a frontline boss slot is important?

Yup.

But the collection of frontline bosses as asset number one?

NO!
NO!
NO!

(Not getting this is a *strategic* mistake of the first order.)

14.2 ASSET #1 = ASSET #1

FRONTLINE BOSSES:
Principal determinants of enterprise productivity
Principal determinants of employee retention
Principal determinants of product/service quality
Principal carriers/embodiments of corporate culture
Principal visible "spear carriers" for Excellence
Principal champions/enablers of sustained employee
    development

Is this list extreme?

After years of observation of organizations of all flavors and sizes, I do not think this is overstatement. In fact, it is almost tautological.

(I reiterate: Full complement of chiefs—we should always think in terms of the *population* of first-line bosses collectively, not just Ms. Smith or Mr. Jones.)

14.3 FIRST-LINE CHIEFS UNEQUIVOCALLY DRIVE EMPLOYEE RETENTION/ SATISFACTION/PRODUCTIVITY

Marcus Buckingham is acknowledged as one of the shrewdest analysts of enterprise effectiveness. He also has had access to a treasure trove of data at the Gallup organization. His book, with Curt Coffman, *First, Break All the Rules: What the World's Greatest Managers Do Differently*, is considered by many (including me) to be a masterpiece.

Mr. Buckingham also is as rabid on the topic of frontline leadership as I am, maybe more so. And, as I said, he's collected and analyzed the data that back up his assertions. In *Break All the Rules*, he concludes that the variables that matter most to the organization, such as productivity, quality, and employee retention, are overwhelmingly based on the first-line manager.

Another shrewd, longtime organizational observer whom I "met" at tompeters.com, Dave Wheeler, commented, **"People leave managers, not companies."**

A couple of years ago, our former farm manager in Vermont decided he needed a bit more stability in his life (we were considering selling the farm, which we eventually did). He was a gem. He could have invented the word *reliable*, and he had an unslakable thirst for picking up new skills. He got a job in a flash at an excellent local company with a great reputation for all the right stuff. And yet he left after six months. We talked about it a lot, but in the end, he could not deal with the constant whining of his first-line boss. "The work was great," he told me over the course of a series of conversations, "but I came home half the time with a headache." He was not a whiner in the most adverse of situations, but his boss was at the best of times. Score one for Mr. Wheeler's assessment immediately above—people leave managers, not companies, no matter how good the company.

Take together these assertions by Mr. Buckingham, Mr. Wheeler, and my former farm manager and you end up with a solid case for my **Asset #1** assertion.

SERIOUS ABOUT FIRST-LINE LEADERS: YES
SERIOUS ENOUGH: NO

I'm openly pushing here for nothing short of a very visible obsession with our full portfolio of first-line chiefs.

Among the many things I've championed in my work in recent times, this emphasis on first-line chiefs seems to have had the most resonance with top bosses. And led to the most serious reassessment and action. One big bank CFO said to me, "I typically ran my department by working with my direct reports [senior middle managers], but after your nudge, I have changed my approach. I have individually and collectively—and directly—reached out to our first-line supervisors, and as a result I have gotten a different feel for the organization as a whole and a real appreciation for that group. As I move forward, we're constructing, for one thing, an intensive mentoring program for our frontline leaders."

The CEO of a major chemical company echoed the bank exec: "After your session with our top team, we started talking more about the frontline leader role. We discovered we were frighteningly casual about both selection and development. And through surveys we were stunned at the variable quality of the [frontline bosses]. We're not just working on 'fixing things,' we are taking a proactive role in, thinking, as you suggested, in terms of major corporate asset. I'll let you know how it works out, but awareness is a big step forward."

14.4 FIRST-LINE CHIEFS EXCELLENCE AS A CORE CORPORATE VALUE

Suggested addition to your statement of core values: **We are obsessed with developing a cadre of first-line managers that is second to none—we understand that this cadre is arguably one of our organization's most important strategic assets.**

14.5 SEVEN KEY QUESTIONS ABOUT YOUR FIRST-LINE CHIEFS

1. Do you absolutely understand and act upon the fact that the first-line boss is THE KEY LEADERSHIP ROLE in the organization?
2. Does HR single out first-line supervisors individually *and* collectively for special, over-the-top developmental attention?
3. Do you spend gobs and gobs of time selecting first-line supervisors?
4. Are you willing, pain notwithstanding, to leave a vacant first-line supervisor slot open until you can fill the slot with someone spectacular?
5. DO YOU HAVE THE ABSOLUTE BEST TRAINING AND CON-

TINUING DEVELOPMENT PROGRAMS IN THE INDUSTRY FOR FIRST-LINE SUPERVISORS?

6. Do you formally and rigorously and continuously MEN-TOR first-line supervisors?

7. ARE YOUR FIRST-LINE SUPERVISORS ACCORDED THE ATTENTION AND ACKNOWLEDGMENT AND RESPECT THAT THE IMPORTANCE OF THEIR POSITION MERITS?

14.6

14.6.1
SUGGESTED STEP #1 TOWARD FIRST-LINE BOSS EXCELLENCE: "GETTING TO KNOW YOU . . ."

Make it a point in the next month to spend a big dose of quality time with each of your first-line chiefs.

14.6.2
SUGGESTED STEP #2 TOWARD FIRST-LINE BOSS EXCELLENCE: PROGRAMMATIC REALLOCATION

CONSIDER: Cut your executive development budget by 25 percent or more. Put every penny of the savings into frontline manager training and development. If my assessment in this chapter is accurate, such a reallocation of resources will have a significant mid- to long-term strategic payoff.

15 TWENTY-SIX TACTICS TO SPUR LEADERSHIP EXCELLENCE, GUARANTEED TO WORK

MY STORY

IT WAS PREDAWN IN MANHATTAN, JANUARY 27, 1983.

Bob Waterman and I were in the NBC green room waiting to be interviewed for *The Today Show* by Bryant Gumbel concerning the surprising success of our new book, *In Search of Excellence*. Bob turned to me and said nonchalantly, "Well, who gets to say it on national television?"

I had no idea what he was talking about and answered with, "Huh?"

"MBWA," he replied. "Who gets to say 'MBWA' on national TV?"

Bob was senior.

He said it.

Thirty-five years later, I still haven't gotten over the fact that *I* didn't get to say to Mr. Gumbel, "Let me tell you about MBWA . . ."

But let's go back to 1979. The research for what became *In Search of Excellence* was in its infancy. The title of our work was undistinguished, the McKinsey Organization Effectiveness Project. We were interviewing folks here and there. On our list of candidates were execs from our near neighbor in Palo Alto (we were berthed in San Francisco), a feisty, still relatively youthful, innovative company called Hewlett-Packard.

The extraordinary experience with HP began with my effort to secure an interview with the president, John Young. I called the main HP phone number and assumed, as would be the case with the giant firms we were used to dealing with such as Chase Manhattan, that I would be passed through a string of secretaries and executive assistants who just *might* schedule an interview in the *distant* future. I reached company reception and asked to speak to Mr. Young. In what must have been all of ten seconds, a gruff voice came on the line, "This is John Young. Who's this?"

Ye gads.

In a flash, with no muss and fuss, an interview was arranged two days hence.

Bob and I took the twenty-five-mile trip to Palo Alto and were soon seated in John's cramped "office" (the president's abode was an eight-by-eight half-walled cubicle) amid the engineering spaces. At some point early in the conversation, "MBWA" spilled out of Mr. Young's mouth. I think he was talking about the famous "HP Way" (it would be called "culture code" or some such today) and said that the cornerstone was this odd (to us) thing labeled "MBWA."

Bob and I didn't know it then, but as of that utterance, everything changed in our professional lives.

MBWA, as it seems half the world knows today, is Managing by Wandering Around. And it meant Managing by Wandering Around. The real meaning was that you can't lead from your office/cubicle. You lead on the shop floor or, for that matter, in the customer's or vendor's place of business.

You lead, damn it, by staying in direct touch with the action that matters. And it gets harder and harder and harder as the company gets bigger and bigger and bigger. (HP had just passed the $1 billion revenue mark when we made our initial visit; indeed, alas, their special character has taken a big hit as their size has exploded.)

To stick with 1979, the United States was getting hammered by the Japanese. As mentioned at the outset of the book, MBAs and their ilk were in the driver's seats at most giant U.S. companies and the extant practice was MBTN or MBSP or MBMP or all three: Management by the Numbers and/or Management by Strategic Plan and/or Management by Marketing Plan. Decisions were effectively made in the analysts' offices—the shop floor, or even the engineering spaces, were foreign soil. The Japanese, on the other hand, were in direct touch with their product and with the people who made it, and it damn well was reflected in, say, superior automobile quality, which was sinking Detroit's Big Three.

MBWA was and is a peerless idea. And the faster things change (think 2018), the more important MBWA becomes. In fact, MBWA for me has become not a "thing to regularly do" but a metaphor for a way of life and style of leadership fit for eternity and, especially, fit for these crazy times. MBWA means jumping directly into the fray, not via spreadsheets (which are important to the extent that they are realistic—few are) but through conversation at the proverbial "coal face"—where the grubby digging is done.

Bob got to say "MBWA" on *The Today Show*, and I've subsequently gotten to say it over a dozen times in over a dozen books and twenty-five hundred times in twenty-five hundred speeches. And, alas, it remains news, in the truest sense of the root word, *new*. The average harried manager remains tied to her or his desk or screen and over time loses touch with reality. Advanced artificial intelligence may be reading faces on screens and assessing moods with some accuracy, but being "in touch" with all one's senses and with every sort of player in the organization remains of the utmost importance, remains the heart of the matter.

This leadership chapter is written in the spirit of MBWA. Nothing fancy. No vision. No charisma. Just practical TTDT—Things To Do Today. Get out and about . . . do your MBWA. Say, "Thank you" a dozen dozen times over. Ask, "What do you think?" to anyone whose path you cross. Take someone interesting and off your normal radar to lunch today. Don't push Send until you've allowed the content of the e-mail to percolate. And about twenty-one other items that come under the heading of "stuff." True transformation (a word I usually avoid like the plague) will mainly come from a dozen new little habits, not some bullshit values statement that nine out of ten employees find laughable because the isolated boss is so unaware of the degree to which it has no impact or veracity in the field . . . where, to re-re-repeat myself, the real work, as always, is done.

THE LEADERSHIP TACTICS NARRATIVE

15.1

15.1.1
MBWA

A desk is a dangerous place from which to view the world.
—John le Carré

A body can pretend to care, but they can't pretend to be there.
—Texas Bix Bender

As you might guess from the chapter introduction, MBWA earns pride of place in this leadership chapter. It is the epitome of stuff to do guaranteed (yes, guaranteed!) to make you a more effective leader. And, alas, stuff that all too often falls by the wayside in the midst of the chaos of a normal day at work. The good MBWA intentions are not fulfilled (for "good" reasons), and you end the day one more degree out of touch than you were when the sun came up. Soon, alas, you will become a MBM—Managerial Blind Man. Awash in numbers and spreadsheets, clueless about the real world—and, believe it, big data and algorithmic voodoo ain't gonna save you, my friend. (I am bullheaded on this topic—and proud of it.)

15.1.2
MBWA: THE RULE OF . . . 25

I'm always stopping by our stores—at least 25 a week. I'm also in other places: Home Depot, Whole Foods, Crate & Barrel. . . . I try to be a sponge to pick up as much as I can.
—Howard Schultz, Starbucks
(*Fortune*, "Secrets of Greatness")

There is no doubt that Howard Schultz has a dozen dozen pressing issues to deal with every day. And yet by hook or by crook, he . . . **FORCIBLY MAKES TIME** . . . to get out and into a bushel of his shops.

His staff is doubtless first-rate. And God alone knows how many terabytes of data Starbucks collects on a daily basis—and considering earlier commentary on the likes of the "augmented memory" flavor of AI, the data may well go so far as to record the second-to-second mental status of every one of Starbucks' gazillion shop employees.

And yet Schultz puts aside the crucial meeting on the next $70 million supply-chain software upgrade and hits the road. He said to me that when Starbucks got in trouble a few years ago, a large part of *his* problem was that he had stayed home plotting the future and in the process lost touch with the intangibles, the feel of what it was like to be one of his customers or employees.

There are no sinners in this MBWA saga. The boss is paid to deal with problems. And every day presents, via, say, the morning report and a dozen dozen new e-mails, two or three or nine unexpected crises. And as she should, she dives in and deals with them. In a flash, it's 5:45 p.m. or 6:45 p.m., and the visit she'd planned to the distribution center, or even the drop by with the purchasing team down the hallway, has gone by the boards.

No MBWA today, alas.

BOTTOM LINE: SCHULTZ (>TWENTY-FIVE SHOPS PER WEEK!!) PROVES INTENSIVE MBWA CAN BE WEDGED INTO THE BUSIEST OF SCHEDULES.

15.1.3
MBWA/GRAMEEN-STYLE

Muhammad Yunus won the 2006 Nobel Peace Prize for effectively inventing microlending, which has had a significant impact on the world's poorest people. His leading vehicle was the Grameen Bank.

Yunus shares with us, in *Banker to the Poor*, an important aspect of his approach:

> **Conventional banks ask their clients to come to their office. It's a terrifying place for the poor and illiterate. . . . The entire Grameen Bank system runs on the principle that people should not come to the bank, the bank should go to the people. . . .**
>
> **If any staff member is seen in the office, it should be taken as a violation of the rules of the Grameen Bank. . . .**

It is essential that those setting up a new village branch have no office and no place to stay. The reason is to make us as different as possible from government officials.

To use my overused term, I do out and out love this. The "bankers" should "have no office and no place to stay." Call it: MBWABYHNA: MBWA Because You Have No Alternative.

Bravo!

15.1.4
MBWA: FUN

Sure.
You do MBWA to stay in touch with the action.
(I just said that—demanded it and commanded it, in fact.)

But there's a much better reason to do it:
It is FUN.

Yes, FUN.
Hang out with the folks doing the work.

WHAT THE HELL ELSE IS THE REASON TO BE IN BUSINESS?
IT'S FUN—OR DAMN WELL SHOULD BE—AT 1:00 A.M. TO SPEND AN HOUR ON THE LOADING DOCK, CHATTING UP THE TEAM.

Yes, you collect invaluable impressions, but hanging out with the team?

"Fun at 1," or you're in the wrong job.

Doing MBWA will, I hope, remind you of why you got into business in the first place.

(Not to mention that the residual of the walkabout—a workforce jazzed up by the acknowledgment and care you've given them—is contributor number one to the bottom line.)

The origin of my MBWA-as-fun assertion was a beach walk in New Zealand in February 2017. I got to thinking about why one goes into business. And got to thinking—as I often do—about MBWA. There was a "Duh!" moment after all these thirty-plus years since I came across the term: **"Holy crap, you do MBWA because it's fun."** And everything else you get out of it is a side benefit—albeit, as it was for Howard Schultz when he'd gotten out of touch, one helluva game-changing side benefit.

15.1.5
MBWA: THE DEVIL (AS ALWAYS) IS IN THE QUALITY OF THE EYE CONTACT

Yes, I rant and rave about the importance of doing your (daily) MBWA. But missing is the all-important how-to-do, or even more important, how-**NOT**-to-do. The topic merits an extended discussion, but space here permits only a passing comment or two, aimed in particular at senior execs:

- Sin #1: **MBWA as Head-of-State Visit.** Remember, you are on the shop floor to **LISTEN** and **ENGAGE.**

You are not there to pontificate and show off the tie you got as a birthday gift.

- Sin #2: **The Retinue Problem**—the big boss accompanied by a passel of bored-stiff, overdressed underlings. The personal touch evaporates, and often as not, you induce terror—or, worse, smirks—which likely makes the visit a net-negative. (Easy solution: GO BY YOURSELF.)

- Sin #3: **The Distracted Look.** People can tell in a flash exactly where your mind is. When you have a distracted look or are antsy, you, once again, turned a huge potential positive into a net negative.

On and on I could go. Instead, I'll conclude with a pair of examples of MBWA when it really counts:

General Ulysses S. Grant's MBWA was what I label CWVA. In Grant's words, "I can **C**ommand **W**hile **V**isiting and traveling **A**bout." His approach, on the morning before a skirmish, is described by Jean Edward Smith in the book *Grant*: "Above all the troops appreciated Grant's unassuming manner. Most generals went about attended by a retinue of immaculately tailored staff officers. Grant usually rode alone. Another soldier said the troops looked on Grant 'as a friendly partner, not an arbitrary commander.' Instead of cheering as he rode by, they would 'greet him as they would address one of their neighbors at home.' 'Good morning, General,' 'Pleasant day, General.'"

(The respect General Grant showed for his troops also extended to the enemy. Here is an excerpt in Smith's book from a Confederate soldier's diary following surrender to Grant's army. The other Union officers had ridden "smugly" past the defeated soldiers. Then, the diarist reports: **"When General Grant reached the line of ragged, filthy, bloody, despairing prisoners strung out on each side of the bridge, he lifted his hat and held it over his head until he passed the last man of that living funeral cortege. He was the only officer in that whole train who recognized us as being on the face of the earth."**)

General Dwight D. Eisenhower . . . took a page from Grant's book. Find a photo of Ike from the night before or morning of D-day. He, too, ventured out alone and in a uniform as plain as that of the private first class or corporal he was addressing. His face was a model of the genuine empathy for which he was known, and the exchange was one-on-one, just a few words usually uttered in a near whisper with his hand invariably on the young soldier's shoulder. This is MBWA at its most potent.

The Grant and Eisenhower examples are a long way from the distribution center or IT team's space, but the idea is exactly the same.

15.1.6
MBPA/MANAGING BY PHONING AROUND: THE RULE OF SIXTY

I call sixty CEOs [in the first week of the year] to wish them happy New Year. —Hank Paulson, former CEO, Goldman Sachs/former U.S. secretary of the treasury

For what it's worth, since 1973—and without fail—I have practiced a version of this. I religiously make between twenty-five and fifty thank-you calls at Christmas and New Year's. The positive feedback is nothing short of astounding—which, of course, confirms the rarity of the practice.

(Addenda: "THERE ARE NO GUARANTEES IN LIFE" IS A COMMON SAYING. AND I AGREE. MOSTLY. BUT IN THIS INSTANCE, I WILL BREAK THE RULE. MAKING YOUR TWENTY-FIVE TO FIFTY THANK-YOU CALLS AT YEAR'S END INCLUDES A GUARANTEE. I GUARANTEE IT WILL PAY OFF—PROFESSIONALLY AND PERSONALLY—A HUNDRED TIMES OVER. [AND AS A BONUS, IT'S IMMENSELY PLEASURABLE. I GUARANTEE THAT, TOO.])

15.1.7
MBFFA: MANAGING BY FREQUENT FLYING AROUND

I am continually told that "this MBWA stuff" is not practical (i.e., not even possible) in the age of dispersed/e-managed teams. To some extent, and by definition, sure. But let's not throw in the whole towel.

If I were leading an important, dispersed project team, I would find some way—*begging, borrowing, stealing, or using personal funds if necessary*—to make the rounds. For want of a better term, I'll call it MBFFA—Managing by Frequent Flying Around.

Maybe quarterly?

LEADERSHIP 1818 OR 1918 OR 2018: **FACE-TO-FACE IS IMPERATIVE. (DAMN IT.) IN 2018. (DAMN IT.)**

I am told by "old people"—say thirty-five-year-olds—that "young people" just don't get this. For heaven's sake, messaging across the breakfast table is more or less the norm. I understand, but precisely because of this, I believe more strongly than ever that face-to-face *is* priceless. My conversations with commanders of big projects almost unfailingly support my view. (And it sure as hell works for me in my professional affairs.)

Bosses of bosses: In this age of dispersed teams, **DO NOT CUT THE TRAVEL BUDGET REGARDLESS OF HOW CASH-STRAPPED YOU MAY BE.**
MBWA.
MBFFA.
PERIOD.
DAMN IT.

15.2 THE (MIND-BLOWING) . . . RULE OF FIFTY

Most managers spend a great deal of time thinking about what they plan to do, but relatively little time thinking about what they plan not to do. As a result, they become so caught up in fighting the fires of the moment that they cannot really attend to the long-term threats and risks facing the organization. SO THE FIRST SOFT SKILL OF LEADERSHIP THE HARD WAY IS TO CULTIVATE THE PERSPECTIVE OF MARCUS AURELIUS: AVOID BUSYNESS, FREE UP YOUR TIME, STAY FOCUSED ON WHAT REALLY MATTERS. LET ME PUT IT BLUNTLY: EVERY LEADER SHOULD ROUTINELY KEEP A SUBSTANTIAL PORTION OF HIS OR HER TIME—I WOULD SAY AS MUCH AS 50 PERCENT—UNSCHEDULED. . . .
Only when you have substantial "slop" in your schedule—

unscheduled time—will you have the space to reflect on what you are doing, learn from experience, and recover from your inevitable mistakes. Managers' typical response to my argument about free time is, "That's all well and good, but there are things I have to do." Yet we waste so much time in unproductive activity—it takes an enormous effort on the part of the leader to keep free time for the truly important things.

—Dov Frohman and Robert Howard, *Leadership the Hard Way: Why Leadership Can't Be Taught—And How You Can Learn It Anyway* **(from chapter 5, "The Soft Skills of Hard Leadership")**

FIFTY PERCENT may seem utterly absurd to you. I surely agree it's a big stretch. Yet the overall case Frohman (a superstar Intel exec and godfather of Israel's high-tech industry) makes is unassailable.

The idea is well worth substantial consideration. And, I'd say, if your unscheduled number hovers around 5 percent or 10 percent—as it does for many of us—you've (we've!) got a big issue and opportunity.

PLEASE DO ME THE GREAT FAVOR OF NOT DISMISSING THE 50 PERCENT DICTUM OUT OF HAND.

Remember, Frohman labeled this the leader's **#1** soft skill—and soft skills for leaders are the all-important first 95 percent of their effectiveness. How about aiming for 20 percent? And monitoring your progress? And finding a coach who will beat you about the head and shoulders if you fall short?

15.3 YOU ARE YOUR CALENDAR

You = Your calendar*

*The calendar **NEVER** lies.

So, what does your calendar say about your true priorities?

You may (will VERY likely) be surprised. And, alas, probably not pleasantly.

One's espoused priorities and one's lived priorities frequently have frighteningly close to a ZERO correlation.

SUGGESTION: Hold a FORMAL weekly/monthly "calendar review" with yourself. (*And* hold an informal DAILY review.) Having a trusted adviser do it with you would be preferable; you are not likely trustworthy—which is to say you are UNtrustworthy—when it comes to self-assessment.

It is axiomatic:

Your calendar *never* lies.

Your calendar *always* knows. (Do you?)

The way we spend our time *is* our priorities.

The way we spend our time *is* our strategy.

The way we spend our time *is* what we (really) care about.

The way we spend our time *is* who we are.

(Obviously, there are hundreds—maybe thousands—of books on time management. My coverage here is laughably inadequate.

Nonetheless, the topic must *always* be broached. And my goal is to remind you . . . IN UNEQUIVOCAL TERMS . . . that it is no exaggeration whatsoever to say: YOU = YOUR CALENDAR. And to guess that your time-allocation management process is likely to far undershoot the importance of the issue. AT THE END OF THE DAY, TIME IS—NOT NEWS—THE ONLY RESOURCE THAT REALLY MATTERS. Act accordingly. Indeed, that *DAILY* review is a must!)

15.4

15.4.1
MEETINGS AS PRIMARY PLATFORM FOR LEADERSHIP EXCELLENCE

Like it or not, meetings are and will be, no matter how hard you try to change things, what we (leaders) do—so why not make those meetings paragons of excellence, rather than treating them as a necessary nuisance?

Meetings = LEADERSHIP OPPORTUNITY #1.

(By definition: Most of your time = Meetings = Leadership Opportunity #1.)

Meeting: **Every meeting that does not stir the imagination AND curiosity of attendees AND increase bonding AND cooperation AND engagement AND sense of worth AND motivate rapid action AND enhance enthusiasm is a PLO/Permanently Lost Opportunity.**

Hyperbole?

I strongly disagree.

Why the hell shouldn't this be the goal if meetings are, as they unquestionably are, your primary leadership platform?

(Please pause and consider this statement.)

(I am all in favor of eliminating unnecessary meetings, et cetera, et cetera, but the fact is you *will* have a lot of meetings under any circumstance. Period.)

15.4.2
MEETING = THEATER

A meeting is a public performance. Quarterbacking GREAT/ EXCELLENT meetings is a performing art. Thinking about meeting-as-theater should inform your every twitch or utterance, in terms of substance and style in equal measure, throughout the course of the meeting in question.

15.4.3
A FEW RANDOM MEETINGS "RULES"

- Start on time. Finish on time. The boss must never be as much as fifteen seconds late, even if she has to cut her boss off in the middle of a call or another meeting. Make it crystal clear that you respect others' time!
- Beginnings and endings overwhelm middles. Start with a bang. Finish with a bang. NEVER launch a meeting with something insipid like, "Let's get going."
- Very early on, work in a few thank-yous for "small"

things that attendees have gotten done recently—
establish a positive and appreciative tone!

- Make sure that 100 percent of attendees participate,
  particularly the quiet ones and the ones with frowns.
  Pepper the meetings with, "What do you think about this,
  Martin?" (Immediately after the meeting, take a moment
  or two to question the frowners—find out what's bug-
  ging them and attempt to deal with it, including, "Let's
  talk about this right now.")
- At the close, acknowledge each person's contribution
  with a thanks and substantive comment.
- Follow up in short order with a thank-you e-mail (or call
  or drop by) that refers to the contribution the individual
  made.
- WATCH YOUR DAMN BODY LANGUAGE. The boss's
  smallest sign of distraction or boredom can be read in a
  flash by one and all.
- Blast any personally directed criticisms with a bazooka.
- Make to-dos crisp, short, and unequivocal.

15.4.4
CONCLUSION: PREPARE. PREPARE. PREPARE.

1. **PREPARE** for every meeting as if your professional life
   and legacy depended on it.
   IT DOES.

In no way an exaggeration!

(In my experience, meeting prep by bosses is contemptibly
low.)

2. See #1.
3. A meeting is a PERFORMANCE.
4. "Meeting EXCELLENCE" is NOT an oxymoron.

(NOTE: This far-too-brief section is in no way about "running better meetings." It *is* about a 180-degree reconception of meetings as premier platforms for the exhibition of leadership EXCELLENCE.)

15.5 THE RULE OF ONE

If there is any ONE "secret" to effectiveness, it is concentration. Effective executives do first things first . . . and they do ONE thing at a time. —Peter Drucker

Strong language—just **ONE** secret to effectiveness, Mr. Drucker asserts. **WOW**. Strong words from the master. And, indeed, few things make me laugh harder than a unit plan featuring "Our Six [or, for that matter, three, or four or five] Strategic Initiatives For 2018."

Fat chance!

The by-product of initiative-itis is confusion, frustration, lost credibility, demoralization, and, ultimately and inevitably, failure (i.e., three hearty cheers—as usual—for Mr. Drucker).

15.6

15.6.1
ALLIES I/THE RULE OF EIGHTY: THE LEADER'S GUIDE TO GETTING THINGS DONE

Spend 80 percent of your time finding and developing and nurturing ALLIES of every size and shape in every nook and cranny—especially the out-of-the-way nooks and crannies—of the organization.

Aiming to accomplish something new and different that goes against the grain?

Getting blowback from the powers that be?

Trying to figure out how to win over those who are putting up roadblocks?

There is actually a simple answer:

Forget about "opponents." Absolutely positively forget about 'em.

Don't waste precious time or emotional energy trying to "remove barriers" and "win over" those who disagree.

Instead, search far and wide for people who buy your act:

Spend virtually all your time—indeed, approximately 80 percent—seeking out and building a base of ALLIES.

Then spend more gobs and gobs (and gobs) of time nurturing* your ALLIES.

Then urge your allies to spend the lion's share of *their* time finding even MORE ALLIES.

*Nurture, above, is a huge word. **NEVER, EVER, EVER, EVER TAKE AN ALLY FOR GRANTED.** It is a common-as-dirt **STRATEGIC ERROR**—that is, you assume your allies are on board, when in fact they are often facing blowback themselves and need constant encouragement. Perhaps spend half of your "Allies time" (50 percent of the 80 percent) on nurturing.

BOTTOM LINE:

LOSERS focus on (waste inordinate amounts of time and emotional energy on) enemies.
WINNERS focus on allies, allies, and more allies.

LOSERS focus on removing roadblocks.
WINNERS avoid roadblocks and focus on small wins that are positive demos of the new way.

LOSERS make enemies.
WINNERS make friends.

LOSERS focus on negatives.
WINNERS focus on positives.

LOSERS stick out like a sore thumb.
WINNERS work via allies and are largely invisible.

LOSERS favor brute force and relish bloodshed.

WINNERS surround those who disagree with allies and "innocent" small wins by the bushel.

LEADERS GETTING THINGS DONE MESSAGE #1:

ALLIES.
ALLIES.
ALLIES' ALLIES.
MORE ALLIES.

(THIS IS PERSONAL: The program I developed at McKinsey that led to *In Search of Excellence* and, according to the book *The Firm*, resulted in no less than the rebranding of the firm, flew directly in the face of McKinsey's core beliefs [strategy first, people/culture a distant second]. Hence, my de facto enemies were the fabled organization's power players, and I was definitely *not* a power player. My eventually successful strategy was to sidestep the bad guys and recruit allies—in the spirit of the suggestion here, ally recruitment and maintenance absorbed the lion's share [indeed, about 80 percent] of my time over the entire four years I was involved in the Excellence project.)

15.6.2
ALLIES II: "SUCK DOWN" FOR SUCCESS

LOSER: "He's such a suck-up!"

WINNER: "He's such a suck-down."

In the saga reported in *Charlie Wilson's War*, CIA midlevel staffer Gust Avrakotos made miracles happen far above his pay grade. Author George Crile put it this way:

He had become something of a legend with the people who manned the underbelly of the Agency.

Gust knew every top-floor CIA executive secretary by name and had helped many of them sort out personal or professional problems. The folks in the mailroom (this was over thirty years ago) and in the bowels of computer operations were also the subject of Gust's intense and personal attentions.

In effect, you could say that Gust Avrakotos was commander in chief of the invisible 95 percent of the agency, which allowed him to make extraordinary things happen despite furious resistance from his bosses and bosses' bosses sitting atop a very rigid organization.

Translation: **"Suck down for success!"**

Wanna get help in a flash with this or that or the other in finance or purchasing or marketing? If you have a fabulous and encompassing network "down below," the waters will—almost literally—part.

Message:

"DOWN" IS WHERE THE REAL WORK IS DONE. INVEST (LIKE A MANIAC) IN "DOWN."

(FYI: Most don't get this, which is why it is a particularly valuable strategy!)

15.6.3
ALLIES III: THE GETTING THINGS DONE IMPLEMENTATION AXIOMS

THE SHORTEST DISTANCE BETWEEN TWO POINTS IS NEVER A STRAIGHT LINE.

IMPLEMENTATION IS A MESSY PROCESS.
IMPLEMENTATION IS AN EMOTIONAL PROCESS; LOGIC PLAYS NO MORE THAN A BIT PART.
IMPLEMENTATION IS A 24/7 POLITICAL PROCESS.
REVEL IN THE MESS.
REVEL IN THE POLITICS.
OR FORGET ABOUT GETTING DIFFICULT AND/OR CONTROVERSIAL THINGS DONE.

15.7

15.7.1
DISPENSE ENTHUSIASM

I am a dispenser of enthusiasm.
— Ben Zander, symphony conductor and management guru

Zander's quote readily translates into a significant leadership requirement:

DISPENSE ENTHUSIASM!

Amen.

But there's also a subtle point. Mr. Zander's primary trade is as a symphony conductor; I've had the privilege of watching him perform. At first blush, at least to a musical amateur like me, a piece of music is a piece of music. A score is a score. The parameters are locked in. Moreover, musicians either know their stuff or they don't.

Of course, that's nonsense. A magical presentation of a favorite symphonic piece stirs your heart because of the emotion and power it transmits in the particular performance you saw.

For example: a 2016 visit to the symphony hall in Boston. I've always loved Bach's Goldberg Variations, but that night's performance took me to the moon. Being "taken to the moon" is where the conductor's dispensing enthusiasm comes in. **Call it the last 90 percent of the quality of the performance.** (That's probably a pretty accurate number.)

All this translates one for one into leadership in the first-grade classroom, the nine-person training department, and the eleven-person project team.

The leader's enthusiasm and her skill at *dispensing enthusiasm* is the . . .

Great Leadership Differentiator.

(Hard research on education supports this. One major study concluded that pedagogic approach—lecture, small-group engagement, and the like—had effectively no impact on the students' post-course learning and engagement with the subject matter.

What made all the difference was the teacher's passion for the material.)

15.7.2
ENTHUSIASM: THE SHOWMANSHIP MANDATE

It's always showtime.

—David D'Alessandro, *Career Warfare*

Key words of equal importance:

SHOWTIME.
ALWAYS.

The old saws, that effective leaders "model the way" or "walk the talk" are 100 percent accurate. For example, leaders must live—moment to moment—the desired culture. And *moment to moment* means just that. The day-to-day stuff and big stuff matter far less than the micro-embodiments of "the way we do things around here" (e.g., the boss's thirty-SECOND exchange with Jane or Jack in the hall on the way out of the meeting).

Leaders **ARE** showwomen (showmen).

ALL leaders are showwomen.

All leaders are showwomen **ALL** the time.

(ALL = ALL)

NO option.

NEVER off stage.

(To restate a critical point made earlier: showwoman/showman does *not* mean louder or extroverted or, surely, long-winded.)

FOR LEADERS, IT'S ALWAYS SHOWTIME AND ALWAYS HAS BEEN.

It had been a scene that those in the room would long remember. Washington had performed his role to perfection. It was not enough that a leader look the part; by Washington's rules he must know how to act it with self-command and precision. John Adams would later describe Washington approvingly as one of the "great actors of the age."

—David McCullough, *1776* (When the situation in Boston during the early days of our Revolutionary War was most dire, Washington convinced the British through a studied demeanor, a carefully constructed tableau, which made his HQ look grand and his army hale and hearty and well equipped, that the Americans were a formidable force to be reckoned with.)

Yes, it's always showtime!
Thee.
Me.
George Washington.

15.7.3
HIRE FOR ENTHUSIASM

Enthusiasm.
Hire for it.
Promote for it.
Reward it.

Be explicit.

15.7.4
ENTHUSIASM: GET THE WEEK OFF TO A ROUSING START

Next Monday: Script your first five to ten plays (i.e., *carefully* launch *every* day or week in a *purposeful* fashion).

NFL coaches carefully script the first few plays of the game, aiming to get off to a good start. Of course, the details of the plan will likely fall through long before play number ten. But the script aims to set the course.

Beginnings are everything.

> A solid research finding, not a slogan.
> So start the week off on the right foot.

Do NOT—come hell AND high water—let the first forty-five minutes of the week slip by without decisive impact.

A week is a precious unit of measure. And a week is a story, a novella—it has a beginning, middle, and end. Sweating—BIG-TIME—on the beginning is crucial to all that follows.

15.8 BODY LANGUAGE: THE 5X RULE AND MORE

Research indicates the pitch, volume, and pace of your voice affect what people think you said about FIVE TIMES as much as the actual words you used.
—Deborah Gruenfeld, *Stanford Business*, spring 2012

In the election in 1994, Mandela's smile was the campaign. That smiling iconic campaign poster—on billboards, on highways, on streetlamps, at tea shops and fruit stalls. It told black voters that he would be their champion and white voters that he would be their protector. It was the smile of the proverb "tout comprendre, c'est tout pardoner"—to understand is to forgive all. It was political Prozac for a nervous electorate. —Richard Stengel, *Mandela's Way: Fifteen Lessons on Life, Love, and Courage*

As I exited a crowded plane after a five-hour flight, I asked the flight attendant how many people bothered to say, "Thank you" as they walked past her on the way out. Her response took me (*the* professional thank-you fanatic!) by surprise:

"The 'Thank you' doesn't really matter," she said. "What matters is a smile and eye contact."

One more time: BODY LANGUAGE TAKES FIRST PRIZE!

The smiling airplane passenger is hardly equivalent to the enormity of the Mandela commentary. On the other hand, it is a marvelous example of the importance of body language in ordinary daily transactions—professional or personal.

Look one more time at the number at the top of this section: 5X.
THIS IS SERIOUS BUSINESS.
Become a formal student of body language.
Little is more important.

Good news: There is a truckload of hard research and guidance on the application thereof available to aid and abet your effort.

Note:

STUDY.
PRACTICE.

(I frequently use some variant on the term above: "Become a formal student of . . ." The reason is that when the talk turns to the likes of body language, I would not be surprised if you took the idea seriously. But experience suggests that your response will in practice be, "Good idea. I'll pay more attention to that." Fine and dandy. AND A HOPELESSLY INADEQUATE RESPONSE. The point is that topics like this *are* subject to formal study. They *are* marked by significant research verification. I am *not* asking you to "pay more attention to," say, body language. I *am* asking you to become a formal student of body language—much as you would if the topic was biochemistry, rose gardening, or taking up the flute.)

15.9 LOVING LEADING (OR NOT)

I had left out one **(BIG)** thing . . .

"Tom, it was a fine speech, but you left out the most important thing . . . leaders enjoy leading!"

I'd given a speech in Dublin titled "The Leadership 50." Afterward and over a Guinness, of course, the head of a sizable marketing-services firm made the above remark about what I had omitted.

As I reflected, I agreed he was right. Simply put:

Some people get off on the people and politics puzzles and the inherent messiness of human affairs that are at the heart of effective leadership.

Some don't.

Leading is its own thing.

And that thing may or may not be your thing.

Think long and hard about this.

This applies to a four-week assignment as project leader of a four-person team as much as it does to a "big" job.

(Obviously, the hope of authors like me, you can learn a thing or two here that will abet your leadership skills, and you may well find that you increasingly enjoy the job; that was the mini-tale in chapter 5 about the Limited's Les Wexner coming to take premier pleasure in the people-development aspect of his enterprise. Still, at some point, and I've by now seen it a dozen dozen times, it may become clear that "this people-politics stuff" just isn't for you for whatever reasons, at which juncture it may be wise to turn to something else.)

15.10 EVERY DAY IS A START-UP: THE RULE OF ZERO

Every year, for 25 years, is a start-up. For that matter, every event we produce is a start-up. When the doors open, our reputation is left outside. We start with not one single satisfied customer! I take nothing for granted.
—José Salibi Neto, HSM Group

I have worked with my Brazilian colleague JSN for thirty years; this truly is his attitude, and I'd judge Key #1 to his sustained success. He does indeed take *nothing* for granted. EVER.

15.11 THE RULE OF TEN

Every day brings at least ten leadership opportunities for every one of us.*

*Perhaps everyone over the age of twelve?
Leadership is not limited to formal roles. While we all know that, it doesn't hurt to offer a reminder. Simply put, every day offers up a plethora of leadership opportunities. When you are busy beyond measure but take a half hour, or even fifteen minutes, to

help someone who is also up against a crushing deadline, well, that's leadership of the first order!

The bigger idea is to instill and reinforce the idea of . . . **"leaders all . . . all the time"** into everyone in your organization.

TEN SAMPLE LEADERSHIP ACTS FOR NON-BOSSES

- BRING GOOD SPIRITS TO WORK. ESPECIALLY, SAY, ON A RAINY DAY. (THIS IS NUMBER ONE ON THE LIST FOR GOOD REASON; OUR ATTITUDE IS OURS TO CHOOSE.)
- Busy as hell? Take ten minutes and help someone with a dreary task.
- Listen intently ("fiercely," see chapter 13) when someone is talking to you. Don't interrupt.
- Repeat: Listen intently when someone is talking to you. Don't interrupt.
- Thank someone for being helpful with a tiny task.
- Chat up someone in another function with whom you accidently cross paths; three to five minutes is fine.
- Take a new hire or two-day temp out for coffee.
- Volunteer for a crappy little task.
- Read an intriguing industry blog post; discuss it with one or two people.
- When you are heading out the door and home, stop for a moment and chat with someone about the day—point to a positive.

This list is directly inspired by Betsy Myers's exceptional book *Take the Lead: Motivate, Inspire, and Bring Out the Best in Yourself and Everyone Around You.* Key message (as here): **LEADERSHIP IS EVERYBODY'S BUSINESS**.

15.12 LEADING: RELATIONSHIPS COME FIRST/ROIR (RETURN ON INVESTMENT IN RELATIONSHIPS >> ROI/RETURN ON INVESTMENT)

The capacity to develop close and enduring relationships is the mark of a leader. Unfortunately, many leaders of major companies believe their job is to create the strategy, organization structure and organizational processes—then they just delegate the work to be done, remaining aloof from the people doing the work.

—Bill George, *Authentic Leadership*

Bill George, former CEO of Medtronic, makes a profound—or is it tragic?—point here. It is in a way the subtext of this book. ("Hard is soft. Soft is hard.") Leaders view their jobs in terms of the mechanics—strategy, processes, and so on—and shortchange the devilish "people bit" or, as Mr. George suggests here, assign it to others. Dealing with this often hard rock roadblock to leader success has preoccupied me for five decades.

Allied commands depend on mutual confidence; this confidence is gained, above all through the development of friendships.

—General Dwight D. Eisenhower, from the magazine *Armchair General,* which offers leadership "secrets" from the most renowned officers (Perhaps DDE's most outstanding ability [at West Point] was the ease with which he made friends and earned the trust of fellow cadets who came from widely varied backgrounds; it was a quality that would pay great dividends during his future coalition command.)

General Eisenhower was the architect and builder of the D-day landing and subsequent campaign that brought World War II in Europe to an end. Dealing successfully with the likes of prickly personalities such as Roosevelt, Churchill, De Gaulle, Patton, and Montgomery was arguably Key #1. It required unimaginable interpersonal skill and, frankly, was far more important than effective strategic planning.

SYSTEMATICALLY IMPROVE YOUR ROIR

Track and Manage your investments in relationships/your relationships portfolio as closely as you would track and manage budget numbers.

What precisely is this week's Relationship Investment Plan?

This *is* the ball game, per the Bill George and Dwight D. Eisenhower comments above.

This is **NOT** a "catch as catch can" topic!

Speed is all. **NOT.** New tech tools allow us to cast a much wider net than ever before, which is invaluable in many ways. But relative to this discussion, speed is not the key to the most valuable relationships. Quite the contrary. Yes, it is 2018, and yes, the world is spinning, spinning, spinning faster and faster every day. But return to Bill George: Getting things done that matter requires friends and colleagues you can trust and who routinely throw themselves in front of the train for you. Accumulating and maintaining a rich network of such friends is a matter of time— that is, a time-consuming investment.

GREAT NETWORK = SIGNIFICANT TIME INVEST-MENT = NO SHORTCUTS.

15.13

15.13.1
ACKNOWLEDGMENT!

The deepest principle in human nature is the craving to be appreciated. —William James

In the classic *How to Win Friends and Influence People*, author and self-improvement icon Dale Carnegie offers the above quote and urges us to pay careful attention to James's word choice:

"*Craving*, not merely *wish* or *desire* or *longing*."

(The desire for acknowledgment is universal and runs as deep as can be.)

Employees who don't feel significant rarely make significant contributions.
—Mark Sanborn, sales training guru

Yes, it *is* a clever quote. But I sincerely hope that you will see it as so much more—a profound statement of surpassing importance to leaders. Making your team members feel that what they do matters (i.e., feel significant) is a worthy candidate for "Leader Job #1."

While giving acknowledgment is a most desirable human trait, I'd add that it is also a first-class profit/growth booster. Customer engagement is a direct product of employee engagement, and, it should go without saying (ha!), those who feel significant are far more likely to go the extra mile (or nine) for their teammates and their customers.

NUMBER ONE:
NO EXAGGERATION
ACKNOWLEDGE is perhaps the most powerful word in the leadership lexicon!

Strong language.
I have observed the power of acknowledgment a hundred times.
A hundred hundred times.
In any damn context you can name.
In any damn culture you can name.

It matters.
It works.

ACKNOWLEDGMENT:
ME = CENTER OF THEIR UNIVERSE

When I left the dining room after sitting next to Gladstone, I thought he was the cleverest man in England. But when I sat next to Disraeli I left feeling I was the cleverest person.
—Jennie Jerome (Winston Churchill's American mother)

When you are talking to [Bill Clinton], you feel like he doesn't care about anything or anybody else around but you. He makes you feel like the most important person in the room.
—Mark Hughes, screenwriter, *Forbes* blogger

Is this an inherent trait or a developable skill? I contend it is both. Some may have more of a proclivity than others for making you or me feel the center of things. But recall that I believe that becoming a "listening professional" is indeed a learnable skill—albeit one that takes time and practice, practice, practice.

15.13.2
ACKNOWLEDGMENT: WDYT

The four most important words in any organization are . . .

"WHAT DO *YOU* THINK?"
—Courtesy of Dave Wheeler, posted at tompeters.com

WDYT: First, it is acknowledgment of the fact that I am worth listening to—a grand certification of my worth. Also, not so incidentally, the collective WDYT answers provide a Niagara Falls of good ideas.

Suggestion: **COUNT YOUR DAILY WDYTs.**
Start: **TODAY.**

(Call it the engineer still in me, but you truly can measure things like this.)

15.14

15.14.1
THE 30K RULE: SO, SO, (SO, SO) EASY TO DO . . .

SO WHY OH, WHY OH, WHY DON'T WE DO IT MORE OFTEN?

THAT IS, SAY "THANK YOU"

CEO Doug Conant sent 30,000 handwritten "Thank you" notes to employees during the 10 years he ran Campbell's Soup.
—*Bloomberg Businessweek*

That amounts to approximately . . .

Twelve thank-you notes every weekday for ten years.

Ye gads.
And you?

"Thank you": WHY THE HELL DOES IT SEEM TO BE SO DAMN DIFFICULT FOR SO MANY PEOPLE, INCLUDING MANY/MOST LEADERS, TO UTTER THESE TWO WORDS? THAT THANK-YOU DEFICIENCY, FOR ME, IS ONE OF LIFE'S GREATEST MYSTERIES.

I have many things to thank my mother for, including love. But near the top of the list—perhaps second, right after love—was her insistence (AND SHE WAS AN ALL STAR AT INSISTING) that the words *thank you* be used on a VERY regular basis. That insistence has not just served me well—it has made all the difference.

At this point, I could regale you with a dozen dozen anecdotes I've gathered over the years testifying to the staggering power of a simple thank-you. This one is typical: A woman I chatted with at one of my seminars interviewed for a midlevel managerial job and subsequently wrote a note thanking the interviewer for his time and consideration. She was the only one of thirty-some candidates who did so. She got the job. (And the interviewer later told her there were several qualified candidates but the thank-you note was the factor that tipped the scales.) There are many more like vignettes, but suffice it to say that most are hard to believe—such a simple gesture, such a disproportionate response.

(Even Twitter: I am a regular Twitter user. Some number of people retweet this or that remark I made. Not a big deal. As a matter of course, I often as not write "Thank you" in response. Often as not, my thank-you results in a line or two (or three) response saying that it was great that I said thank you. And I bet that on a hundred of those thank-you-for-the-thank-you occasions, the response was along the lines of "Thank you for bothering to say, 'Thank you.'" *Bother* is a big word: acknowledging that I went out of my way to take the time to say thank you. Yes, even Twitter.)

15.14.2
THANK YOU: LITTLE >> BIG

It's not the thank-you for making the million-dollar sale that matters. (Praise for that's going to happen regardless!) It's, to use Ken Blanchard's (*One Minute Manager*) phrase, "catching someone doing something [some little thing] right."

To the recipient, the spontaneous kudo for the "little ones" has higher impact than the biggies.

It means that the boss (or peer) noticed the wee gesture. You have made the recipient—recall the earlier quote—feel significant. Significant = BIG word.

15.15

15.15.1
CIVILITY/COURTESY

From a Twitter conversation on civility/@tom_peters:

Tim Brander: **"Internal courtesy sets the tone for external relationships."** (Oh my, is this ever true!)
Dave Wheeler: **"MBMR. Management by Mom's Rules. Good Home Training applied can be a performance multiplier and persona 'differentiator.'"**
Sunny Bindra: **"You're not 'running late,' you're rude and selfish."**

More (not from Twitter):

MRI means "most respectful interpretation" of what someone's saying to you. I don't need everyone to be best friends, but I need to have a team with MRI. So you can say anything to anyone as long as you say it the right way. Maybe you need to practice with, "Can you help me understand why you don't want to do this or why you wanted to do that." . . . I just make it so it's a human environment.
—Robin Domeniconi, CMO, Rue La La,
a flash sale website (from Adam Bryant,
Quick and Nimble: Lessons from Leading
***CEOs on How to Create a Culture of Innovation*)**

Civility is a good human strategy AND an excellent bottom-line strategy. Simply put . . .

THERE IS NO ITEM DISCUSSED IN THIS BOOK THAT WOULD NOT BE TEN TIMES EASIER TO IMPLEMENT IN AN ENTERPRISE WHERE UNWAVERING CIVILITY WAS A KEYSTONE OF ORGANIZATIONAL CULTURE.

15.15.2
CIVILITY/CARING

The one piece of advice which will contribute to making you a better leader, will provide you with greater happiness, and will advance your career more than any other advice . . . and it doesn't call for a special personality or any certain chemistry . . . and anyone can do it, and it's this:
    You must care.   —General Melvin Zais

This excerpt is from a National War College address by General Zais to midlevel officers. I once gave the annual Forrestal Lecture at the U.S. Naval Academy. I handed out, on my own nickel, four thousand copies (CDs—ye olde days) of the Zais speech that featured this quote. I thought it was that important.

15.15.3
CIVILITY: K = R = P

KINDNESS = REPEAT BUSINESS = PROFIT

K = R = P/KINDNESS TO PATIENTS IS KIND AND COST EFFECTIVE:

There is a misconception that supportive interactions require more staff or more time and are therefore more costly. Although labor costs are a substantial part of any hospital budget, the interactions themselves add nothing to the budget. **Kindness is free.** Listening to patients or answering their questions costs nothing. It can be argued that negative interactions—alienating patients, being non-responsive to their needs or limiting their sense of control—can be very costly. . . . Angry, frustrated or frightened patients may be combative, withdrawn and less cooperative—requiring far more time than it would have taken to interact with them initially in a positive way.

—Jo Anne L. Earp, Elizabeth A. French, Melissa B. Gilkey, *Patient Advocacy for Health Care Quality: Strategies for Achieving Patient-Centered Care*

Regarding kindness and its impact: Press Ganey Associates is the premier source of hospital patient satisfaction measures. One study included 139,380 patients from 225 hospitals. Remarkably, *none* of the top fifteen factors determining patient satisfaction referred to patients' health outcome. Instead, patient satisfaction was effectively determined by the quality of patient-staff interactions and the way patients observed staff members behaving toward one another.

(Source: Susan Frampton, Laura Gilpin, Patrick Charmel, *Putting Patients First*.)

Hospital patient count is shown to be directly related to patient satisfaction evaluations. Hence, kindness, not to minimize the spiritual value thereof, has a positive impact on hospital revenue and profitability.

KINDNESS:
Kind.
Thoughtful.
Engaged.
Listening.
Appreciative.
Open.
Honest.
Responsive.
Profitable.

Kindness = "Soft"?
NEVER!

15.15.4
CIVILITY VERSUS SPEED

Civility and speed can (often) be at odds. If relationships are everything (AND THEY ARE), then civility beats speed!

The "speed is everything" crowd has a good point. But so does—equally—the "civility is everything" crowd.

Think about this. Do **NOT** be conned by the speed-is-all adherents, including, historically, me.

Read! Study!
Little > Big/Civility/Kindness

The Manager's Book of Decencies: How Small Gestures Build Great Companies by Steve Harrison

The Power of Small: Why Little Things Make All the Difference by Linda Kaplan Thaler and Robin Koval

The Power of Nice: How to Conquer the Business World with Kindness by Linda Kaplan Thaler and Robin Koval

15.16 HELP[ING]: WHAT LEADERS DO FOR A LIVING/AN ART AND SCIENCE TO BE MASTERED

What do leaders *do* for a living?

They **HELP!**

(Aid and abet their team members' pursuit of personal, professional, and organizational goals.)

Right?

Next question: How many of us could say we're **"professionals at helping,"** meaning that we have *studied* and *mastered*—like a professional mastering her musical craft—helping?

My experience says: Damned few merit the "professional at helping" designation. Helping is "one of those things": "Helping? Sure, I know how to help people. What's the big deal? What's so complicated?"

HELPING . . .

1. Helping *is* a big deal—in fact, a VERY big deal.
2. Most of us are rank amateurs when it comes to effectively helping.
3. In my opinion, true excellence in "helping" is much more delicate than neurosurgery. (I believe it with heart, head, and soul.)

PURE GENIUS: *Helping: How to Offer, Give, and Receive Help* by Ed Schein

MIT professor Ed Schein is the acknowledged master on this topic. Relative to the discussion here, his book demonstrates that you can treat helping as a standalone topic that can be subject to scientific study.

HELPING/LAST CHAPTER: SOME KEY PRINCIPLES

- "Effective help occurs when the helping relationship is perceived to be equitable." (Full partners in moving forward.)

- "Everything you say or do is an intervention that determines the future of the relationship." (Everything = Everything. Small > Big.)
- "Effective helping begins with pure inquiry." (Questions, *not* prescriptions, first.) (See also Schein's book *Humble Inquiry: The Gentle Art of Asking Rather Than Telling*.)
- "It is the client who owns the problem." (Words matter, e.g., "client": There's a quote in *Helping* from a National Football League player turned lawyer turned professional football coach; he calls his players "my clients." Think twice or thrice on this: FOOTBALL PLAYER AS THE COACH'S CLIENT. NICE.)

SUMMARY
- "Helping" is what we/leaders do for a living!
- Employee as CLIENT!
- STUDY/PRACTICE helping as you would neurosurgery! (*Helping* IS your neurosurgery!)

Obviously, I have no more than scratched the surface. My goal is simply to raise the level of attention to this topic. I do hope I have adequately demonstrated that this is indeed what leaders do for a living and that it is supremely difficult to do it well. The good news: It *is* a topic that can be dissected and an area in which we can improve through assiduous STUDY and PRACTICE. (The parallels with "listening professional" in chapter 13 are almost exact.)

15.17 READ!

CEO Failing #1: "If I had to pick one failing of CEOs, it's that they don't read enough."

—The cofounder of one of the world's
largest investment companies to TP

The conversation was a casual one. This and that. Out of the blue, my dinner companion said, "Do you know what's the number-one shortcoming of CEOs?" I made a smart-aleck response along the lines of, "Well, I can think of ten major shortcomings, but, no, clue me in on number one."

The response he gave—see immediately above—could have knocked me over with the proverbial feather.

As I subsequently thought about it, it made more and more sense.

Recall the quote by physicist Albert Bartlett: "The greatest shortcoming of the human race is our inability to understand the exponential function." We are all under the gun; keeping up is nigh on impossible, but one must try, age twenty-one (last year's university graduate) or age seventy-five (me).

And the best weapon circa 2018: **READ! READ!! READ!!! READ!!!!**

Note: The above exchange took place at a private party, and it is inappropriate to name my dinner companion. It was not Warren Buffett. But speaking of Buffett . . .

In my whole life, I have known no wise people (over a broad subject matter area) who didn't read all the time—

none. ZERO. You'd be amazed at how much Warren [Buffett] reads—and how much I read.

—Charlie Munger, vice chairman,
Berkshire Hathaway (Munger is Buffett's number two)

READ!!!

15.18

15.18.1
WAIT!

Rarely does a book have the personal impact of . . .

Wait: The Art and Science of Delay by Frank Partnoy.

Speed, speed, speed is the plea—by me and pretty much everyone else. And the times surely are a-changin'. Yet Mr. Partnoy, in a thoroughly researched book, persuasively argues that to slow down and think about it is the very definition of what it means to be human.

Consider, from *Wait*:

Thinking about the role of delay is a profound and fundamental part of being human. . . . The amount of time we take to reflect on decisions will define who we are. Is our mission simply to be another animal, or are we here for something more?

Life might be a race against time, but it is enriched when we rise above our instincts and stop the clock to process and understand what we are doing and why.

Computer programmer, investor, writer, painter Paul Graham wrote, "The most impressive people I know are all terrible procrastinators."

No commandments from me will be forthcoming. I am simply suggesting that you take a deep breath (yes, that's permissible in 2018) and reflect on this idea and seriously consider reading Partnoy's book.

15.18.2
WAIT AND EXCELLENCE: FIRST-ORDER PARTNERS

Here's where I come out on the topic of waiting:

THE DAY PATIENCE DIES IS THE DAY THAT EXCELLENCE DISAPPEARS. ACHIEVING EXCELLENCE IS BY DEFINITION A PAINSTAKING PROCESS.

WHILE THE TIMES REQUIRE EXTREME URGENCY, PEERLESS QUALITY OF WORK WILL ALWAYS DEMAND CARE AND THOUGHTFULNESS, WHICH BY DEFINITION, CANNOT TO ANY SIGNIFICANT EXTENT BE RUSHED.

IN FACT, IT IS PRECISELY SUCH "PEERLESS QUALITY OF WORK" AND "CARE" THAT ANIMATE THIS ENTIRE BOOK. EXCELLENCE IN ALL WE DO IS BY FAR THE MOST, AND PERHAPS ONLY, EFFECTIVE RESPONSE TO THE COMING TECHNOLOGY MAELSTROM.

15.19

15.19.1
EFFECTIVE SELF-MANAGEMENT: LEADER VIRTUE #1?

**Being aware of yourself and how you affect everyone around
you is what distinguishes a superior leader.**
—Edie Seashore

Edie Seashore knew few if any peers in the world of organizational development. Her assertion here is a strong one: When it comes to effective leadership, self-knowledge is the number-one distinguishing trait.

In her excellent book *Take the Lead: Motivate, Inspire, and Bring Out the Best in Yourself and Everyone Around You*, Bentley University's Betsy Myers echoes Seashore:

**Leadership is self-knowledge. Successful leaders are those
who are conscious about their behavior and the impact it
has on the people around them. They are willing to examine
what behaviors of their own may be getting in the way. . . .
The toughest person you will ever lead is yourself. We can't
effectively lead others unless we can lead ourselves.**

15.19.2
SELF-MANAGEMENT PROBLEM #1: MISPERCEPTION

In *The New Leaders*, Daniel Goleman (the EQ guru) and his colleagues get to the heart of the matter. Leaders' self-perception stinks, and the smell gets worse as one climbs the hierarchy steps:

How can a high-level leader like _____ [Goleman et al. do not provide the name] be so out of touch with the truth about himself? It's more common than you would imagine. In fact, the higher up the ladder a leader climbs, the less accurate his self-assessment is likely to be. The problem is an acute lack of feedback [especially on people issues].

This quote is consistent with a very substantial body of research on leaders' misperceptions in general. In one quantitative study, for instance, the researcher counted the number of times a leader interrupted others in the course of a typical meeting and the number of times the leader himself was interrupted. I'm sure you can imagine the results: The leader felt that he had rarely interrupted but that he had frequently been interrupted. The data unequivocally say the reverse—to a degree, nearly an order of magnitude, that would be laughable were the topic in fact not so serious.

15.19.3
SELF-AWARENESS/VOICES OF THE MASTERS

Ben Franklin: "There are three things that are extremely hard: steel, a diamond, and to know one's self."

Dale Carnegie: "The biggest problem I shall ever face: the management of Dale Carnegie."

I'm afraid I've never been keen on self-reflection. "Just get on with it" is more or less my motto. Yet virtually all, if not all, of the top leadership thinkers—and the likes of Messrs. Franklin and Carnegie—are clear that self-knowledge ("leading ourselves," per Betsy Meyers, above) is an imperative for effective leadership.

Who am I to disagree?

15.20 LEADERS (AND THE REST OF US) BEWARE: YOUR JUDGMENT, WELL, STINKS

The first principle is that you must not fool yourself—and you are the easiest person to fool.   —Richard Feynman

Psychologist Daniel Kahneman was awarded the Nobel Memorial Prize in economic sciences in 2002 for his studies of cognitive biases. He and his colleague, the late Amos Tversky, began their study of errors in human judgment in 1973 at Tel Aviv University. The work the two produced is encyclopedic and of the most profound importance.

In 2011, Kahneman produced his summa, *Thinking, Fast and Slow*. It is effectively a chastening 499-page catalog of the errors we make in judgment. Our use of intuition comes in for a particularly severe drubbing. In a word or three, our intuition (thinking fast) by and large stinks. Though, truth be known, slowing down our thought processes also results in its own flavors of errors.

Kahneman summarizes in his introduction: "My aim for watercooler conversations [regarding the book]: improve the ability to identify and understand errors of judgment and choice, in others and eventually in ourselves, by providing a richer and more precise language to discuss them. In at least some cases, an accurate diagnosis [of our biases] may suggest an intervention to limit the damage that bad judgments and choices often cause."

BOTTOM LINE:

Cognitive biases cloud every decision and judgment we make. Awareness is not "the answer," but it helps. In the face of our limited cognitive processing skills, I am hardly endorsing paralysis; we must move forward. I am, however, urging study, reflection, and awareness.

How often is our judgment twisted by cognitive biases? One hundred percent of the time.

Not a joke line.

Not a rounding error.

Read! Study!

I surely don't imagine that you will read all these. The goal is simply to offer you a certified (by me) sampler. *Thinking, Fast and Slow* is a must, as is *The Invisible Gorilla* (about one of the most famous social psychological experiments in recent decades, in which the large majority of observers did not see a gorilla walk in front of them because of a simple distraction created by the researchers).

Thinking, Fast and Slow by Daniel Kahneman

Mistakes Were Made (But Not by Me): Why We justify Foolish Beliefs, Bad Decisions, and Hurtful Acts by Carol Tavris and Elliot Aronson

The Invisible Gorilla and Other Ways Our Intuitions Deceive Us by Christopher Chabris and Daniel Simons

Why We Make Mistakes: How We Look Without Seeing, Forget Things in Seconds, and Are All Pretty Sure We Are Way Above Average by Joseph Hallinan

Everything Is Obvious: How Common Sense Fails Us by Duncan Watts

The Drunkard's Walk: How Randomness Rules Our Lives by Leonard Mlodinow

Fooled by Randomness: The Hidden Role of Chance in Life and in the Markets by Nassim Nicholas Taleb

Predictably Irrational: The Hidden Forces That Shape Our Decisions by Dan Ariely

How We Know What Isn't So: The Fallibility of Human Reason in Everyday Life by Thomas Gilovich

Being Wrong: Adventures in the Margin of Error by Kathryn Schulz

A list of 159 cognitive biases can be found at: http://en.wikipedia.org/wiki/List_of_cognitive_biases

15.21 WOMEN RULE

In chapter 12, I discussed women's overwhelming market power and the failure of most businesses to address with rigor the strategic opportunity this presented. And, via the **"Squint Test,"** I suggested that an exec team ought to more or less look like the market being served. That is, there is an important market-size argument for sky-high female representation at the top—over half would be a logical conclusion.

But that's the least of it—or at least far from the whole story.

The point in this section goes far beyond gender-based market power. The point here is that it appears that women are . . . IN GENERAL . . . more effective leaders than men. As I say farther along, that does not amount to a suggestion that male leaders should be shown the door. It does amount to a forceful suggestion that if women are not solidly represented in top management (and in the leader portfolio in general), you are making an enormous strategic mistake.

You are, well, being stupid.

15.21.1
WOMEN RULE/THE RULE OF FIFTY-SIX

McKinsey & Company found that the international companies with more women on their corporate boards far outperformed the average company in return on equity and other measures. Operating profit was 56 percent higher.

—Nicholas Kristof, "Twitter, Women, and
Power," *The New York Times*

FIFTY-SIX is a rather formidable number, eh? (*Formidable*, hell. It boggles the imagination.) And the source, extensive McKinsey & Co. research, is as close to unimpeachable as it gets.

15.21.2
WOMEN'S DEMONSTRATED LEADERSHIP PERFORMANCE

What immediately follows is a small but powerful sample of evidence and opinions of women in leadership roles:

1. *Harvard Business Review*:
   "Women are rated higher in fully **12** of the **16** competencies that go into outstanding leadership. And two of the traits where women outscored men to the highest degree—taking initiative and driving for results—have long been thought of as particularly male strengths."

Comment: Twelve of sixteen

2. Lawrence A. Pfaff & Associates:
   - Two years, 941 managers (672 male, 269 female); 360-degree feedback
   - Women: better in **twenty** of **twenty** categories; fifteen of twenty with statistical significance, including decisiveness, planning, setting standards (typically considered male strengths)
   - "Men are not rated significantly higher by any of the raters in any of the areas measured."

3. "AS LEADERS, WOMEN RULE: New Studies find that female managers outshine their male counterparts in almost every measure."
   —Special Report, *Bloomberg Businessweek*

4. "Research [by McKinsey & Co.] suggests that to succeed, start by promoting women." —Nicholas Kristof, "Twitter, Women, and Power," *The New York Times*

5. "In my experience, women make much better executives than men." —Kip Tindell, CEO, Container Store, *Uncontainable: How Passion, Commitment, and Conscious Capitalism Built a Business Where Everyone Thrives* (A few years ago, Container Store was named the number-one "Best Company to Work for in America"—it invariably finishes in the top ten. And its financials are more than sound.)

6. Women's strengths match new economy imperatives, as reported in Stanford professor Judy B. Rosener's book *America's Competitive Secret: Women Managers*:

   Women's typical leadership style: "Link [rather than rank] workers; favor interactive-collaborative leadership style [empowerment beats top-down decision making]; sustain fruitful collaborations; comfortable with sharing information; see redistribution of power as victory, not surrender; favor multi-dimensional feedback; value technical & interpersonal skills, individual & group contributions equally; readily accept ambiguity; honor intuition as well as pure 'rationality'; inherently flexible; appreciate cultural diversity."

**Rosener's research is of particular note in 2018: The posi-
tive assessment of women's leadership skills in general is
likely to be far more pronounced given emerging changes
in organizational structure and overall economic and social
network structure. In today's topsy-turvy settings, where
traditional, rigid hierarchy is no longer ubiquitous, and is
often downright counterproductive, women's demonstrated
relative strengths are more important than ever.**

15.21.3
REFLECTION: A TWENTY-YEAR-PLUS ENTERPRISE PERFORMANCE OBSESSION

This topic has been a passion of mine since 1996—two full
decades and then some. My reasons have little or nothing to do
with social justice. (Social justice issues concerning women are
very important to me, but not a principal dimension of this business analysis.) My interest has everything to do with organization
effectiveness per se—my career obsession.

The attributes more likely to be found among women than men
are especially fit for our emerging times/organizational forms—
forms which de-emphasize "command and control" regimes for
getting things done and increasingly emphasize cooperative, jum-
bled "forms." And, recall, as discussed in chapter 11, women do
indeed buy more or less everything, in both the consumer and, in
the United States, commercial categories.

Everything argued here, and I've said this before but it bears
repeating, requires the words *more likely to be found* or *typically*.
There are many men who deal brilliantly with ambiguity. But
"typically," women are more comfortable with convoluted, non-

linear situations than men are. (E.g., at a seminar I attended on this topic, I clearly remember a remark made by a prominent movie director. It went like this: "*When I read a script by an unidentified writer, I guarantee you I can predict the author's gender nine out of ten times—frankly, ten out of ten times. Women authors' products includes twists and turns and hopelessly tangled human relationships and so on. The men's scripts are down the center of the road, linear to a fault—and it often is a fault.*")

MY AHA MOMENT

There was more or less an aha moment that, in retrospect, started me down the path to examining women's leadership tendencies that differ from men's. It occurred at one of my company's four-day Northern California executive seminars. One attendee, a senior exec at the travel services giant, Rosenbluth International, had made his bones doing (with great success) big systems sales for AT&T.

The conversation went like this:

Him: "Tom, I had one secret."

TP: "Which was . . . ?"

His response, which I remember quite clearly, hence close to verbatim:

> *I hired women!*
> *You see, all the real purchase decision analysis is effectively made two or three levels "down" in the client organization by fairly junior staffers. My guys were typically all hung up on hierarchy and rank; they wouldn't dirty their hands with the denizens of the lower reaches. The women I brought on*

board couldn't care less about name, rank, or serial number;
org charts were for dummies. So the women would invest
immense amounts of time developing relationships in every
nook and cranny in the bowels of the client organization.
In nine out of ten cases, that "investment" iced the sale.
The [client] VP of purchasing almost without fail did
whatever his staff proposed that he do. All the guys had
wasted God alone knows how much time trying to suck
up to "the man," but "the man" was essentially irrelevant.

Thence, though I didn't know it at the time, my career as a performance-based women's advocate had begun!

15.21.4
TECH, TOO

Tech has historically been a wasteland for women. One hopes that things are changing. But there is data, a sample of which is presented here, that paints a rosy picture of women in tech.

Women-led private tech companies: 35 percent *higher return on investment than male-led firms*

Women-led tech companies with venture backing: *Revenues 12 percent higher than male-led venture-funded companies*

Twenty-five thousand Kickstarter projects: *Women-led crowd-funding candidates more likely to get fully funded than male-led candidates* —*Inc.*, October 2015 (cover, "Will the Next Steve Jobs Be a Woman?")

15.21.5
SMALL BUSINESS SUPERSTARS: WOMEN-OWNED BUSINESSES

The growth and success of women-owned businesses is one of the most profound changes taking place in the business world today.   —Margaret Heffernan, *How She Does It*

More relevant data from Ms. Heffernan:

- U.S. firms owned or controlled by women: 10.6 million (48 percent of all firms)
- The number of American employees of women-owned businesses exceeds the total number of domestic employees of the bellwether Fortune 500
- Growth rate of women-owned firms versus all firms: three times higher
- Rate of jobs created by women-owned firms versus all firms: twice as high
- Likelihood of women-owned firms staying in business versus all firms: greater than 1.0
- Growth rate of women-owned companies with revenues of >$1 million and >100 employees versus all firms: two times higher

15.21.6
WOMEN'S STRENGTHS AS NEGOTIATORS, SALESPERSONS, INVESTORS

NEGOTIATION

From Horacio Falcão's cover story in *World Business*, May 2006, "Say It Like a Woman: Why the 21st-Century Negotiator Will Need the Female Touch":

- Ability to put themselves in their counterparts' shoes
- Comprehensive, attentive, and detailed communication style
- Empathy that facilitates trust-building
- Curious and active listeners
- Less competitive-for-competitiveness' sake attitude
- Sense of fairness
- Ability to persuade
- Collaborative decision-makers

SALES

From the back cover of Nicki Joy and Susan Kane-Benson's book, *Selling Is a Woman's Game: 15 Powerful Reasons Why Women Can Outsell Men*:

TAKE THIS QUICK QUIZ:

Who manages more things at once?
Who puts more effort into their appearance?

Who usually takes care of the details?

Who finds it easier to meet new people?

Who asks more questions in a conversation?

Who is a better listener?

Who has more interest in communication skills?

Who is more inclined to get involved?

Who encourages harmony and agreement?

Who has better intuition?

Who works with a longer to-do list?

Who enjoys a recap to the day's events?

Who is better at keeping in touch with others?

INVESTMENT

From the Motley Fool's LouAnn Lofton, in her book *Warren Buffett Invests Like a Girl: And Why You Should Too*:

WOMEN . . .

1. Trade less than men do
2. Exhibit less overconfidence—more likely to know what they don't know
3. Shun risk more than male investors do
4. Less optimistic, more realistic than their male counterparts
5. Put in more time and effort researching possible investments—consider details and alternate points of view
6. More immune to peer pressure—tend to make decisions the same way regardless of who's watching

7. Learn from their mistakes
8. Have less testosterone than men do, making them less willing to take extreme risks, which, in turn, could lead to less extreme market fluctuations

FYI: Mr. Buffett gave Ms. Lofton's book a sterling review!

The evidence just reviewed, then, suggests that women are frequently, in fact more often than not . . .
BETTER NEGOTIATORS.
BETTER SALESPERSONS.
BETTER INVESTORS.

15.21.7
MORE TO COME?

Girls/young women's rate of outpacing boys/young men on the education front is staggering. Headlines like this one are becoming commonplace:

THE NEW GENDER GAP: From Kindergarten to Grad School, Boys Are Becoming the Second Sex
—Cover story, *Bloomberg Businessweek*

This topic is of supreme importance; widespread male disenfranchisement could have severe economic and social consequences. And the male-female gap will surely grow at, given the "tech tsunami," a particularly politically volatile time.

15.21.8
NO, DON'T TOSS ALL THE MALES OVERBOARD

The point of these quotes and assessments, collectively, is not to suggest that tomorrow morning you should demote or dismiss all your male managers. Among other things, the research is remarkably clear:

The winning formula is **GENDER BALANCE.**

What the evidence presented here does unmistakably suggest is that women are exceedingly effective leaders, especially in the context of the times. If you do not have top-to-bottom gender balance, with perhaps even a lean toward a female majority, you are missing the boat. The name of the boat is Organizational Effectiveness/Business Effectiveness/Excellence.

15.22

15.22.1
COMMUNICATION: THE 100 PERCENT RULE

The problem with communication is the illusion that it has been accomplished.   —William H. Whyte

Leaders: Communications failures are . . . One hundred percent your fault!

Many bridle at this.

Tough.

You will never get me to budge.

You (leader) are paid—first and foremost—to get this right.

15.22.2
THE UNIQUENESS COROLLARY: 14 = 14

Suppose you have fourteen direct reports. It's your job to figure out why Ms. Smith or Mr. Jones didn't listen or engage; it is up to you to craft an "engagement strategy" for each individual:

14 people = 14 different, carefully crafted engagement strategies.

Concocting these 14 differentiated approaches is how you earn your pay.

OR DON'T.

For example, 14 = 14 is what we routinely expect of teachers:

14 kids = 14 (very/RADICALLY) different learning trajectories. Right? How often? ALWAYS.

(Which is hardly to suggest that the average teacher gets an A+ on this. But the notion [14 = 14] is unassailable.)

BOTTOM LINE: IT'S WORSE THAN YOU THINK.

One size doesn't fit all. One size never comes within ten country miles of fitting all. In fact, one size doesn't fit one person over the course

of, say, a week. Tom Monday is (very?) different from Tom Thursday.

15.23

15.23.1
APOLOGY

I regard apologizing as the most magical, healing, restorative gesture human beings can make. It is the centerpiece of my work with executives who want to get better.

—Marshall Goldsmith, *What Got You Here Won't Get You There: How Successful People Become Even More Successful*

Most.
Magical.
Healing.
Restorative.
Centerpiece.

Those are extraordinarily powerful words, and Marshall Goldsmith is an extraordinarily powerful voice; he's generally considered the top executive coach.

Well, Mr. Goldsmith and I are in complete agreement. But, as is so often the case in this book, it's not rocket science, and I am stumped:

WHY IN THE HELL IS IT SO HARD TO SAY, "I'M SORRY"?

A short set of apology "rules":

Apology Rule #1: Do it NOW. Don't delay. An issue comes up today, and at a meeting, you are a bit more abrupt than you might have been with Joe in front of his peers. So before you go home, drop by Joe's cubicle—not for a heart-to-heart or any such grand thing, but just for a thirty-second nod and acknowledgment that wires may have gotten crossed and that you were the guilty wire crosser. Trust me, please, please, please trust me: **YOU JUST PERFORMED AN ACT OF IMMENSE—AND LASTING—POWER**.

Apology Rule #2: Do it IN PERSON. Obviously, this may not always be possible. But if it is, do it face-to-face. E-mail is a big no-no. A phone call is ten times better than an e-mail. But in person—dropping by the cubicle—is ten times or a hundred times better than the call. An apology is an intimate act; your body language will speak many times more than your words.

Apology Rule #3: See Rule #1. Do it NOW. THE APOLOGY IRON LAW: NOW. NOW. NOW. **THERE ONCE WAS A TIME WHEN YOU COULD HAVE HEADED OFF A FIRST-ORDER FIASCO WITH A NINETY-SECOND DROP BY OR A FIVE-MINUTE PHONE CALL WITHIN A FEW MINUTES OR HOURS OF THE ISSUE ARISING OR COMING TO YOUR ATTENTION.**

Apology Rule #4: SHUT UP! Effective apology is mostly about LISTENING. You are mainly, with your "I'm sorry," acknowledging that something went awry; remember our discussion of the power of acknowledgment. Then let the other person speak until they wear themselves out. Isiaah Crawford, president of the University of Puget Sound, brilliantly said,

"It's hard to listen your way into trouble."

(Obviously, this command is paradoxical. You are there to apologize, but please shut up. Well, the true apology is your presence; that's the acknowledgment bit. The words are secondary. So: SHUT UP.)

Hence my complete guide to apology:

DO IT NOW.
DO IT IN PERSON.
DO IT NOW.
SHUT UP.

15.23.2
APOLOGY PAYS: BIG-TIME!

From John Kador, *Effective Apology*:

1. "With a new and forthcoming policy on apologies . . . Toro, the lawn mower folks, reduced the average cost of settling a claim from **$115,000** in 1991 to **$35,000** in 2008—and the company hasn't been to trial in 15 years!"
2. "The VA hospital in Lexington, Massachusetts, developed an approach, totally uncharacteristic in healthcare, to apologizing for errors—even when no patient request or claim was made. In 2000, the systemic mean VA hospital malpractice settlement throughout the United States was **$413,000**; the Lexington VA hospital settlement

number was **$36,000**—and there were far fewer per patient claims to begin with."

I am not in the least surprised by either of these examples. (FYI: Mr. Kador offers dozens more.) As I said above, it is virtually impossible to overstate the power of apology, even when the topic is the likes of a lawn mower accident or a medical error, where the consequences could be grave physical injury or worse.

Read! Study!

Yes, there *are* entire books on the topic of apology (and this is a very good one). It is another one of those things in the leadership arena that sounds obvious but in fact is a subject worthy of deep, formal study.

Effective Apology: Mending Fences, Building Bridges, and Restoring Trust by John Kador

15.24 LEADERSHIP REVIEW: THE RULE OF FOUR

Leaders: Embrace the BIG FOUR big words:
"THANK YOU."
"I'M SORRY."
(How ya doin' with the BIG FOUR?)
(How ya doin' **TODAY** with the BIG FOUR?)

15.25

15.25.1
E-MAIL/WHOA: TAKE A DEEP BREATH, WAIT . . . THE SIN OF SEND

1. Do **NOT** push **SEND.** Pause. Five minutes. An hour. Overnight. (The world will not come to an end.)
2. Do NOT immediately respond to that IM (unless it is a car accident involving spouse or child). PAUSE. **REFLECT.** (The world will not come to an end.)
3. Responding to that e-mail **CAN** wait an hour or two or even three. Can wait a **DAY.** Pause. Think. Counsel with others. (The world will not come to an end.)

When I introduced the riff above at the top of a speech, I said, "I want to earn my fee times ten in the first 120 seconds. If you pay attention to this, I guarantee I will have indeed covered my fee—times ten or times a hundred."

I was very serious!

There is no honest reader of this book who will not admit to having pushed SEND prematurely.

RUSH.

RUSH.

RUSH.

RUSH.

Oh, shit!

(RIGHT?)

15.25.2
E-MAIL/IM/EXCELLENCE WHY NOT?

1. Anyone who puts anything in any e-mail/IM that might embarrass him or her next week, next month, in 2024, is a DAMN FOOL.

2. A sloppy* e-mail (etc.) is a **TOTAL PIECE OF CRAP**. *Sloppy: Ungrammatical. Poorly argued. Equivocal— could be interpreted multiple ways. Flippantly critical of someone/anyone. Rude, etc., etc.; i.e., unprofessional.

3. Assume your boss's boss (OR your boss's boss's boss) will read any e-mail you write.

4. Assume your least supportive colleagues will read any e-mail you write.

5. Assume one or more than one customer will read any e-mail you write.

6. Assume that any "clever" e-mail you write will go viral.

7. MY PERSONAL RULE: Every e-mail I send is a complete representation of who I am as a professional and, more broadly, who I am as a human being.

Medieval times (1999): Oral hissy fit would mostly evaporate in four or five days. Modern times: No matter how limited the distribution, any e-communication may go viral in a matter of minutes—maybe even seconds. (Not news. Just a reminder.)

Hasty, emotional response is the nightmare scenario!

Same rules for "personal" e-mails as "professional" ones. Personal e-mails frequently end up not being personal.

E-MAIL.
EXCELLENCE.

Make this duo a tautology, not an oxymoron.

15.26 DECONSTRUCTING LEADERSHIP

REDUCTIONIST LEADERSHIP TRAINING

In general, I am an avowed enemy of reductionist thinking. I prefer wholes to parts. And yet I have come to think that leadership training as it is ordinarily conceived is not reductionist enough; we assume away the key components of leadership as almost too obvious to bother with.

BOTTOM LINE: Leaders need to be good at an extensive set of discrete things that account for 90 percent of their effectiveness.

Effective leadership = Doing specific tasks well

SUGGESTED LEADERSHIP SKILL SET

Avid practitioner of MBWA/Managing by Wandering Around

Aggressive ("fierce") listener (student of listening excellence)

Expert at questioning

Expert at helping (so, so difficult)

Expert at building matchless first-line management

Expert at holding productive conversations

Fanatic about clear communications that acknowledge (radical) individual differences

Master of social media

Master of/obsession with acknowledgment

Effective at fast, proactive apology

Excellent presenter

Conscious master of body language

Master/student of hiring

Master of evaluating people

Time manager par excellence/vigilant regarding over-scheduling

Avid student of the process/psychology of influence

Student of organizational politics

Student of decision-making/student of cognitive biases that derail decision-making

Brilliantly schooled student/practitioner of negotiation

Fanatic about employee development for 100 percent of staff

Student of the power of diversity on any and every damn dimension you can name

Aggressive in pursuing gender balance

Insistent on instilling business sense in one and all

Have at it.

Effectiveness at such discreet activities must not be avoided or evaded.

They are the essence of what you do.

They are how you spend your time.

They can be studied.

They can be practiced.

That's it. Leadership chapter completed. No "vision." But a bunch of stuff that is (virtually) guaranteed to work—getting better at several of these twenty-six items will improve your leadership effectiveness.

Pick one or two or three or four or five . . . and work on 'em.

Start: Today

Good luck!

CODA 2018

MY STORY

I TEND TO DRIVE A LOT OF PEOPLE CRAZY.

I wave my arms like a wild man when I give public presentations to groups of ten or ten thousand.

I say **"WOW!"** [always ALL CAPS] a lot.

I use exclamation marks as if there's no tomorrow**!!!!!!!!!**

There isn't really. Today is all we have. Live it to its fullest. Be of service. **NOW.**

Trite but true: No one knows what tomorrow will bring, and yesterday is dust.

My company logo is a standalone, no-text-added red exclamation mark**!**

I consider myself, in effect, a red exclamation mark.

Tom Peters is the Red Bull of management thinkers.
—Bo Burlingham, *Inc.* (2013)

A human exclamation point who no longer needs his last name. —Nancy Austin on Tom Peters

W. Ross Ashby was the author of the Law of Requisite Variety, referred to earlier and introduced in his classic 1956 book, *An Introduction to Cybernetics*. The science surrounding the LRV is of the highest order—and mostly beyond my ability to comprehend. Nonetheless, I am able to loosely translate Ashby's law into a principle prescription for these nutty times: CRAZY TIMES CALL FOR CRAZY SOLUTIONS.

2018.

Crazy.

Me.

You.

Our organizations.

Crazy.

Or bust.

Not optional.

THE NARRATIVE: AVOID MODERATION!

KEVIN ROBERTS'S CREDO

1. Ready. Fire! Aim.
2. If it ain't broke . . . break it!
3. Hire crazies.
4. Ask dumb questions.
5. Pursue failure.
6. Lead, follow . . . or get out of the way!
7. Spread confusion.
8. Ditch your office.

9. Read odd stuff.
10. **Avoid moderation!**

(Mr. Roberts was most recently CEO of Saatchi & Saatchi. His book *Lovemarks* is on my "best business books ever" short list.)

Insanely great.   —Steve Jobs's new product standard

Radically thrilling.   —BMW, ad for a new model

Astonish me.   —Sergei Diaghilev, to a lead dancer

Build something great.
                            —Hiroshi Yamauchi, Nintendo president,
                                       to a senior game designer

Make it immortal.   —David Ogilvy, to a copywriter

Every project we undertake starts with the same question: "How can we do what has never been done before?"
                                      —Stuart Hornery, Lend Lease

Let us create such a building that future generations will take us for lunatics.   —The church hierarchs at Seville

You can't behave in a calm, rational manner. You've got to be out there on the lunatic fringe.   —Jack Welch

We are crazy. We should only do something when people say it is "crazy." If people say something is "good," it means someone else is already doing it.
—Hajime Mitarai, former CEO, Canon

We all agree your theory is crazy. The question, which divides us, is whether it is crazy enough to have a chance of being correct.
—Niels Bohr, to Wolfgang Pauli

"There's no use trying," said Alice. "One cannot believe impossible things." "I daresay you haven't had much practice," said the Queen. "When I was your age, I always did it for half an hour a day. Why, sometimes I've believed as many as six impossible things before breakfast."
—Lewis Carroll

To hell with "well behaved." . . . Recently a young mother asked for advice. What, she wanted to know, was she to do with a 7-year-old who was obstreperous, outspoken, and inconveniently willful? "Keep her," I replied. . . . The suffragettes refused to be polite in demanding what they wanted or grateful for getting what they deserved. Works for me."
—Anna Quindlen, *Newsweek*

The reasonable man adapts himself to the world. The unreasonable one persists in trying to adapt the world to himself. Therefore, all progress depends upon the unreasonable man.
—George Bernard Shaw, *Man and Superman: The Revolutionists' Handbook*

Life is not a journey to the grave with the intention of arriving safely in one pretty and well preserved piece, but to skid across the line broadside, thoroughly used up, worn out, leaking oil, shouting, **"Geronimo!"**

—Bill McKenna, pro motorcycle racer

**MODERATE TIMES CALL FOR MODERATE RESPONSES.
IMMODERATE TIMES CALL FOR IMMODERATE RESPONSES.
GERONIMO.**

There you have it.
Thank you and good luck!

ACKNOWLEDGMENTS

I am lucky enough to spend the northern hemisphere midwinter months in New Zealand. In 2013, I was invited to visit the University of Auckland Business School to give a lecture. The initial one-shot event has grown into an annual weeklong affair and appointment as an adjunct professor. In February 2016, prior to my annual Auckland visit, I got serious about pulling together fifty years of material for a string of class sessions and lectures. The result, pure and simple, is this book. Hence, my first acknowledgment goes to my colleagues at the University of Auckland Business School, Professor Darl Kolb and Dean Jayne Godfrey in particular, for getting this ball, now called *The Excellence Dividend*, rolling.

After the material had taken roughish shape by the fall of 2016, my wife, Susan Sargent, said out of the blue, "It's a book. Call Esther and Sonny." I had intended to self-publish this memoir of ideas in the most low-key way possible. But Susan almost literally threw me on the Amtrak Acela from Providence, Rhode Island, to Manhattan for a morning meeting with my longtime agent and friend, Esther Newberg, and a lunch with my longtime publisher and friend, Sonny Mehta, and his wife, Gita. And another week or so later I was back in New York, this time for a meeting with my new editor and publisher within the Penguin Random House family, Edward Kastenmeier and Anne Messitte. "Bottom line": My heartfelt thanks to Susan, Esther, Sonny, Gita, Edward, and

Anne for making "all this" possible—or making it "necessary" as Yogi Berra once put it.

Donna Carpenter Lebaron and I have been working together since *The Tom Peters Seminar* was born in 1993. And she once again has been of priceless assistance as editor and general sounding board. Donna in turn (and thence I) has been abetted by writer and newspaper editor Ken Otterbourg; Ken has gone through every page herein at least four times and, among other things, edited out "de facto" at least 444 times.

The book, as noted in the introduction, is constructed around three hundred or so quotes that capture my beliefs better than I can. So my thanks to Richard Branson, Herb Kelleher, John DiJulius, and a few hundred others (including Napoléon and Lewis Carroll) for helping me see the light and for putting the beliefs animating this book into memorable words.

Shelley Dolley and I have been a team now for more than fifteen years. There are a million strategic and operational, academic and logistical tasks that she performs with unflagging zest—and, yes, excellence. On a raft of editorial issues and more, Shelley (and I) are supported by another longtime colleague and deliverer-of-excellence, Cathy Mosca. Thanks on top of thanks to Shelley and Cathy.

"My" team of supporters at Penguin Random House, to whom I am eternally grateful, include editorial assistant Andrew Weber, who made this book project his own to my benefit, publicist Kate Runde, and the Vintage team of Eddie Allen, Chris Zucker, Quinn O'Neill, Barbara Richard, Melissa Yoon, and Jessica Dietcher.

Of special note: This is a book about "excellence." There was another book about excellence that I was associated with and which appeared on the scene in 1982. I want to take the occasion of the publication of *The Excellence Dividend* to thank for the umpteenth time my *In Search of Excellence* coauthor and soul mate, Bob Waterman. In the course of this book, McKinsey & Co. has come in for occasional criticism—but the bottom line is that the firm gave me the prestigious platform from which the "excellence book" was launched.

Each chapter of the book starts with a personal vignette. The first one singled out my first "boss"—namely the late Richard E. Anderson, commanding officer of U.S. Naval Mobile Construction Battalion 9 in 1966 and 1967. "Captain Andy" guided me through ten months in Vietnam—clearly my most formative life experience. I have, simply, never encountered a more effective leader or a leader more committed to his people and to excellence.